CW00546781

FLYING
TO THE LIMIT

Other books by the same author:

Phoenix into Ashes William Kimber
Typhoon and Tempest at War (with Arthur Reed) Ian Allan
Testing Years Ian Allan
English Electric Canberra (with Arthur Reed) Ian Allan
English Electric P1 Lightning Ian Allan
Fighter Test Pilot PSL
My Part of the Sky PSL
Testing Early Jets Airlife
Tempest over Europe Airlife

As part of our ongoing market research, we are always pleased to receive comments about our books, suggestions for new titles, or requests for catalogues. Please write to: The Editorial Director, Patrick Stephens Limited, Sparkford, Near Yeovil, Somerset, BA22 7JJ.

FLYING
TO THE LIMIT

Reminiscences of air combat,
test flying and the aircraft industry

ROLAND BEAMONT

Patrick Stephens Limited

© Roland Beamont CBE, DSO*, DFC*, DL, FRAeS 1996

All rights reserved. No part of this publication may be reproduced, stored in a retrieval system or transmitted, in any form or by any means, electronic, mechanical, photocopying, recording or otherwise, without prior permission in writing from Patrick Stephens Limited.

First published in 1996

British Library Cataloguing in Publication data
A Catalogue record of this book is available
from the British Library.

ISBN 1 85260 553 7

Library of Congress Catalog Card Number 96-75832

Patrick Stephens Limited is an imprint of Haynes Publishing,
Sparkford, Nr Yeovil, Somerset, BA22 7JJ.

Designed & Typeset by J. H. Haynes & Co. Ltd
Printed in Great Britain by Butler & Tanner Ltd, London and Frome

Contents

For Pat

Dedication

To the test pilots and observers whose task remains vital and often dangerous. In the 30 years from 1949 eight aircraft were lost on test from Warton and Samlesbury. Six aircrew were killed and four injured. T. B. O. Evans, T. H. Durrant, Alan Love, Roy Bigland, R. 'Russ' Pengelly and John Gray did not return.

Acknowledgements

The author expresses grateful thanks for the assistance received from many sources in preparing this book. In particular to Joan Moores for her invaluable and enthusiastic support in interpreting and typing my manuscripts; to British Aerospace for quotations from the author's Warton test reports, and to Chrys Butcher and Warton's photographic department. To Haynes Publishing for quotations in Chapters 1 and 13 from the author's *Fighter Test Pilot* (PSL, 1986); to Lionel Howarth; to No 3(F) Squadron Association; to IPC Magazines, to Jimmy Dell, my test flying friend and colleague of many years, for his reminiscences on Lightning and Jaguar testing, and to the Society of Experimental Test Pilots, USA.

Finally, as always to my wife Pat, for her formidable criticism and resolute proofreading, and for putting up with it through all the years with such steadfastness.

Author's note: The opinions expressed in the following chapters are the author's and do not necessarily reflect those of any other authority referred to in the text.

Glossary

A&AEE	Aeroplane and Armament Experimental Establishment
ADGB	Air Defence of Great Britain
AFDU	Air Fighting Development Unit
AFTS	Advanced Flying Training School
ALG	advanced landing ground
AoA	angle of attack; angle between wing chord line or other fore-and-aft axis and direction of local undisturbed airflow
ASI	airspeed indicator
CAP	combat air patrol
CFE	Central Fighter Establishment
CFI	Chief Flying Instructor
CG	centre of gravity
CHT	cylinder-head temperature
compressor surge	gross breakdown of airflow through the compressor
departures	disturbances which increase without oscillation, or situations involving unpremeditated loss of control
downwash	angle through which a fluid stream is deflected down by an aerofoil
DR	dead (or deduced) reckoning
E(R)FTS	Elementary (and Reserve) Flying Training School
ETA	estimated time of arrival
flutter	high-frequency oscillation of structure owing to the interaction of aerodynamic and aero-elastic forces
fly-by wire	flight control system using electric signalling instead of mechanical linkages
G	acceleration due to Earth gravity
IAM	Institute of Aviation Medicine
IAS	indicated airspeed
IMN	indicated Mach number
intake buzz	high-frequency and often violent pulsation of airflow at the intake of a supersonic air-breathing engine
JPT	jet-pipe temperature
MoD	Ministry of Defence
MoD.PE	Ministry of Defence, Procurement Executive
MU	Maintenance Unit

neutral point	CG point at which an aeroplane's stability would be neutral
Nh	the r.p.m. of the high-pressure (HP) stage of a turbine
OAT	outside air temperature
OCU	Operational Conversion Unit
OP	oil pressure
OT	oil temperature
PIO	pilot-induced oscillation(s)
pitot-static	relating to a system of instrumentation fed by a combination of pitot-tube pressure and local static pressure, the difference giving the airspeed indicator reading
PPS	partial pressure system
pro-spin	tending to enter a spin from the stall
PRU	Photographic Reconnaissance Unit
QDM	one of the 'Q' code series of basic three-letter telecommunications codes, meaning 'Will you indicate magnetic heading for me to steer towards you, with no wind?'
QFE	another basic telecommunications code (see above), meaning 'To what should I set altimeter to obtain height above your location?'
RAE	Royal Aircraft Establishment
ramjet	an air-breathing jet engine which has no mechanical compressor or turbine, compression being achieved entirely by increasing pressure as a result of the vehicle's speed through the atmosphere, and which therefore cannot be started when the vehicle is at rest
reheat	the injection and combustion of additional fuel in a specially designed turbojet jetpipe called an afterburner, to provide augmented thrust. Also referred to as afterburning.
SAM	surface-to-air missile
Sleeve-valve	piston-engine valve gear using one or two concentric sleeves between the piston and cylinder with suitably shaped ports in the walls that line up intermittently with inlet/exhaust connections on the cylinder
spoilers	hinged or movable surfaces on the upper rear surface of a wing which reduce lift when opened and usually increase drag. Used to steepen angle of descent or augment roll, and sometimes the only form of roll control in supersonic combat aircraft.
surge-line	boundary between gas-turbine operating region and region where surge of the compressor (i.e. a gross breakdown of airflow through the compressor) is certain
TAF	Tactical Air Force
torque	twisting or turning moment or couple
VFR	visual flight rules
V_{ne}	never-exceed speed
wet wing	wing in which the structure forms an integral fuel tank (as opposed to a wing in which fuel tanks are fitted)

Introduction

'The Test Flight'! The term used throughout the media by cub reporters and columnists, and by radio and television news and 'defence experts' to describe the beginning and, as far as they are concerned, the end of the testing of a new type of aircraft, has become almost accepted usage on the subject.

If it is successful on flight one a new aircraft then becomes non-newsworthy until it crashes, or until some years later when it can become the subject of another news story — 'new fighter delayed again — massive cost overrun', etc.

In fact the first flight of a prototype merely marks a significant point in the evolution of a new military aircraft or civil transport. Before this event many years of intensive activity will have gone into specification, design, wind tunnel and rig testing, fabrication, unit assembly, final assembly, total systems ground testing, structural and resonance testing, ground engine running and systems functioning, design and crew-training simulator programmes, and finally runway trials of steering, braking, nosewheel lifting in response to pitch control, and drag 'chute or reverse thrust testing. Only when all these have been proved to programme acceptance standard can the aircraft be 'cleared for Flight'.

This marks the beginning of the second and often longer phase of intensive activity — flight development and flight clearance.

In the first experimental phase, which can last for some years, the full design envelope is explored progressively, first to the limits of the customer's specification and subsequently to the absolute design limits to establish safe margins beyond the customer's requirements. In military aircraft this involves ultimately flying into areas of known 'high risk' when combinations of maximum speed, normal acceleration (G) and rate of roll have to be achieved simultaneously, and these are not 'one-off' points but have to be repeated at increasing Mach number from sea-level to maximum operating altitude.

Then the slow-speed, high-angle-of-attack characteristics have to be thoroughly explored and safe margins against 'departure' (i.e. spinning) established. In current and future generations of military aircraft the effectiveness, safety and reliability of the spin-prevention mode in the Flight Control System computer have to be explored and confirmed.

In parallel to these basic airframe trials engine/intake compatibility, performance and 'suitability' have to be established, often entailing a heavy programme if a new engine design has been matched to a new airframe.

When the basic test programmes are well under way, specialised systems testing is carried out on early development aircraft and these lead to the vital weapons system trials and, finally, to evaluation of weapons delivery.

This massive continuous effort from initial contract through to entry into service of a safe, reliable and effective operational aircraft calls for a decade or more of intense effort from many thousands of dedicated people in the main and support companies in the industry, and in all this the test pilot still retains the key to success or failure.

If he identifies a major defect or potential danger or delaying factor in good time he can save the whole programme; and the automatic data transmission from his aircraft direct to the flight test computers by no means always identifies trouble first.

Alternatively, if he is insufficiently alert or critical enough to identify trouble, or subsequently not resolute enough to demand urgent action despite inevitable opposition from commercial influences on the Board, this can result in programme failure when the customer ultimately rejects the product or, worse still, in a fatal accident, possibly his own.

The media idea of 'The Test Flight' is in fact a continuing farce. Only when the first series production example is accepted by the customer, many years and thousands of testing hours after the prototype first flight, and after the aircraft has survived ten years or more of the extensive test programme and the checks and balances of company appraisal, Ministry of Defence, Procurement Executive (MoD.PE) approval and Service Trials at the Aeroplane and Armament Experimental Establishment (A&AEE), Boscombe Down, can the experimental test pilot be said to have done his job; and along the way there will have been some close calls and, sadly, possibly fatalities.

Contrary to the widespread prediction by many engineers in the 1970s, 'fly-by-wire' control systems have not brought in an era of totally predictable and therefore 'safe' flight development. The experimental test pilot's work remains vital and, by comparison with most other professions, dangerous. But when this subject arises some engineers are likely to say: 'What are you worried about — you've got a good escape system!' And thanks to the late Jimmy Martin and his world's most successful ejection seat system, the test crews of today do have such a system.

The fact remains that the advanced computer technology of the 1990s has not increased the safety of flight testing. It has actually introduced a new hazard factor — the possibility of main controls computer malfunction which leaves the crew no alternative but to crash-land or abandon the aircraft, as seen in the recent crashes of the American YF–22 prototype, the Swedish SAAB Gripen prototype and, after two years of remedial redesign, the second 'improved' Gripen series production aircraft. Thankfully all these disasters were without loss of life.

When all these phases have been completed successfully the military aircraft can then be sent for its final 'Service' trials by the A&AEE Boscombe Down, but on the way at every stage it is likely to be subjected to media sniping inspired by politicians, environmentalists or just plain headline seeking journalists. A classic example was one of the endless attacks on the great Concorde programme in the 1970s when a well-known woman commentator in a BBC broadcast said that the best thing that could happen to Concorde would be for it to crash on its first flight. But she did not feel it necessary to mention the probable fate of the courageous test crews who had no ejection seat escape system on that civil airliner.

So, the First Flight is only an early stage, but an important one, in the arduous process to entry into service of a new aircraft which may take ten years of dedication and determination by all those involved.

From first flight to into-service experimental and development trials and production service acceptability, tests continue to involve from 2,000 to 3,000 hr of intensive testing. Most of this work is progressive and routine in nature (inasmuch as any fast-jet flying in the ever changing skies can be 'routine') once the full flight envelope has been explored and established satisfactorily in relation to specification and customer requirements. But there is always an element of the unpredictable which must be taken into full consideration in the planning for each sortie, no matter how mundane the requirements on the test schedule appear to be.

In over 40 years of flying, from Hurricanes to Tornados, I can recall many instances of the unplanned and unexpected encroaching into the professional calm of a test flight. For example:

The starboard undercarriage of a Hurricane II self-lowering during a production schedule 400 m.p.h. dive, tearing off the brake hydraulics as it went, at Langley in 1942.

A Tempest V airscrew overspeeding (failure of an hydraulic seal) just after take-off at Langley in 1943; and aileron overbalance with geared tabs on the first production Tempest at 500 m.p.h. indicated airspeed (IAS).

A Meteor IV encountering compressibility pitch-down at very low level during flight envelope expansion from Moreton Valence in 1946.

A canopy failure resulting in explosive decompression at 43,000 ft in a Vampire on clearance tests at Samlesbury in 1947 (no pressure suit was available at that period).

The first experience of incipient elevator flutter coupling with 'eight-cycle' airframe natural frequency in the prototype B.3/45 Canberra on flight 3 from Warton in 1949.

Canopies coming off the P.1 at high speed (trans and supersonic) from Warton 1955 (one with the author and two with Desmond de Villiers).

Repetitive fire warnings and engine bay fires in the P.1B Lightning programme, 1957–65.

Catastrophic fin failure in high Mach number, roll-yaw coupling on Lightning T.4 and T.5 prototypes, in the 1960s at Warton (J. W. C. Squier and J. L. Dell ejected safely).

Near losses at Warton of the Canberra B. Mk 5 prototype (Hillwood) and the second Tornado prototype (Millet) in bird strikes.

Repetitive undercarriage malfunctions on the TSR.2 prototype, resulting in an emergency landing on flight 5.

Near losses of development Tornados at Warton and Turin in landing pilot-induced oscillation (PIO) incidents in the 1970s; and the tragic loss of another with its crew over the Irish Sea in 1979; and so on.

The high-technology era of the 1990s, with its dependence on advanced computer control of the total operation, shows no sign of eradicating human error as a source of potential danger in flight development. There is a continuing need for test pilots to be trained and alert for any possible eventuality in their work, and even some that 'experts' will inevitably say are not possible!

The testing of the whole capability of a new aircraft is a fascinating task with clearly definable targets and still, for the test pilots, some intriguing and possibly dangerous unknowns. Much of this work is repetitive and routine but it is sometimes enlivened by unexpected arisings, some of which are described in the following pages.

The clear professional aims of testing and military flying contrasted sharply with the uncomplicated tranquillity of the open-cockpit biplane flying of the 1930s, and with the administrative and philosophical turmoil encountered subsequently in the industry in the late 1960s and the 1970s. But it all added up to a fascinating 40 years for me.

Chapter One

Fledgling

The chalk downs of Stoke Clump, Goodwood's Trundle Hill and Halnaker's conical mound with ancient windmill atop shimmered in the heat-haze of a late June summer day. The only sounds were a whispering breeze waving the grasses on the bank and in the field beyond, and the wonderful continuous chorus of skylarks, so dense that no individual bird could be identified. Sussex in the 1930s was so different from the farm-chemical ravaged countryside of the 1990s.

It was perfect peace. No vehicles had passed down the lane behind for over an hour, but suddenly there came a distant sound, rising and falling for a time and then a continuous exciting note — the Rolls-Royce Kestrel engine of a Hawker Fury! A search of the sky, glaring with the morning sun in the south-east, failed to reveal anything and then there, a flash of light on burnished aluminium cowling and silver-doped biplane wings! A Fury biplane fighter returning to Tangmere, the RAF base of Nos 1 and 43 Squadrons for the strategic defence of Portsmouth Naval dockyard to the west and London to the north.

This was what a 14-year-old had bicycled six miles from home at Summersdale near Chichester to see. The silver biplane curved easily overhead towards the easterly wind and then right-handed back towards the west and began a gentle descent. It was going

Author making a Hawker Fury model, 1932. (Author)

Hawker Furies of No. 1 Squadron at Tangmere in the 1930s. (Author)

to make its landing approach right over where I was lying in the grass! Now completing the final turn, the Fury seemed a little high and then down went the inside wing in a strong sideslip (a technique which I would learn in years to come with firm use of crossed controls and the slipstream pummelling the face from one side in the open cockpit).

Now the thin silver wings and shining engine cowling were only hundreds of yards away, with the throttled engine popping and banging, and then with a swoosh of exhaust-fume-laden slipstream and an elegant fish-tailing with flailing rudder the Fury flashed overhead at about 50 ft, the pilot's helmeted and goggled head leaning left to see the grass ahead of his exhaust stubs and the long shining Kestrel engine cowling.

The wheels touched before the tailskid — bounce! Then another and finally one more small one and the beautiful biplane was slowing down in the green but already slightly browned grass, leaving a small trail in the air of dust, grasses and exhaust smoke.

He stopped with the big wooden propeller slowly ticking over and then with a burst of throttle to swing the tail round began to taxy back straight towards my point of vantage on the airfield boundary. Here was a bonus! Perhaps the pilot was not satisfied with his bumpy arrival and was going to try another!

So it was that this beautiful biplane fighter, gleaming silver with the red bars of No. 1 squadron on its top wing and fuselage sides, swung round and stopped not 30 yd from a fascinated boy. Then joy of joys the pilot waved to him, swung again into wind with a burst of power and rudder, and then with full throttle raised the tail and accelerated away to take-off again in a cloud of dust, leaving a scent of hot engine exhaust and sunwarmed grasses that would remain with the boy for the rest of his life — which, in the event, turned out to be much longer than he could have subsequently reasonably expected.

First flight for RPB. An Avro 504 at Sommersdale near Chichester in 1927. (Author)

Goggles rather too large for this aircrew member. (Author)

Second Flight. Fox Moth, Selsey 1932. Pilot C. W. A. Scott – England–Australia record holder. (Author)

Interest in flying was not for me a sudden urge or a desperate teenage mood to 'do something'! It began with a first flight in a 'barnstorming' Avro 504 near my home at Chichester in 1927. My father seemed a little apprehensive at my demands to go and see 'the aeroplane in the field'; but when he had negotiated the fare for a flight, five shillings, he said: 'You'll be quite all right, I'll come too' (the Avro carried the pilot and two passengers). I said that would not be necessary at all, but he was determined and came anyway!

The rush of wind in the open cockpit, and the sight of our village and home below in that short flight left an indelible impression. This was followed in 1932 by a flight in a de Havilland Fox Moth flown by the famous Charles W. A. Scott, who had only recently made a record solo flight to Australia. A red-letter day indeed.

By now my regular trips to Tangmere, supported by my dear mother with endless supplies of sandwiches and lemonade, were becoming a feature of our family life. I suspect that my mother was quite happy to have me well-occupied and out of the house!

At this period the RAF, with enlightened government support, had a well established policy for encouraging recruitment. Under the Schools Assistance scheme a father need only apply to his nearest RAF Station for an 'air-experience' flight for his son. This my father did and I duly reported to the adjutant of No. 1 Squadron at Tangmere to fly on a brilliant clear day, and again joy of joys, with him in a D.H. moth over Portsmouth and the great battleships of the Royal Navy.

By now, the mid-1930s, I could see no future occupation for me other than the Royal Air Force. In the environment of those times no question ever arose on the subject of if the son of the house was going to leave home after schooling. Of course he was, and he was actively encouraged to think about his future from an early age.

In my case I could not wait. My school days at Eastbourne had not been satisfying. I had not worked and knew it so this was on my conscience, and my preference for the RAF over the predominant career advice at school* of Army, the City, or the Church, in that order, was not met with any enthusiasm by my house-master or the 'Careers' master.

My father, continuing with quiet, steady support, arranged for another air-experience flight, this time at Halton in an Avro Tutor with a friend of his, Flt Lt Walkington. This time at the age of 16 I was allowed to take the controls, and that did it! Apparently I had paid attention to Walkington's briefing for I felt a great surge of

---

* Eastbourne College

Fourth flight. An Avro Tutor at RAF Halton in 1936, pilot Flt Lt Walkington. (Author)

confidence and enjoyment as the Tutor responded to my movements of the controls. It did not seem easy but it was not at all daunting. I wanted more, much more.

Walkington told my father that I had 'good hands and natural ability'. Neither of us could know that some eight years later his son John would serve as a fighter pilot in my Wing of Tempests in the hard fighting at Volkel in Holland in the battles for Germany.

So now a path was forming for the future. With sufficient 'credits' in the appropriate subjects in the Schools Certificate examination (the equivalent of GCSE in the system of the 1990s) I could apply for the RAF College at Cranwell and a permanent commission, but when I failed to obtain all the necessary passes I left Eastbourne and spent two terms cramming at Brighton to retake the exam. This time in 1938 I just managed enough passes at 'Credit' level to permit an application for a Short Service commission of five years in the RAF, but then another complication arose.

After the Munich crisis of 1937 it was rapidly becoming evident that Neville Chamberlain's 'Peace in our time' was no more than a pious hope. The clouds of war were gathering over Europe and for my parents (and all other parents) this was a dreadful situation. They had lived through the horror of the First World War only 20 years before and now, were we to face another probably even more terrible war?

My father had served through the Great War and now would serve again in the Active Reserve; and it seemed that their son would be caught up immediately in the air war of which none really understood the implications. Would it not be better, they said, for me to change direction and go into the Army? As I imagined that thoughts about my survival were uppermost in their reasoning I said, with the cheerful confidence of youth, that war in the air would be much safer than war on land or at sea. I was not sure why, but it sounded a good argument. And so it was settled!

In September 1938 my father drove us in our little Morris Ten up to London from our Chichester home through the leafy lanes of Sussex. With virtually no traffic we reached Hammersmith Bridge in under two hours, and the Aldwych half an hour later where we parked directly outside the Air Ministry at Adastral House for my interview. He said he would wait for me, and was still there with no problems when I came out three hours later.

Though somewhat overawed by the weighty headquarters atmosphere, coupled with the dawning feeling that I was suddenly committing myself from the relative freedom of teenage life at home to an unknown future which would most likely involve responsibility, discomfort and not a little danger, there was only a brief momentary thought that I could still walk out of the door before it was too late, and then I was into the physical examination by monosyllabic specialists followed by interviews with some rather paternal officers who, it seemed, were more interested in what I had done at school (which was not much) than anything else. To their final question: 'Why do you want to join the Air Force?', I said something to the effect that it was the finest of all the Services and that I wanted to fly more than anything whether or not there was a war, and that if necessary I wanted to fight for my country in the air. That seemed to do, and the senior interviewer said: 'You will hear from us in two weeks'.

After a quick meal in a Lyons Corner House we drove back out of London in the 'rush-hour' which in those days merely consisted of rather more traffic than there had been in the morning. As we climbed over the tranquil South Downs at Duncton Hill in the dusk I wondered at the ease with which it had been possible to go in apparently one step from a secure home and teenage freedom directly into a potentially demanding adult life. But that had indeed been the easy bit.

A Tiger Moth of No. 13 EFTS at White Waltham in January 1939. (Author)

Pupil pilots at White Waltham.
Author left front. (Author)

Promptly two weeks later a buff-coloured envelope with the Air Ministry seal on the back arrived with instructions that I had been provisionally selected for a Short Service Commission in the General Duties branch (flying) and that I was to report for *ab initio* flying training, still as a civilian, to No 13 Elementary and Reserve Flying Training School (EFTS) at White Waltham on 2 January 1939, and that a subsequent Commission would be dependent upon my successfully passing the White Waltham course.

The remaining weeks of 1938 flew by in preparation for leaving home and in taking what seemed like last opportunities for fishing the Avon at Braemore and combining wildfowling with birdwatching on the marshes and mudflats of Chichester Harbour, both activities in bitter weather with early snow which, I explained to my worried mother, was a good toughening process for what lay ahead. I also put in a strenuous

The author walking to his Tiger Moth in the mud and snow of January 1939. (Author)

run almost every evening for two months to improve my general fitness, which had not been enthusiastically commented on at the Air Ministry medical!

Then came the day in January 1939 when I piled my few belongings, which included trout rods, a twelve-bore and field glasses and my treasured fishing and bird diaries, into the slightly worn, bright red four-year-old MG which had been my father's generous response to my late plee: 'By the way I expect to be posted all over the place and I won't get much leave, so I don't suppose I'll be able to get home often unless I can get a car!' He said 'How much have you saved?' '£20' I said. 'OK,' he replied 'here's another £20, see what you can find.' In two days we found the MG for £45, and it made possible home visits for the next six months, including one '48 hr leave' from near Edinburgh to Chichester and back, night driving both ways. I arrived back at dawn at 5 a.m. with just time to change and get on parade at 6 a.m. for the morning PT run! But that was all in the future. Now the weeks at White Waltham were a blur of 6 a.m. PT parades, 30 min for breakfast, classroom lectures on theory of flight, aerodynamics, aircraft construction and engine design until 10 a.m. Then kitting up in ungainly Sidcot flying suits before waddling out to the line of Tiger Moth biplane trainers on the slippery, muddy field, or from mid-month onwards on the crinkling white covering of snow which made those January open-cockpit flights extremely cold and added complication to the student's already difficult tasks of judging the moment to flare for landing!

It was cold and uncomfortable, but every day was challenging and I enjoyed the flying. However my mentor, a very experienced and well respected Reserve instructor, Flt Lt Selby Loundes, did not appear to share my enjoyment and towards the end of January when I had some 10 hr dual some of the quicker learners of the course had already gone solo.

I seemed to be managing with basic aerobatics, spinning, and practice forced-landings, but the quality of my landings was clearly not meeting with approval in the front cockpit. They therefore began to get worse!

I perceived that a crisis was approaching. We had been informed that the cut-off point was 15 hr dual. If after that the student had not soloed he was 'up for a bowler hat' — that is, discharge.

Worried and puzzled by this I could only see each flight going well enough, but ending with a poorly judged approach, or a bad 'hold-off' and a bouncing 'arrival'. No particular comment came from the front cockpit, and the silence was even more unnerving!

Then came the day when I had had 14½ hr instruction and on 'the Flights' notice board my name was down not with my instructor but the Chief Flying Instructor (CFI). If this was to be the final curtain there was no doom in the manner of the CFI, the much respected 'Pan' Cox, of whom we were all rather in awe. With a friendly smile he said: 'Now, we'll just do a standard circuit and landing — imagine I'm not here'

I settled into the now familiar narrow cockpit, pulled down the Sutton harness, connected my 'Gosport' speaking tube and said: 'Ready to start, Sir'. 'Go ahead' he said, 'she's all yours'.

Carefully following the approved starting drill I finally called to the mechanic standing in front of the propeller: 'Switches off, suck in'. He repeated the words and then pulled the propeller over twice. I said 'Switches ON, contact' moving the ignition switches to ON and setting the throttle. The engine caught at the first swing of the propeller and once it was running smoothly I waved away the chocks from under the wheels (the Tiger Moth had no brakes).

I taxied out over the rough and by now familiar field towards the take-off point at

Number 13 EFTS White Waltham from the Tiger Moth's cockpit. (Author)

the far (eastern) boundary, swinging the nose from side to side to watch for other aircraft, and then stopped 'cross-wind' to run-up to full throttle and check each ignition switch for magneto drop. All was normal. I throttled back and then scanned the sky to ensure no aircraft on the approach (there was no air traffic control on training airfields in 1938) and said through the voice tube: 'All set Sir, no aircraft on approach or on the take-off run'. 'Off you go' said the voice.

Turning into wind with a burst of throttle and hard right rudder to kick the tailskid round on the rough grass I opened the throttle fully, eased the stick forward until the tail began to lift, checked back at about 50 m.p.h. and the bumping ceased.

Hold her straight, climb at 65 to 800 ft. Turn left 90°, level out and check all round for other aircraft — one Tiger Moth crossing ahead on the Downwind pattern. He was going to land ahead of us and would need watching.

Approaching the wood beyond the south-west boundary, turn left 90° downwind. Well placed for the cross-wind leg turning point, a house beyond the south-east boundary. Check engine instruments — all OK. Now turn 90° over the house, on to the base leg and reduce power to 70 m.p.h.

Tiger Moth ahead banking into its final approach — follow it, but not too close. Check height 800 ft for final turn — turn left 90°, throttle back to gliding and line up for landing run — the aircraft ahead landing and should be clear for us.

Airspeed indicator (ASI) back to 60 m.p.h. and hold — a little high so left stick and right rudder into a gentle sideslip to lose about 100 ft — about right; level up.

Remember a short burst of throttle to clear plugs in case of need to overshoot. OK, throttle right back 'over the hedge'. The Tiger Moth ahead now well clear. Don't flare too early and drop it! At 50 ft the grass below starting to blur. Ease the stick back smoothly — don't 'seize' on it. Back more, the nose rising high into the forward view. Watch the field ahead over the left side forward of the lower wing.

Then a gentle pitch forward from the tailskid and the main wheels started rumbling. No bounce, a perfect 'three-pointer'.

It was miraculous. I realised that I had not only made my first decent landing but that I had not thought once of the voice in the front cockpit which had not said a word throughout.

As the Tiger Moth trundled to a halt the front cockpit said: 'Turn round and go back to the boundary', and nothing more. What had I done wrong? Was I going to have to do it all again? These and other worries teemed through my head as we bumped with gusts of exhaust smoke back to the east side of White Waltham. 'Stop here' said the voice, and then the front cockpit harness straps flipped back as the CFI climbed out. He took off his helmet, hair blowing in the slipstream, and leaning into my cockpit with a beaming smile said: 'Nothing wrong with that — one circuit just like that. Then come in. Off you go!' He turned and walked away as if he had no further interest, which I knew was not the case.

So I did what he had told me, and in a few moments, again at 800 ft and turning into the standard landing pattern, I realised that for the first time there was no-one in the front cockpit. This traditionally should have produced instant feelings of uncertainty and insecurity, but with much still to do and only the briefest thought: 'There's no-one here but me to land this thing!', I felt nothing but growing confidence and determination that the coming landing would not only be safe but as good as the last one.

Well, it was not! It was safe enough but it bounced a bit so that when I taxied in it was without a triumphant silly grin. But I need not have worried and heard no more of a possible 'bowler hat'. The next few weeks of intensive solo flying interspersed with periodic checks with a new instructor were times of enormous enjoyment and rising confidence. Stalling, spinning, loops and rolls, engine off (throttle closed) forced-landing practice and then the big one — the solo cross-country flight; all 50 miles to Yatesbury and back and the immoderate feeling of self-confidence when sauntering across the Yatesbury tarmac from my parked Tiger Moth to report in and log my arrival, the return destination and estimated time of flight.

Then suddenly it was over and the course results were posted. My name appeared in the 'Passes' column (there had been five failures) with a posting to RAF Uxbridge the following week for induction and parade ground (squad drill) training as an acting pilot officer. My shortfall, I learnt much later, had been a classic case of instructor/student incompatibility. I had not inspired my initial instructor with confidence in me, and gradual awareness of this had progressively reduced my own self-confidence to the point of failure. I never looked back but became aware that I was a slow learner and fundamentally allergic to close supervision, a condition which I never completely overcame in a long career and lifetime! But I have always been so grateful to 'Pan' Cox.

The First World War atmosphere of Uxbridge with its old wooden hutted quarters, red-brick officers' mess and main buildings and wide asphalt parade grounds, together with the daily round of 6 a.m. PT runs followed by squad drill and then lectures on RAF regulations, responsibilities of junior officers, etiquette and mess rules, was not

A Hawker Hart trainer at Drem in 1939.   (Author)

unfamiliar to those of us who had experienced school Officer Training Corps training, though it was clearly puzzling to some of the others. But I think we were all surprised one day, some indignantly so, to be subjected by an aggressive and clearly resentful NCO to a diatribe with full barrack-room expletives, mostly unimaginative, on what we should not do when 'walking out' and, apparently more importantly and in great detail, what we should do when reporting back to 'the prophylactic room' at the Guard Room on our return!

Hawker Audax, Drem 1939.   (Author)

The Course was soon over and our posting notices appeared, mine to No. 13 Advanced Flying Training School (AFTS) at Drem near Edinburgh. Whether my beat-up MG could make such a long journey remained to be seen, but the following morning with one of my new friends on the Course, Hilary Edrich, we piled our few belongings behind the seats in the MG and headed for the north.

After night-stopping at a bed-and-breakfast near Boroughbridge it was a revelation to leave the smoke of the industrial Midlands behind and drive through the rolling hills of Northumberland and the Lammermuirs in sparkling air with visibility clear to the horizon in all directions. 'We're making good time' said Edrich. 'Oh yes', I said, showing off. 'I keep to a steady 50 m.p.h. — that's the way'. 'I don't know how you do it'! said Edrich.

And so down towards the conical hill of North Berwick Law with the waters of the Forth and Craiglieth Island ahead and the Bass Rock standing high out of the North Sea in the east. This was going to be good flying country indeed.

Turning into the main entrance at Drem was something of a surprise. This was no modern permanent RAF base, but rows of new wooden hutments against a background of ancient and run-down First World War hangars all indicated that it was a new development. The old grass airfield and buildings had until very recently been a pig farm and this we learned was all now being reactivated under the prevailing RAF expansion scheme. We were in fact to be the opening No. 1 course of the new FTS.

The author under training at Drem. No 'wings' yet. (Author)

Waiting for my instructor in a Hawker Hart at Drem. (Author)

The author taking off from Drem in a Hawker Audax, 1939. (Author)

We students soon found that there would be little time for grousing about minor discomforts such as cold, unheated hutted quarters, mud everywhere and bare, unfurnished crew rooms where in the total absence of chairs and ash trays we students sat on the fag-end-strewn floor between flights.

As before, our days began with a 6.30 a.m. run this time from the aerodrome to Gullane village and back; a brisk experience in every sense in what seemed to be the prevailing bitter north-easterly wind, often rain or sleet laden, straight off the North Sea.

Then to the classroom for navigation, more theory of flight and basic studies of the Hawker Hart and Audax biplanes on which we were to qualify; and so down to 'the Flights' for the day's instruction.

With nothing remotely resembling modern changing facilities we kitted up in the concrete floored open-ended and windswept new hangar where we were each allotted a tin 'flying clothing' cabinet for our blue airman's dungaree overalls (no dignity of a flying suit at that stage), leather helmet and 'Gosport' speaking tube, goggles and leather gauntlets.

My first sortie in a Hawker Hart was eagerly anticipated although with a little

Climbing away from Drem in the Audax. (Author)

apprehension. After the 140 h.p. frailty of the little Tiger Moth the 500 h.p. Hart looked impressive, heavy and possibly quite a handful.

It is probable that in my eagerness I may not have taken in the instructor's first briefing because nothing of it has remained with me, but the first sortie really was memorable. Unlike the rear seated pupil in the Tiger Moth, the Hart Trainer was flown by the student from the front with his instructor in the back. The pupil looked ahead along the Kestrel engine cowling between the centre-section struts — there was no other head — you were in charge!

The voice from the back restored a more balanced view and commanded that we taxied out on the rough grass to the 'downwind' take-off point, watching for other aircraft and taking care not to use the wheel brakes too harshly (to avoid tipping up on the nose).

The big biplane rumbled easily down the field feeling much more substantial than the Tiger Moth, and then we were ready for the run-up checks. The Rolls-Royce engine belched exhaust smoke on either side as it cleared the plugs, and the big Watts laminated wood propeller became a blur in front.

Checks of the left and right magnetos showed mag-drops within limits. Pressures and temperatures OK. Control checks all round and then: 'Ready to go, Sir'.

North Berwick harbour photographed in a vertical dive by Allan Bishop over the author's shoulder. (Author)

With its castoring tailwheel the Hart turned easily into wind using the stick-lever with rudder pedal differential brakes, and then full throttle, raise the tail slightly and almost at once the rumbling ceased. Now here was the difference. The gusting 15 m.p.h. wind did not seem to affect the Hart, which sailed smoothly into the climb at 65–70 m.p.h. It felt immediately stable, smooth and 'solid'. Here was a real aeroplane and its response in bank and pitch were precise and sensitive, giving immediate confidence. Directionally it was so firm and true as to seem to render the rudder unnecessary.

I cannot recall the exercises on that sortie but retain a vivid impression of power, stability and ease of manoeuvre and of the growing enjoyment of being in the open cockpit of this fine aeroplane on this splendid sunny day among broken cumulus clouds, with the Lammermuirs' purple heather all around, the green farmlands sweeping down to the shining Forth and far to the north beyond Perth the white capped mountains of Tayside. The air was like champagne (though I would not have described it thus, not having experienced the beverage at that time) and this was real flying.

The voice from the back eventually said: 'Take her back and land. Remember the Rad cooler, watch out for other traffic and for the green light. In this wind you'll want to be dead into wind — check the windsock.'

In following all this I began to realise that the Hart almost flew itself, and that setting up the final glide approach was almost deceptively easy. So much so that as we approached the boundary I was a little too high and I said: 'Shall I sideslip or overshoot Sir?' 'Your decision' said the voice, so I sideslipped off a little height, throttled right back 'over the hedge' and with exhausts popping and the big propeller windmilling slowly in front, levelled out above the grass — too high and too fast I was sure! Here was the vital decision point. To open up and go round again or hold level until the speed dropped.

With commendable restraint as we arrived at mid-field still airborne there was no voice from the back. I eased the stick back at about 55 m.p.h. and 'rumble', we were

Returning to land the Audax at Drem. (Author)

down with plenty of room ahead to the boundary. In the event the Hart had almost landed itself, and I was soon to appreciate that it would do this repeatedly as long as you got it right on the approach.

The voice from the back said: 'That wasn't bad but you will have to get your approaches right — too high and fast on that one'.

From then on I was in a new world. The early cold spring merged into green-leafed summer with all too often the brilliant northern skies closing down to very low cloud and sea mist — the North Sea 'harr' which made flying and training more difficult but of course in the long term more effective.

Flying the Hart was a wonderful experience and then came the ultimate thrill of solo in the Audax light bomber (now relegated to the training role).

If I had ever had doubts they were now dispersed by the winds in the open cockpit in the Drem circuit, or sometimes on 'ceiling climb' to 15,000 ft (no oxygen). On a clear day the wonder of the whole of the Highlands spread out to the Western Isles and to Sutherland in the north, or we sometimes indulged in illegal and surreptitious solo low flying below the cliffs and over the rocks down the coast past the Bass Rock with its wheeling white clouds of gannets.

This sense of fulfilment, even euphoria, was sharply subdued one day when one of my new-found friends, Australian Allan Bishop, failed to return from a flight in the back (gunner's) cockpit of an Audax. Not wishing to miss any time in the air, he had gone as a passenger with another student who had then decided to 'beat up' his girl friend at a nearby house in the country and had crashed, killing them both.

I had the week before taken Allan for a break-neck dash in the MG down to my

Hawker Hart cockpit instruments. (Author)

home at Chichester in Sussex for a '48 hr leave', night driving both ways. Allan had said afterwards that flying Harts was a much safer occupation!

With his colleagues I escorted Allan's coffin at the Drem cemetery, and then came another shock. Apparently my course examination results had not reached the required academic standard, and I was up for a 'CFI's check'.

History was repeating itself, but this was different. At White Waltham I had been unsure of my flying, but now I was quite absolutely sure. This was something I could do, and do well I thought.

I need not have worried. The Second World War had just been declared and after a brief and unmemorable address by the CO at a station parade in which we students were told we were now at war, and a certain amount of subsequent banter about 'nice timing for the course — cannon fodder!', we had got straight on with the remaining syllabus to finish the course by the end of September.

This war emergency of course meant that the powers were going to retain anyone who could fly almost regardless of their academic standards. But I of course did not understand this and felt that I was again, and at this vital moment, on the point of discharge. The thought of having to join the Army or the Navy just did not occur to me. I just had to fly. Although I was not aware of much else other than my close circle of friends, our daily flying, and the awe-inspiring qualities of the instructing staff, I could not imagine what was coming next.

The CFI, whom we all regarded as God, was John Grandy, soon to become a distinguished Hurricane squadron commander in the Battle of Britain and much later Chief of the Air Staff, eventually retiring from the RAF to become Governor of Gibraltar. In fact he was one of our all-time most distinguished aviators who, when we walked out to the Hart Trainer, said with a great cheerful grin: 'Blowed if I know what this is about but let's see what you can do'.

The sortie included all the manoeuvres I had been trained in and had enjoyed in the Hart, and when Grandy said: 'Take her home', I felt that it had not gone badly as I set up the standard approach, eased the Hart gently over the hedge, checked back with the stick and rumbled smoothly on for a three-pointer.

Back at the tarmac I completed the shut-down procedures and waited for the CFI to climb out. Doing this with what I was to know in the future was his inevitable ruddy-complexioned broad grin he said: 'That was fine but you will have to sit the Nav exam again. Off you go'.

Reprieved at the eleventh hour together with fellow student Peter (Dutch) Hugo, who had also failed the first exams, we were the last on the course to receive our 'Wings'. Hugo went on to do great things in Fighter Command, becoming one of our most distinguished Spitfire wing leaders and at one time the youngest Group Captain in the Royal Air Force.

The final stages of the Course included more demanding and advanced exercises including the 'cross-country under the hood'. In this exercise the pupil was shut off from the outside world by the closing before take-off of a folding fabric-covered cockpit hood and he was required to fly by sole reference to the rudimentary (in those days) instruments over a triangular course with 40-mile legs, calculating his position and turning points by deduced reckoning (DR) navigation. Without radio, wind information or any means of cross-checking position this was always a tall order, but it probably gave some indication of the student's determination in uncomfortable, claustrophobic and rather unnerving conditions.

My 'blind' cross-country occurred on a day of unfavourable weather with low cloud, rain and quite severe turbulence, and once my instructor had set us up over the starting

Hilary Edrich and the author at Drem. Summer 1939.
(Author)

point south of Drem he said: 'You've got her' and I gingerly turned on to the first heading for Turnhouse. The second leg would be to Perth and the final leg back across the Forth to Drem, in all about one hour's 'blind' flying time at 130 m.p.h.

It was not long before the turbulence rocking the aeroplane and the unaccustomed heat in the hooded cockpit with no cooling slipstream began to tell and I soon felt nauseated. This led to disorientation and it needed intense concentration to maintain height, attitude and airspeed together with the 'air-plot' which should be giving our position relative to the flight plan.

With the first turning point time coming up I said: 'Turning starboard over Turnhouse for Perth' through the voice tube. There was no reply, so I struggled on until the cockpit chronometer indicated overhead Perth. I called the turn but there was still no reply. I began to wonder if there was anyone there.

Heading south and trying to steady the wildly swinging compass I realised that I had

The author and Allan Bishop and the red MG at Drem. (Author)

no real idea of where we were and could only continue and hope. Eventually in some particularly heavy 'bumps' the time was up — we should be at least somewhere near Drem! Then I made my big mistake.

Through the voice tube I said: 'ETA (estimated time of arrival) up Sir, where are we?' Back came the apparently reincarnated voice: 'How the Hell should I know — we've been in cloud for the last half hour!' Then he said: 'I've got her', the throttle came back and the altimeter slowly unwound from my tenaciously held 2,000 ft. There was quite a risk element at that point I thought, because the cloud base had been low when we started and the Lammermuir hills ten miles to the South of Drem were quite high. But apparently the instructor had calculated where my sightless wanderings had led us to, and we broke cloud only a few miles to the south-west of the aerodrome. In the circumstances I felt that my performance in difficult conditions had not been all that bad, but the instructor made no comment.

The term ended with the traditional 'dining-in night' with instructors and pupils in mess-dress — the last wearing of mess-kit for the duration of the war — the haggis was piped in and downed with the traditional dram, and the brandy that followed the port was enough to put the pupils at least on to a higher plane of social activity. In the rising hubbub in the ante-room after dinner a sudden silence was followed by a roar of approval and there, through the swing doors, appeared my red MG propelled by it seemed the majority of my colleagues on the Course!

What the Station Commander and staff thought of this was not immediately apparent, but someone said: 'Where are the keys Bee?' and I said: 'No you don't', climbed into the car and started it up with a roar and a cloud of blue exhaust smoke. Keeping the revs going I slipped in first gear and moved forward towards the ante-room fireplace with blue and gold mess kits peeling off on all sides.

'That will be enough' said a stern voice from the CO 'Take the bloody thing outside!'

With willing hands all round the MG started backwards through the swing doors, and then got stuck. The combined initiatives of the directing staff and pupils then failed to resolve how to swing it round back the way it had come' in, down the steps and through the main entrance doors, until someone had a brainwave. 'Shove it across the hall into the instructors' ante-room', he said. And so it was that when the instructors came in in the morning, probably with sore heads like the rest of us, they could not have a quiet five minutes with the newspapers because there was a red car in the way!

During the final week at Drem I was walking one evening with Hilary Edrich round the short promenade bordering the little bay at North Berwick when we sighted the figure of a girl running along the tideline with a dog. From a distance she looked attractive and Edrich said: 'I bet you daren't speak to her!' 'I'll bet I will' I said and, jumping down on to the sand, walked over towards her feeling slightly incongruous in 'best blue' uniform and highly polished black shoes on the wet sand.

The girl appeared not to notice my arrival and chased the labrador further into the wavelets. With my black shoes now immersed I said: 'Hello, lovely dog'. She turned with a smile that lit up the evening and said: 'Yes isn't he!' Frantically seeking an impressive or even adequate follow-up I said: 'I've got an MG over there — like to have a ride?' Doubtfully she replied: 'There are two of you' looking over to where Edrich was monitoring progress. 'Oh not now' I said, 'when I've got rid of my friend sometime.' 'Well perhaps I could manage next Sunday', she said. 'I'll pick you up at your home' I said. 'No' she answered firmly, 'here at 2.30. Now I must go' and with another smile which took my breath away she ran off with the dog.

I watched her slim upright figure, flowing golden hair and swinging tartan skirt as she darted like a sandpiper through the shallows but with the grace of a swan. She seemed about seventeen. Edrich said: 'You're on to something there Bee' in a tone that suggested that he had missed the boat. I confirmed that he had.

Promptly at 2.30 p.m. on the Sunday I parked the MG just where I liked on the front — no parking problems in the 1930s! She appeared along the tideline but with no dog. This was encouraging. She thought it would be nice to just go round to Berwick Law and climb it. So we did, and this supposedly fit young officer was soon blowing hard up the steep slope of the Law with the tartan skirt swishing through the heather ever further ahead. She was sitting serenely on the top looking out across the sparkling Forth when I arrived, and said sweetly: 'What kept you?'

We talked and talked the afternoon away in the sun and wind, watching the gannets wheeling over the coastline, and it was clear that she was a country lover as I was. Far too soon she said: 'I must go. Take me back.' 'Where do you live?' I asked. 'No, back to the beach. I'll be in trouble if I am seen with a strange man' she said. 'I could get you into a lot more trouble than that', I said. 'You wouldn't get the chance' she said with peals of laughter. At that moment I thought she was the loveliest creature in the world.

Leaving her at Berwick I told her that I was soon to be posted away and 'how about the flicks (cinema) on Wednesday?' She said she would love that and would be there at seven.

Arriving much too early and parking the MG outside the cinema I waited for her, and waited some more. After an hour I went back alone to the aerodrome, wondering. In the next few days I went down to North Berwick as often as I could, but she never appeared.

Then came the Course posting to Armament Practice Camp at Evanton in the far north on the edge of the Cromarty Firth. This was to be ten days of magic, of biplane wings in formation winding through the glens of Tayside between towering cloud-topped and snow-capped mountains. Then letting down over the river Lossie to the coast and on past Findhorn and Inverness to the Cromarty Firth, with the mountains of Easter Ross dominated by Ben Wyvis rising ahead towards Sutherland on the far horizon.

Landing in loose formation behind my section leader and taxying in from the small grass aerodrome to the line of Harts, Audaxes and a Hawker Fury fighter. On climbing down from the cockpit with the Kestrel exhausts ticking as they cooled, the sound of curlew, redshank and geese from the salt marshes just beyond the boundary and the air a heady mixture of heather, pine and salt estuary.

Days spent flying solo along the mountain-edged coast past Invergordon to the Tain range, there to dive on 15 ft gunnery targets, sighting through the ring-and-bead sight in front of my windscreen and firing my Vickers 0.303 in machine gun with its recoil mechanism hammering away in my cockpit, all too close to my left knee.

An adequate number of hits recorded by the 'range party', then air-to-air attacks on the drogue target towed by another Audax. Great care was needed to establish a line of attack which would not shoot down the towing aircraft!

Finally and most exhilarating of all, dive attacks on the white 'bombing circle' with '4½ lb bombs practice smoke'. The method was to approach the target circle at the briefed height and direction until the target was in sight to port and just forward of the left lower wing centre-section. Then, throttle back, wing-over and down, rolling out to wings level in a 45° dive (or thereabouts!). Centre the target in the ring-and-bead gunsight and press the bomb release. My first missed by too much, but the second was on the edge of the ring and the third and fourth inside it. This was good for morale; especially so when a second sortie produced similar results.

Then the short homeward flight along the slopes of the high hills with the spate rivers Glass and Alness below shining with foaming invitation to this frustrated young fisherman with no time or opportunity to try them.

Later a few beers in the mess and early rising next morning often in sharp frost and crystal clear air to the spectacular horizon in every direction, and always the curlews and the salt tang of the Firth.

On one such beautiful morning it was my turn as Station Duty Officer to take 'Colour Hoisting' parade at 7.30. This, my first solo and non-training ceremonial, was a slight ordeal, but it was successfully steered by the awe-inspiring but strangely understanding and helpful Station Warrant Officer. Then breakfast, and leap into the cockpit for the new day's flying.

No thought of war or of anything but the magic of those days. On one of these, a Wednesday and still regarded as 'Sports Afternoon', I elected to walk up the glen past the tumbling, foaming river Glass towards the mountains inland. After an early white frost the sun was hot on the heather and the air itself sweeping down from the north-west through the mountains was part of the magic of the day.

I walked the glens around dramatic Cnoc Ceislein all day and, returning to Evanton too late for dinner, went to bed hungry but full of wonder. This country, this flying and now the surging feeling of confidence that I could indeed fly well, enjoyed every second of it, and would be able to handle that department whatever the future might bring, was all magic. I knew it could not last but enjoyed it to the full right through to our last flight at FTS.

The day came in early October when we flew back from Evanton to Drem, solo this time as an indication that being qualified we no longer needed leading by an instructor. There was cold, grey overcast on the day and a little worry on reaching Lossiemouth that the dark clouds ahead with mountains rising into them on either side would make it difficult to find and fly through them.

We had not yet been trained in over-weather flying and the standard procedure was 'under-the-weather', but I found and flew down the majestic Tay where, in times to come with my dear wife of so many years, we would catch some majestic salmon. Then down to the coast of Fife and out across the grey foam-flecked Forth towards Craiglieth, and finally in the mist and rain the North Berwick Law of recent poignant memory.

Touching my Audax down easily on the Drem grass for the last time and taxying towards our north-west tarmac area by the new hangars I saw a line of monoplane fighters dispersed along the northern boundary — Spitfires! With my friends we crowded round these surprisingly small, lithe and beautiful fighters — could we have skill enough to fly them was the unspoken thought shared I'm sure by all of us. I noticed that these camouflaged fighters had the squadron code 'PR' on their fuselage sides, but I could not know that in only three years' time I would command that squadron.

The notice board had our postings at last, some to bombers, to coastal or training, and some in a short list to fighters. With my friends Edrich, Harriman and Hugo, my name was there on the fighters list and I was posted to RAF St Athan in South Wales.

I had already lost my friend Allan Bishop, and before a full year was out Edrich and Harriman were to die in battle. But now it was all rush to clear ourselves from Drem. The famous Edinburgh-to-London express, the 'Flying Scotsman' was to stop at the Drem halt especially to load up No. 1 Course.

I made quick temporary arrangements to leave the MG for servicing with the Scottish Motor Traction company, and then loaded, with my excited colleagues and our kit into three-tonner Crossley trucks for the station.

There in the cold, gathering dusk we clambered into the for us unprecedented luxury of first-class compartments, all green leather upholstery and shining mahogany. Settling down, I looked out along the platform to where a group of girls were waving, some laughing and some tearfully, at their departing heroes. Then she was there. The girl in the tartan skirt was standing alone, unsmiling and peering into each carriage window. I started to get up but the train was moving. She had not reached my carriage. The train entered a bend and she was lost to sight. I have always hoped that the fates were kind to 'tartan skirt'.

Chapter Two

Hurricane Years

In 1939 I commenced training on the new Hawker Hurricane 'eight-gun' fighters, and flew them in combat in 1940 in the Battles of France and Britain and in the night Blitz of 1940/41. Luckily surviving this, I was then posted to test Hurricanes at the Hawker factory at Langley from November 1941 to June 1942, and some interesting incidents occurred during these 'Hurricane' years.

HURRICANES IN COMBAT AND FLIGHT TEST

In October 1939 No. 11 Group Fighter Pool (Operational Conversion Unit (OCU)) at RAF St Athan was equipped with Hawker Hurricane Mk Is fitted with Watts two-blade fixed-pitch wooden propellers, and after 5 hr dual on Harvards and 2 hr solo the students made their first flight in the fighter which was soon to become famous in the Battle of Britain.

St Athan, near Cardiff, was an almost circular all-grass airfield which proved helpful to most of the students in their early and often unsuccessful attempts to stop their North American Harvard trainers ground-looping in the landing run.

Another advantage of having no runway was of course that the take-off could always be made directly into wind as indicated by mandatory prior reference to the windsock, already standard procedure for the students fresh out of training on Hawker Hart and Audax biplanes.

A North American Harvard trainer of No. 1 Fighter Pool, St Athan, in October 1939. (Author)

A Hurricane I in the markings of 1939/40. (Author)

The author with his first Hurricane, St Athan October 1939. (Author)

One's first flight in a Hurricane was always going to be memorable. This, the Messerschmitt Bf 109E and the Spitfire represented the highest state of fighter technology and performance in the world at that time and only recently a Hurricane of 111 Sqn had gained world-wide acclaim by averaging over 400 m.p.h. from Edinburgh to London — the pilot, the squadron CO, was not known as 'Downwind Gillan' thereafter for nothing!

To a student with experience only of 100 m.p.h. Tiger Moths, 170 m.p.h. Harts and now 185 m.p.h. Harvards the Hurricane with its 1,000 hp Rolls-Royce Merlin engine and eight 0.303 in Browning machine-guns seemed a menacing giant of an aircraft — and there would be no instructor on board. This would be going in at the deep end!

The Harvard had in fact given me brief experience of the increased inertia of a heavy, all-metal aircraft with cleaner aerodynamics resulting in much quicker acceleration in the dive than that of the biplanes; but the reality of the Hurricane was still impressive.

First impressions on strapping in were that the cockpit was similar in layout to that of a Hart with only the added undercarriage and flap controls as additions to the vital actions; and of course the reflector gunsight in the windscreen. The engine panel was very similar, and engine starting after correct action with the Ki-gas pump was straightforward.

Taxying with the familiar control-stick mounted differential brake lever was easy, and so to the line-up, first checking back to ensure no in-bound landing traffic while awaiting a 'Green' Aldis light from the 'Duty Pilot' (no air traffic control radio control in those days).

With tail trimmer set, throttle and mixture lever fully forward with friction screw tightened and puffs of grey exhaust smoke soon clearing at max r.p.m., then came the surprise! No sudden surge of acceleration but, with thunderous roar from the exhausts just ahead on either side of the windscreen, only a steady increase in speed as the Hurricane lurched and bumped over the rough grass pulled by its ponderous fixed-pitch propeller.

Now to concentrate. Smooth forward stick to raise the tail, but not too far bearing in mind Mike Lister Robinson's (OCU flight commander) kindly instruction: 'Don't get the tail too high or you'll break the bloody prop'! But already the far boundary was rapidly getting near with the ASI only rising slowly past 50 m.p.h. It had to be 65 for take-off and that hedge ahead looked enormous. Then 65 at last and with more a snatch than an ease-back on the stick the Hurricane leaped over the boundary and settled into the climb towards the mountains of Wales with an immediate feeling of solid stability and assurance. Here was an aeroplane that felt secure and at ease with itself, and not in any sense 'knife-edged' in controllability.

Now to the briefed sequence: change hands to left on the stick and right to select the undercarriage UP gate and then press and hold down the hydraulic retraction lever. Awkward this, and some disturbance in pitch and roll while holding the climb at 120 m.p.h. with the left hand until retraction was complete.

Throttle back to cruise r.p.m. at 2,000 ft and check navigation, and then the next surprise. This thundering fighter was gathering speed prodigiously and the landmarks were disappearing behind at a rate which was becoming disorienting. The cruising speed of 240 m.p.h. IAS was already faster than the diving speed permitted in our old Hart biplanes. It was going to be very easy to get lost in this aeroplane and a turn back towards the South Wales coastline on this clear morning ensured easy map reference for the rest of the sortie.

Now the radiator temperature was dropping and the radiator flap was set to 'closed' (mental reminder to open it for full-power climb if needed). The training schedule called for 'feel of controls in Rate 1 to Max Rate turns at 200 m.p.h. and not below 2,000 ft. Climb to 10,000 ft and slow down to "stall approach", clean and in landing configuration. No full stalls. Dive to 300 m.p.h. and return to base.'

With these exercises completed there was an immediate feeling of relief and then positive enjoyment. This aeroplane responded easily and precisely in manoeuvre at low and high speed — at full throttle it had reached 300 m.p.h. IAS (a terrific speed for a student) in only a shallow dive, and its quoted maximum diving speed, a dramatic 400 m.p.h., IAS seemed no longer a mythical figure — we would soon try this!

With 45 min already on the time-of-flight clock the sortie seemed only to have just begun but it was time to turn back up the coastline from Swansea and, even throttled back in descent from 10,000 ft, the ASI soon rose above 300 again and St Athan appeared ahead in only a few minutes. By now this impression of great speed was leading to some apprehension; how to slow this thing down to land on what now began to look like a far-too-small aerodrome!

Joining circuit at 1,000 ft downwind and giving the required wing-rock signal request for landing resulted in an immediate 'Green — clear to land;' those on the ground being well on the alert for a 'new boy' on his first Hurricane solo.

Slow down to 100 m.p.h. Undercarriage down and locked with accompanying rumbling and trim disturbance. Turn on to long finals and flaps down at 85 m.p.h. Sharp nose-down trim change easily trimmed back on the elevator trim wheel.

Throttle down to near idling to steady at 75 m.p.h. and then the boundary seemed to rush up towards us. Over the boundary a bit high, throttle right back with popping and banging from the exhausts and a clear impression of the great wooden propeller ticking over in front and the feeling that this aeroplane is never going to stop! Then flare out with easy response to stick movement. A long float — are we still too fast? Then the rumble of, miraculously, a three-point-touchdown at about mid-field.

On with the wheel brakes very gently with the long propeller tips in mind, and then the Hurricane was rolling and bumping slowly enough to turn back towards dispersal and taxy in, swinging the nose from side to side with the differential wheel brakes to ensure a clear path to the tarmac. It had all been much easier than a Harvard!

In retrospect that first Hurricane sortie was a moment of elation but also of relief. Apart from the new scale of speeds that the pilot had to adapt to, the Hurricane had all the qualities of its stable, secure biplane predecessor the Hart, but enhanced by livelier controls, greater precision and all this performance. It was not going to be all that difficult to cope with and it was going to be an exciting and pleasurable experience; and so it proved to be in the critical days of 1940. Meanwhile our squadron postings appeared on the notice board and mine was to the British Expeditionary Force at Lille in France!

In the following winter of 1939/40 with 87 Sqn it was difficult to amass flying hours and experience on our Hurricanes owing to long periods of very bad weather, but every achieved sortie led to increasing confidence and by the spring of 1940 close formation flying, formation take-offs and landings (easy with the Hurricane's wide under-carriage and stable, non swing-prone ground characteristics) and limited practice combat were all part of the normal routine and very enjoyable too in this fine aeroplane.

We took our Hurricanes into major combat on 10 May 1940 from an advanced airfield with tented accommodation at Senon near Metz which was bombed and strafed at dawn on that day by low flying Dorniers; and from then until evacuation on 20 May we had little time to evaluate anything beyond the daily reducing chances of coming out of all this alive. What was becoming clear was that our Hurricanes could

No. 87 Fighter Squadron at Lille, Vendeville in November 1939. The author is fourth pilot from the right, running. (Imperial War Museum)

catch Dorniers and Heinkels, and also Junkers Ju 88s just, but they could not catch full-throttle Bf 109s or Bf 110s. But we could out-turn all of those, and we soon found that the Hurricane's gun-aiming accuracy was very good.

In fact confidence in our aircraft increased with every sortie, and the cause of our heavy casualties was put down to the enemy's overwhelming superiority in numbers and not to any superiority in the quality of their equipment or aircrew.

In the intensive combats now occurring every day the Hurricane was seen to be reliable, easy to operate off rough grass fields, easy to fly in formation and extremely capable in close combat manoeuvres against tough, experienced opponents in high-quality aircraft. The only disadvantage that showed up soon was rather restricted vision from the cockpit due to the canopy frames, but vital rear-view scanning was obtainable by sliding back the canopy (which the pilot of the '109 with its side-hinged canopy could not do) and 'clearing the tail' by yawing/rolling left and right.

A Hurricane I of 87 Sqn refuelling in the hard frost, Lille, December 1939. (Imperial War Museum)

In close combat we could not match the '109 in climb or dive but could out-turn it and out-roll it, especially above 300 m.p.h. indicated when the '109 became almost 'locked-solid' laterally. Furthermore, a full throttle 'corkscrew' dive in the Hurricane would get any '109 off your tail. The '110 was no problem in close combat except that it could get away from a Hurricane in a steep dive.

The Hurricane was a steady instrument flying platform day and night, and its easy landing characteristics with wide undercarriage and good, positive elevator made it a very practical fighter for night and bad-weather flying as 87 and other squadrons were to show in the winter of 1940/41 when the Hurricane's role was changed to night defence after the successful conclusion of the mainly daylight Battle of Britain.

With experience came increasing confidence in our aircraft. The Hurricane was superb and met every requirement no matter how extreme some of our 'ops.' orders from HQ No. 10 Group seemed to be, and also some that we devised for ourselves! In the bad days of 1940 throughout the Battle of Britain, 87 had maintained a proficient formation aerobatic team, the precise flying controls and responsive engines permitting precision formation through loops, barrel rolls, 1G semi-stall turns and rolls-off half loops, wing overs and, in suitable conditions, tight 'Vic-3' take-offs and landings on grass or runways.

We were able to achieve as standard drill wingtip overlaps to level with the leader's tailplane tip, although in my first formation aerobatic training sortie I had hit the leader's tailplane (New Zealander Derek Ward, my flight commander) and knocked a piece off it and also off my own wingtip. Saying: 'You won't do that again, we'll have another go', Derek led us off again in two serviceable Hurricanes and he was right — I never did that again!

The author's Hurricane I at the end of the Battle of Britain showing five victories and just fitted with glareshields in front of the windscreen for night fighting, October 1940. (Author)

Obergerfreiter Joseph Bröker and his Bf 109E at Cherbourg Maupertus whom, with another Hurricane, I shot down at Abbotsbury on 25 August 1940. He survived as a POW and we met again 50 years later! (Joseph Bröker)

The author with his father, a reserve Lieutenant Colonel just back from France, at the height of the Battle of Britain, August 1940. (Author)

So precise was this formation practice that it was seen as a means of maintaining high skill standards and of raising squadron morale, especially among our ground crew who took delight in noting that other squadrons did not do this sort of thing at that time.

Perhaps the ultimate demonstration of the great confidence engendered by our Hurricanes came in early 1941 when we extended these activities to formation aerobatics (with Vic-3s) by moonlight, and then in full darkness; and for many months in that winter it was normal for the formation team (Ward, Badger and myself) to take-off for '15 min aeros' when there was an early stand-down from night operations, before going off-base to bed.

My Hurricane was never hit in the Battles of France and Britain, and in over 700 hr on type I never experienced an engine failure although there was one hairy incident when in a pitch dark night take-off the engine coughed and spluttered with orange instead of blue exhaust flames. With clouds of acrid smoke which stung the eyes (canopy open for take-off) the engine lost power and it was only just possible to scrape round in the pitch darkness and back on to the flare-path — in the 'black-out' the fuel bowsers had been confused and the Hurricane had been topped up with paraffin!

In day combat the Hurricane had proved to have excellent gun platform stability and this, and the night flying skills acquired by 87 Sqn were now put to good use in a series of moonlight ground attacks carried out in the spring of 1941 from Warmwell over Normandy to Caen Carpiquet and Cherbourg Maupertus airfields. These were among the first fighter ground-attack operations to be carried out since Fighter Command had gone over to the offensive (in 1941), and they at once demonstrated the practicability of the Hurricane in this new role.

Factory test flying
A posting to the Special Duties list for attachment to the Hawker Aircraft Company for test flying duties came at the end of two years of continuous operations with Hurricane squadrons 87 and 79, from November 1939 to November 1941. It brought with it some marked contrasts.

Fighter pilot training and then the operational experiences of combat in France and the Battle of Britain had produced a heightened enjoyment of all aspects of flying including the risk element, and there was a tendency to disregard the latter and even at times take a chance quite unnecessarily for the hell of it. Getting back unscathed was always good for a laugh and cause for celebration!

At Hawkers I soon found that things were different. The essence of the work, I was told by assistant chief test pilot, Philip Lucas, (George Bulman, the Company's famous chief test pilot, was in America leading a team evaluating American fighters), was: 'No matter what happens on test, always bring it back!' And I was to immediately forget the acquired fighter pilot philosophy — 'When in doubt, bale out!'

The job, whether production schedule testing on Hurricanes or experimental and development work on the exciting new Typhoons and Tempests, was to carry out every flight with the greatest attention to all aspects of safety including the bad weather which, in the days before radar and any other navigational aids, was often a dominating feature. 'Bring back the aircraft and the test results' was the central theme, and one soon got into the swing of it. It was quite different to Service flying and every flight had significant technical interest — not merely chasing after the enemy and when over the sea hoping your engine would not stop, which seemed to a junior fighter pilot to be the core of squadron flying!

But after a few months of this new discipline with plenty of flying every day (on one particular day my log book records 11 Hurricane production test sorties between

9.00 a.m. and 4.30 p.m.) I began to feel an urge to return to squadron life, and so on 16 March 1942 I borrowed Hawker's Miles Whitney Straight two-seater communications aircraft, G-AEUT, and flew down to Westhampnett, the Tangmere satellite where my old friend from 13 FTS days, Pete (Dutch) Hugo, was commanding a squadron of Spitfire Vs.

Pete was most welcoming and said: 'We're just off on a low-level to Cherbourg, want to come?' Before he could change his mind I said 'Sure', and soon after found myself in a delightful but unfamiliar Spitfire, code EB-V, as Hugo's wingman with the rest of the squadron rising and falling on either side behind, very low over the sea and heading towards the enemy coast.

It made a change from test flying, and it was probably just as well that we had no action because there would have been a lot of explaining to do on all sides if I had failed to bring back my most irregularly 'borrowed' Spitfire from a show with a squadron to which I did not belong! But the flavour of the occasion, the operational atmosphere and the casual, humorous but determined style of Hugo's pilots, began to escalate my thoughts of getting back. My tour at Hawker was nominally for six months, and it was already being suggested that I could stay on longer. However the new Typhoon which I had been testing had given me other ideas.

Meanwhile there was all this testing to do every day, and on one beautiful clear early summer morning after completing the Hurricane's 400 m.p.h. dive over Reading I looked down at the Thames winding through the wooded slopes of Henley and Marlow, splendid in their mantle of fresh green leaf and looking most inviting, and decided to go back to Langley (near Slough) along the scenic route!

Down between the river banks at Henley, hopping over bridges as we came to them with the Hurricane at a comfortable 180 m.p.h., round bends and in between islands and the high banks, and then nose-down right on the water for a straight stretch between high trees on both banks towards Marlow — this was better than a sedate cruise home at altitude!

Now ahead a long island with houses on it and high trees on both banks. Right down to water level between the island and the right bank — a narrow channel this!

And then twang — flash! We had clearly gone through something; a telephone or power line, possibly both! What had seemed until then only mildly irregular now seemed positively irresponsible — the Hurricane might even be damaged let alone whatever was behind. Regretfully easing into a gentle climb I noted no problems with the aircraft and set course for Langley while pondering on the possibilities of repercussions!

Deciding that the best course would be to just see what developed, I joined the Langley circuit over the balloon barrage, silver-shining in the brilliant sun, and curved the Hurricane down into the Holmewood approach lane through the balloons. A normal landing and taxying in to the tarmac produced no unusual attention and as the Hurricane was 'off test' I shut down, put on the parking brake and climbed down.

The ground staff foreman then said: 'Hey, what's this?' and pointed to what looked like a fine black line spiralling round the fuselage from nose to tail, and similar marks on the wings! It had clearly been telephone wire at least but, I hoped, not high-tension power cables. There was nothing for it but to report the incident to the boss, and Philip Lucas, calm and phlegmatic as usual, asked: 'Just how low were you?'. I said: 'I thought I was under any phone wires between the banks and the island', and he said 'That low!' He then said we would await developments and not report to the authorities as he had enough trouble already with complaints of aircraft noise from the built-up areas all round Langley, Slough and Windsor.

Eventually a police constable turned up and said that there had been a reported incident at Marlow and did we know anything about it. Philip said: 'Can you identify the aircraft by type, code letters or serial number?' 'No' said the constable, 'Oh well,' said Philip, 'let us know if you can get them and then we'll see if we can help'.

I felt a bit guilty on a number of counts, and it helped me to realise that I was itching to get back to a squadron for some rather more exciting flying, and so I was delighted when the AOC of No. 11 Group appointed me to command 609 (West Riding) Squadron Royal Auxiliary Air Force, one of the first with Typhoons. But my colleagues in the Langley test pilots office maintained that 'Bee had been posted back to operations so that he could do his low flying over France where it would not create so much fuss!'

Hurricane Production Flight Test

Meanwhile, at the Hawker production and experimental factory at Langley in 1942, Hurricane Mk IIs armed with four 20 mm cannon were coming off the production line at 250 per month, and the test schedule for each aircraft was simple but thorough.

On first flight, after engine, hydraulics and wheel-brake checks a full-throttle/fine-pitch climb was made to rated (max power) altitude around 14,000 ft, recording engine figures and trims at 4,000 ft intervals; then straight into a 2 min maximum performance 'level' to record engine figures and IAS at 14,000 ft. This was followed by a dive to 400 m.p.h. IAS reached at about 8,000 ft, to check trim.

Lateral or directional trim asymmetrics would be noted, then straight down to 5,000 ft for stalls 'clean' and then with undercarriage and flaps down. This would be completed over the circuit then straight in to land and taxy in to the 'production' apron and, with engine kept running, call for some inches of trimming tape to be doped on rudder and/or ailerons — then take off and straight back up to 10,000 ft to repeat the dive checks for trims.

The process was repeated if symmetric trim had not been achieved first time; or, if engine or systems adjustments were needed first, the re-trimming would be cleared on the next or final flight. Most machines were 'cleared-test' in two flights, and few defects occurred.

Radio was not used in the test programme at all, apparently because it was judged that the notoriously unreliable TR9d and early very high frequency (VHF) sets would cause serious delays to the delivery programme! Radios were not fitted until after delivery to the maintenance units (MUs) where they were installed and tested for service.

All test flying was done without navigation aids of any kind (except when occasionally one of the Langley barrage balloons remained visible above cloud, which was very helpful to both sides!). But it was by no means only visual flight rules (VFR) — the pilots became very proficient in over-weather DR navigation and the basic weather minima were 1,200 yd visibility, 800 ft cloud base and clear airspace from 14,000 to 8,000 ft for the dive test!

The flying rate at the factory was high and eight to ten test flights per pilot each day not uncommon. For example on 14 March 1942 my log records 11 test flights (in Hurricanes BN953, '896, '976, '979, '978, '902 and '971) between 8.30 a.m. and dusk. A pint at the local was welcome after that!

The Hurricanes seldom gave trouble and in more than 400 test flights on them at Langley I only had one serious defect. On 24 December 1942, while diving Mk IIA Z5075 to 400 m.p.h. IAS, there was a loud bang and a violent lurch and yaw to starboard with a lot of buffeting roughness.

Throttling back sharply and kicking hard left rudder to reduce the yaw, I found the starboard undercarriage red light on and so, slowing carefully, I returned to Langley. Here 'airmanship' failed me — twice! Selecting undercarriage down produced thuds and the port green light, while the starboard remained red. With no radio communication there were no other means of checking the undercarriage, so I set up a careful approach past the edge of the Holme Wood repair factory area towards the south-west landing strip on Langley's quite narrow grass field, still with one green and one red undercarriage light.

At this point I should have checked two things — first the brake hydraulic pressure, and second that what at take-off had been a strong southerly wind was now a strong south-easterly! My main preoccupation of course was what would happen at touchdown if the possibly damaged starboard leg folded. But if that happened I reckoned that the aircraft might swing (or even cartwheel) to the right and well away from all the new production Hurricanes and a few of the new 'experimental' Typhoons parked along the tarmac stretching in front of the main works buildings on the left.

I felt that this was being suitably responsible. After all I was not about to jump out and abandon the Hurricane — I had been told by the chief test pilot Philip Lucas: "No matter what happens, always bring it back".

The next thing that happened was a gentle touchdown on apparently both wheels, and with throttle right back as the aircraft slowed on the rough, bumpy grass I began to think that this was a job well done. Then we began gently but persistently to veer to the left! Full right rudder held the swing momentarily then, as the speed dropped and the rudder lost effectiveness, progressive right brake had no effect at all!

Now I appreciated the wind veer. We were weathercocking into a south-easterly from the port side and the differential brakes were not working! Quite right — the brakes hydraulics gauge showed zero! Things now slotted more clearly into place — the dive incident, which must have been an unselected lowering of the starboard undercarriage, probably tore off the fairing and with it the brake hydraulic lines. We were now weathercocking purposefully round towards all those brand new Hurricanes on the Flight Shed tarmac — and there was not a single way of stopping before hitting them unless I retracted (at least part of) the undercarriage!

There were now only seconds and a hundred or so yards before impact — just time to consider which action would cause the least damage. On balance I thought that retraction could well damage a wing and the propeller and shock-load the engine, while a now gentle trundle at low speed into another Hurricane might result in only light damage; so I switched off the ignition and in silence and a spirit of resignation rolled off the grass on to the tarmac and into clanging collision with another brand-new Hurricane which, I was very soon informed by the Flight Shed foreman, 'had just been bloody well put off-test'!

I learned about flying from that; more especially that one should never concentrate on one brilliant solution to an in-flight problem to the exclusion of due consideration of all other possibly related aspects.

In sum the Hurricane was a rugged, straightforward fighter to fly, good in bad weather and with its wide undercarriage and 65 m.p.h. final approach speed not critical to land in adverse conditions of rain, snow and rough surfaces. The pilots enjoyed flying it and had great confidence in it, knowing that they could not break it by rough handling; and it was not until the Bf 109Fs arrived with improved performance in 1941–42 that the Hurricane's performance became no longer adequate for the major air defence and air superiority roles in the West. But the Hurricane still continued to give good value world-wide in the campaigns where the latest and more powerful fighters were not available to the enemy.

In 1940 those of us who flew Hurricanes enjoyed them hugely and had no reason to feel that they were inferior to the enemy — we just wondered how long the Luftwaffe could go on taking it!

The Hurricane I Compared in 1940 with Spitfire I

The Spitfire's elegance fired the imagination of everyone and the solid, staid-looking Hurricane seemed dull by comparison; but the two types made a much more closely matched pair than had been recognised by many subsequent 'historians'.

The Spitfire had a marginally higher climb rate to 15,000 ft and a steady improvement on up to its operational ceiling at around 32,000 ft which was about 2,000 ft above that of the Hurricane. The Spitfire was 30–40 m.p.h. faster over the altitude range but its practical dive limit was the same at 400 m.p.h. IAS though with a significant difference. A Hurricane could be 'corkscrew' dived at full bore at that speed, vertically and with full aileron still responsive to the limit, and nothing would break then or in the subsequent strong pull-out.

In this manoeuvre or in straight pull-outs from high speed dives there was a strong possibility of pulling the wings off a Spitfire — at least 23 are known to have done it and this was a clear incentive to the Spitfire pilot not to do it, but if circumstances included a '109 on your tail this presented a problem. No such dilemma ever occurred in a Hurricane and this was confidence-making.

The Spitfire I's ailerons became very heavy above about 350 m.p.h. and 'solid' above 400, while the Hurricane I retained adequate rolling power to 400 m.p.h. and beyond. The Hurricane could out-turn the Spitfire and of course the '109 up to 20,000 ft plus, but it ran out of steam in speed and manoeuvre above that by comparison.

The Hurricane I's gun-platform stability was clearly superior to the Spitfire I's, and the pippa could be held spot-on in turbulence, wake and combat manoeuvre better than with the Spitfire whose relatively low directional damping and wing-twist when the guns fired tended to affect its gun-aiming accuracy.

With the Hurricane, taxying vision and the stable wide track undercarriage were much better than in the Spitfire, which had a taxying and landing accident rate in a different scale entirely that became a serious problem throughout the war.

Because of their higher altitude ability the Spitfires were more often launched at the '109 top-cover first — hence some of the Luftwaffe's conviction that only Spitfires mattered; and they became so obsessed with this that there were many recorded instances of German pilots shouting 'Achtung Schpitfuer' when they were actually being attacked by Hurricanes! In fact the Hurricanes, used in larger numbers and mainly at the bomber streams and escorts below 20,000 ft, saw more of the action in the Battle of Britain and achieved a clear majority of the successes.

On a personal note, in November 1940, when it had become apparent that someone was losing the Battle and it was not us, our good friend Mike Lister Robinson, by then commanding 609 Sqn at Warmwell, came to see us at Charmy Down in his brand new Spitfire II which we duly admired. After lunch we went out to see him go knowing that he would give us some splendid aerobatics then, while he was strapping in, my CO 'Widge' Gleed said: "Go on Bee — see him off!" Needing no encouragement, I started my Mk I Rotol-prop Hurricane and took off after Michael, keeping in his blind spot below and behind as he pulled up to wing-over down into his first run. I stayed there for a roll, a roll-off-the-top and then back for an upward roll until he saw me as he came round for another pass — and then it started! With throttles and pitch levers to the firewalls we were soon down to dispersal hut level and behind the trees and hangars, and I remember thinking that this was all getting rather dangerous. But in his tightest turning with wingtip vortices, racking roll-reversals and everything he tried, I had no difficulty in keeping my Hurricane in the 'slot' behind his tailwheel. It must have been quite frustrating until he finally rolled out level and still at full power started to draw away. But before he could do this of course I 'shot him down'!

That convinced us all that for our job at that critical time a Spitfire II could be nice, but that our Hurricanes, and our knowledge of them in combat, were in the prevailing circumstances much safer for us!

In the half-century since the Battle of Britain much contentious verbiage has been put about, in many cases by one-time Spitfire pilots who, not content with singing the praises of their illustrious mount which without question did win the high altitude battle in 1940 on its own, have gone on to claim that the Hurricane was 'shamefully inferior' in that great battle. Of course it never was and it was in fact the highest scoring fighter where most of the battles were fought below 20,000 ft. But over the years the ever enthusiastic media has promoted this falsehood, and now inevitably it has begun to appear as 'fact' in revisionist writings.

The Hurricane was a fine, highly manoeuvrable and rugged fighter and it played a major part in achieving the victory in one of the greatest air battles in history. Together, the Hurricane and Spitfire made a great and victorious team in 1940.

Hurricane Night Operations

The onset of winter 1940/41 was a strange period for 87 Sqn, which had spent the previous six months in the thick of the day fighting in Northern France and Belgium. Pilot losses in France in May and then through July, August and September in major battles over the Channel from Portland to Portsmouth, had totalled more than 50 per cent including two fine commanding officers, 'Johnny' Dewar and Terry Lovell Grieg; but we had given as good as we got or better, and by October with the emerging realization that the Luftwaffe had been defeated by the RAF over the south of England, morale which had been inspiring and unfaltering throughout the summer's battles was sky-high indeed.

At that point surprising movement orders were received to base the squadron at a new satellite airfield of RAF Colerne near Bath called Charmy Down, after some intermediate night operations from the grass airfield at Bibury where we had carried out periodic moonlight patrols over Bristol during the past few weeks.

This looked ominous and it was soon confirmed that 87 was to become a full-time night-fighter squadron! This prospect seemed disastrous to a bunch of day-fighter pilots who had not only survived the two great air defence actions of the war so far but had done so with, they considered, a very positive share in the ultimate victory. As they now saw it they had to give up the inspiring climbs in formation into the brilliant skies above cloud to fight and throw back an arrogant enemy whose black-swastika-clad hordes had daily trespassed over our land and homes, and instead live a life of crouching in the dark in ill-heated huts awaiting the Op's telephone call to 'Patrol Line A at 10,000 ft'; an order which would lead to a lone flight into the darkness in whatever the weather happened to be when the order was issued. 10 Group Headquarters' comforting observation in this connection was already well known: 'If the Hun is flying so can you!'

It was an enormous contrast and it said much for RAF training that as night bombing was seen to be the new threat to this country following the failure of the German air forces against Fighter Command in daytime, 87 and the other squadrons concerned just got down to the new job as best they could.

There were no effective homing aids at the beginning and each sortie had to be conducted by DR (watch and compass) navigation to and from the patrol line which, in theory, could be seen from 10,000 ft as groups of flares at ten-mile intervals. In practice the flares could only be seen on very clear nights, which seldom happen over this country in the winter. So the patrols were flown by timed runs on reciprocal headings and, in the cases of all but the most skilled in pilot navigation, after 1½ hr on patrol on a pitch-dark night and over cloud or mist there were few pilots who had much of an idea of their position.

Then in theory a 'fix' should have been possible by 'triangulation' on radio voice transmissions. In practice the TR9 radios were so unreliable and sensitive to atmospheric conditions that the night-fighter pilot would have to resort to setting the 'safety course' for his home beacon at the end of his '1½-hr patrol and then begin his descent, hoping to break out below cloud at the end of a timed run without first hitting high ground and in sight of the beacon flashing his base signal or any other beacon which would lead him to somewhere to land before his fuel ran out!

Once on patrol it was a case of eyeballing with no radar through a thick armour-glass windscreen surrounded by heavy metal structure (and past the reflector gunsight with its bright aiming spot and graticules when switched on), and the sighting of and holding on to another aircraft in the darkness was supremely difficult. The majority of our few interceptions in that winter were on searchlight-illuminated targets or following fleeting glimpses of bombers silhouetted against the massive fires of the cities of Bristol, Swansea, Plymouth or London burning below.

Nevertheless the job was tackled with intense effort and what would nowadays be called 'professionalism'. Specific training was carried out on every suitable night by pilots not on standby and included local and cross-country formation flying in moonlight and full darkness and, of particular importance, pairs flying to assess each other's limits of night visibility by the No. 2 dropping slowly astern of the leader until firstly the latter's silhouette disappeared at about 400 yd, and then the blue exhaust flames became almost invisible. Inevitably sometimes contact was lost and in all these sorties DR navigation over a totally blacked-out countryside was the sole means of recovery to a safe landing.

The enthralling vistas of the day fighter pilot in wide-open skies had been replaced for us by the confines of the dimly red-lit cockpit with often nothing distinguishable in the total darkness outside. Then our whole existence seemed limited to this and the thunderous vibrations of the Merlin engine on whose continued roar life indeed depended, for as our recent experiences had indicated parachute escape from the Hurricane was by no means an assured way out.

Clear moonlight or even very clear starlight nights were a pleasure as navigation could generally be visual on the outlines of the Severn, or on occasions Plymouth Sound or the Thames; but in all other circumstances of darkness in mist, rain, thick cloud, icing and snow, all of which occurred in plenty in that winter at Charmy Down, the uncertainty was dominant. Sometimes, after casting around in a black goldfish bowl at the lowest altimeter height considered safe relative to the hills one might be over, the mist to one side or ahead began to glow intermittently with the signal of a flashing beacon. Then, one would turn up the cockpit rheostat, check the beacon signal against the beacon card for the bearing to the airfield, set the new course and begin final descent and when below 500 ft the line of shrouded paraffin flares would appear one after the other ahead. Undercarriage and flaps down, sometimes a hurried S turn to line up and then throttle closed, stick back, sparks each side from the throttled engine and then the thump of a hard arrival or less frequently a gentle three-pointer and no more to do but try to keep straight between the flares, which was not all that easy in a crosswind in the wet.

After a brief handover to the loyal ground crew who would service one aircraft after another all through the night in the open whatever the fierce winter weather, it was back to the generally bitter-cold dispersal hut for a hot cup of tea and a lie down under a blanket for the rest of the night or until one's turn for another patrol, this time with luck to return more easily in the light of the dawn.

It was a challenge every night but although the risk of accident was high and many aircraft and some pilots were lost that winter the chances of operational success were low and very few interceptions occurred, and most were inconclusive. I fired at two Ju 88s over Bristol in the searchlights during a five-month period, and both plots disappeared over the Severn and were recorded as 'probably destroyed'. But when 'Splinters' Smallwood (later Air Chief Marshal Sir Denis) saw some navigation lights over the middle of a major raid on Bristol one night and dived to investigate, he found 'a clot of a Heinkel' and shot it down over land.

It was slow going and by the spring of 1941 with the news that the Spitfire wings were taking the offensive and beginning the 'sweeping season' over France, 87 sought other outlets from the dreary round of night 'Politician Patrols'. The energetic CO, 'Widge' Gleed, obtained tentative and rather surprised support from No. 10 Group Headquarters at Rudloe Manor for two experimental operations, the future of either of which was to depend 'strictly on results'. This meant that in the event of initial failure there would be no second chances.

One plan was to send a detachment to a small grass airfield on St Mary's in the Scilly Isles for the purpose of daylight interception of enemy mine-laying and reconnaissance sorties which had been reported in the area in some numbers by Intelligence. The second plan was, for that time, an unusual and some thought extremely radical one of employing our new-found confidence in night operations in ground-attacks by moonlight on enemy airfields.

By the spring of 1941, following its long, hard winter of night operations and a training syllabus which had even included our regular night formation aerobatics, 87 felt ready to extend its new-found expertise and on 9 April the first of these new operations was mounted.

Squadron Leader Ian Gleed led four aircraft to Warmwell at dusk for refuelling, and then followed a long wait until the take-off time planned for the first sortie. The plan involved the CO and his usual No. 2, 'Rubber' Thoroughgood, reconnoitring the area of Caen-Carpiquet airfield south-east of the Cherbourg peninsula and attacking 'targets of opportunity' if the nearly-full moon gave sufficient visibility. If the defences were active and included searchlights, each aircraft would attempt to cover the other by strafing.

No-one knew if ground-attack with 0.303 in machine-guns would be practical by moonlight. The object was to find out and if the CO's sortie was successful Derek Ward and I were to make a follow-up attack. This was to be not only the squadron's first night ground attack but probably the first by any single-engine fighters in the Second World War.

At Warmwell in the stillness of the otherwise deserted aerodrome the moon rose in a cloudless sky over the Purbeck Hills, and the chill of a heavy dew heralded a frost later, leading to practical thoughts of keeping windscreen and wings protected. Then start-up time approached and the first two Merlins crackled into life, shattering the stillness. Presently they taxied out over the rough grass, turned into wind and thundered off in loose formation, extinguishing navigation lights as they turned south under the now bright moon.

Ward and I prepared for a long two -hour wait for the first pair to return and for confirmation that the next sortie would be on, but as we were entering the cold Mess building, deserted but for us on this day-fighter station, the unmistakable sound of a Merlin approaching brought us back to the 'Flights' in a hurry and in time to see

'LK-A', Gleed's Hurricane, swing round and switch-off. He slid back the hood as we climbed up on the wing and said: 'Got a bloody great Dornier off Lulworth! Where's "Rubber"?' But then the other Hurricane curved in down the moon path, and in an hilarious debriefing it transpired that hardly had they settled down on course for Normandy at about 10,000 ft than Gleed had glimpsed a dark shape going past in the opposite direction and turning sharply, had seen exhaust flames against the stars, closed and opened fire on a clearly recognised Dornier Do 17.

Thoroughgood meanwhile had lost his leader in this manoeuvre, but then saw a fire going down and hitting the sea so he also came back.

Gleed, having had one successful sortie and now experiencing delay in rearming, was of a mind to try the offensive operation on another night, but New Zealander Derek Ward with our two Hurricanes armed and ready was not to be put off and it was decided that the second sortie would go ahead as planned. So the second Section would now do the exploratory work!

With a brilliant moon and a stable weather forecast all was favourable and after a loose formation take-off over the undulating Warmwell grass and setting course on the climb for France, station keeping in the moonlight was as easy as in daylight. With 80 miles of water ahead the customary illusion of engine roughness soon occurred, to be disciplined after a close scrutiny of the perfectly healthy engine instruments. Night cross-country formation flying carried no mystery for us and flying No. 2, I relaxed in the comfortable knowledge that Derek Ward's navigation would be accurate. Sufficient to cross-check only at the first visual checkpoint on crossing the enemy coast to ensure a good 'safety course' for the likely solo return because visual contact with the leader would most likely be lost over the target.

The two Hurricanes droned steadily on at 10,000 ft and then, indistinctly at first and soon with final definition, a thin dark line to starboard revealed the Cherbourg coast curving round eastwards towards the Normandy beaches ahead. The enemy coast and time to tighten the harness straps, check engine and fuel gauges, switch on gunsight with rheostat set low hopefully for ground-attack, and then finally turn the gun button on the spade-grip from 'Safe' to 'Fire'.

With the coastline clear below Ward's Hurricane began to lose height gently, holding course for Carpiquet which should come up in four minutes. Down to 2,000 ft, then with final confirmation of target area two brilliant blue searchlights snapped on and weaved almost horizontally ahead in agitated scan.

Breaking radio silence Ward called: 'There's the aerodrome' and dived down to port. Ahead the flak defences erupted in chains of brilliant tracer weaving haphazardly at first, but then one of the searchlights illuminated the leading Hurricane followed by another and it looked for all the world like a moth twisting in a car's headlights.

Here was the No. 2's task. Rolling down on to the source of the nearest searchlight I aimed directly at it and fired a long burst with first the tracer rounds and then the 'de Wilde' flashing explosive rounds confirming accuracy. With breathtaking suddenness the light snapped out leaving a dying glow which helped judgement of pull-up, and then with a snap the other light swung right on from almost dead ahead. In the dazzling blueish glare nothing could be read in the cockpit, and though I was at very low altitude the ground was invisible. Tracer shells now began to whip by with a pronounced 'whoomph whoomph' and the only possible action was to aim and fire straight down the beam knowing that this was the classically dangerous manoeuvre as it would destroy 'night vision' for probably a fatal period if and when the light went out.

After a seemingly endless burst (in reality a very few seconds) the dazzle snapped out to blackness, again with the dying glow of the light helping me to avoid flying right into it. Then a snatched pull on the stick with a fleeting impression of objects flashing by on each side before regaining some sort of reorientation in a shallow climb with the moon in the right place and the altimeter now perceived to read 300 ft and climbing. But where was the target? Over to port converging chains of tracer shells showed where Ward might be and immediately lines of machine-gun tracer pouring downwards showed his attack on something and then a flash of fire on the ground. There were no searchlights now and quickly aiming for the fire and diving down through 200 ft I saw the moonlight suddenly glint on runways, hangars and the shapes of parked aircraft by the now raging fire.

With gunsight aiming-spot near the fire, I made a continuous gun-burst strafing run through what looked like parked Bf 109s and on into a hangar before clearing low over the latter as the Brownings stuttered out of ammunition into silence. Then low down and pursued briefly by chains of tracer shells and bullets I raced over shadowy fields, woods, a railway line with red-lit signals, then a glinting canal and with final relief the light strip of beach at the coast before pulling up at climb power to set course for the planned recovery base, Middle Wallop, with only a single searchlight still weaving behind.

On the climb a disturbing hot smell caused swift study of the engine panel and outside for any signs of battle damage although no hits had been felt. But all was well and the smell was recognized as cordite smoke from the Brownings.

Crossing out had been on planned time and now a revised navigation plan had to be good to find Middle Wallop. A brief radio call to Ward produced only silence and worry. His aircraft should not be far away, so had he been hit?

Under the still clear moon but in haze up to 8,000 ft, the sky and sea below seemed to merge and only in a look back did the moon path on the sea confirm that there was no cloud below. Holding course at 10,000 ft for half an hour seemed ages longer and then in a gentle descent I searched the greyness ahead for a sign of land. A recognizable pin-point was important for confirmation of heading to the Wallop flashing beacon. Suddenly a faint white line appeared to starboard. This seemed wrong as it should have been the chalk cliffs of Purbeck at Swanage's Old Harry Rocks to port. This had to be the Isle of Wight at the Needles and descent rate was increased to ensure a better view of the mainland crossing-in, but in the moonlit haze this could not be seen.

There was nothing to do but hold course until I was within radio range of Wallop and then suddenly, duck! A large black shape loomed ahead and rushed down the starboard side. Then another straight ahead and a third above to port. In the concentration on events I had completely forgotten the Southampton balloon barrage! In clear weather they flew to above 5,000 ft and a glance at the altimeter showed 4,500 ft!

With full throttle and fine pitch the Hurricane was stood on its tail with fleeting glimpses of more balloons. This time their silvered tops were seen from level and above glinting in the moon and the danger was past.

Ahead appeared a beacon flashing the code for Wallop and soon the Hurricane was bumping down the strange grass flarepath. The time was 0200 and at dispersal (John Cunningham's Bristol Beaufighters) no news was to be had of Ward. While 'LK-L' was being refuelled and rearmed, experiences were exchanged with the pilots of the AI equipped Beaufighters, who were intrigued to hear about our attempts at 'eyeballing' enemy aircraft at night and these night ground attacks in the single-engined Hurricane. They thought we were mad on both counts.

After a short, relaxed, 15 min flight back to Bath under the still-bright moon, I landed on the Charmy Down flarepath before dawn to find Derek Ward already there after returning via Warmwell, where he had landed to check for possible flak damage. He said: 'Thanks for shooting that searchlight off me, "Bee". It was great and we must try that again!' As indeed we did on 6 May, again from Warmwell when I led an attack on the Bf 109 airfield at Maupertus on Cherbourg in 'LK-L' (Serial V7285) with Peter Roscoe flying No. 2. On this sortie there was no difficulty seeing runways and buildings in the moonlight, but we could not identify aircraft easily or other detailed targets at first, and the searchlights and flak were very active and accurate. Both aircraft fired at gunposts and searchlights briefly before attacking the parked aircraft finally seen near the hangars, and then disengaged discreetly.

Shortly after crossing out over the coast a brief winking signal light revealed the white 'V' of a fast vessel travelling west close in to the shore. On the assumption that it might be an E-boat, I eased 'LK-L' into a diving turn to line up the target against the moon path. This worked, and at a few hundred feet and an estimated 1,000 yd the low profile of a fast patrol boat could be easily seen in silhouette against the bright moon-path. I opened fire and continued to point-blank range with de Wilde hits sparking all round the bridge area and tracer ricocheting upwards ahead.

The ammunition ran out as the Hurricane cleared close overhead and I held it low in a tight left bank away from the moon as late return tracer fire erupted from one or two gun positions. But these soon fell away behind and course was set for Warmwell which was reached uneventfully.

The most hazardous part of the operation occurred back at Warmwell an hour later after refuelling and rearming. During take-off over white-frosted grass towards the misty Purbeck Hills the right wing dropped violently and heavy vibration set in accompanied by a rumbling roar and nearly full left stick was suddenly required even to hold the wings level. Despite the indistinct light of the moon the cause of the trouble was evident; a large dark hole in the top surface of the starboard wing showed where the whole gun servicing panel on that side had disappeared. The problem was two-fold; how to make a safe landing and where!

Some experimenting showed that with undercarriage down and no flap, aileron control of the wing-drop ran out below 100 m.p.h. and this would mean a fast landing although flap could be lowered once the wheels were on the ground. I therefore decided that the longer runway of Charmy Down, would be better for this sort of arrival and it would also be less complicated to do it at home! So I set course for Bath in gathering moon haze which was not helpful, but after some anxious moments the home beacon was eventually found periodically illuminating the murk ahead. Then a long, flat approach was made from the beacon on the bearing for Charmy Down, whose flarepath thankfully appeared dimly out of the haze at about a mile ahead.

At 110 m.p.h. the left stick load was becoming nearly unbearable, and when the threshold lights flashed by underneath I selected the flaps just as the main wheels touched in a tail-high 'wheeler'. With the red 'glim lamps' of the runway end approaching rapidly maximum possible braking was applied short of nosing over, and then with hard left rudder the Hurricane was slithered sideways to stop off the runway on the frosty grass overshoot area. There was no further damage and after a look at the wing the flight sergeant subsequently passed some crisp advice to the Warmwell station armourers about how to fasten gun panels.

This sortie gave further confidence to the theory that fighters could be used in offensive operations at night and that ground targets could be identified and attacked in good moonlight. The short range of 0.303 in machine-guns and their low lethality meant that these particular operations were of questionable value apart from waking up the enemy, but we had at least shown that with heavier armament it could be a different story.

Chapter Three

Typhoon

The Hurricane was becoming outclassed in the European theatre by 1941 and there was an urgent need to bring forward into service its planned replacement, the Hawker Typhoon. I took part in testing these new fighters when attached to Hawker again, and soon found that I had joined the programme at an interesting time.

Typhoon troubles

The introduction into RAF service in 1941 of Hawker's new 400 m.p.h. fighter was not easy. The Typhoon had proved to have many engineering problems which led to low serviceability and required intensive maintenance effort in the squadrons. So the early flying training rate was slow and soon became further complicated by three emerging factors.

The second Hawker Typhoon prototype at Langley in 1941, showing the zero rear visibility from the cockpit. (British Aerospace)

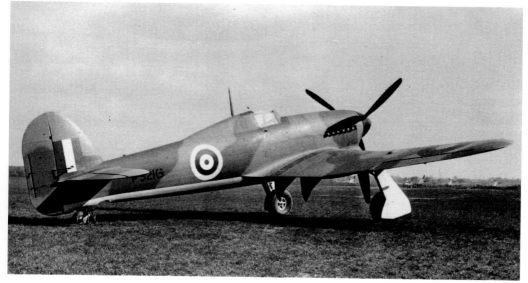

The new Napier Sabre 24-cylinder 2,000 h.p. engines were prone to frequent failure, resulting in a worrying loss rate in forced landings and some fatal crashes. Adding to this problem an unexplained in-flight structural failure occurred in 1942, killing the pilot; and it was followed soon afterwards by two more identical crashes.

In parallel there was mounting concern that the newly discovered and little understood phenomenon of 'compressibility' could be causing these accidents; in addition the heavy vibration roughness typical of early Typhoons was thought to be possibly linked with both engine and structural failures.

My introduction to one of the problems came on 29 February 1942 at Langley, when I took over the 'vibration' programme in Typhoon IA R7684. This aircraft was instrumented with vibrograph sensors in the rear fuselage and tail unit, and in an extended series of tests it was flown over a range of altitudes and speeds and engine settings aimed at covering all the most severe vibration conditions.

In my first sortie the schedule called for maximum continuous cruise at 3,000 ft for 30 min, followed by a repeat at 5,000 ft and again, fuel permitting, at 7,000 ft. This would require a triangular course to bring the aircraft back close to base with just enough fuel for landing.

The background to these tests was that in addition to the mounting concern about the possibility of high vibration levels contributing to the recent structural failures, the pilots in the first Typhoon squadrons were becoming apprehensive about the physical strain of flying these aeroplanes. After the normal 1½- to 2-hr sorties they complained of severe fatigue to the extent that a rumour spread quickly that Typhoon flying was a high risk to the pilots' marital prospects! Accordingly, the rumour continued, it was not long before they set out to prove to their satisfaction, and presumably that of their lady friends, that Typhoon flying was not diminishing their enthusiasm for or performance in their off-duty activities. In due course the birth rate in the neighbourhood of the Typhoon bases was said to have shown a sharp increase!

I therefore approached my first Typhoon test flight with more than usual personal interest. As the Typhoon thundered across Oxfordshire to the west in broken turbulent cloud and light rain, the general level of noise and roughness was certainly impressive and I noted that heavy vibration could be felt through the stick and wherever one touched the cockpit structure or controls. Also the windscreen frame seemed alive when touched and then, in a momentary shaft of sunlight, I could actually see the car-type wind-up side windows oscillating. After 1½ hr of this tedious cruising it was a relief to land back at Langley; and after two more of these 'vibrograph' sorties that day I could see what the squadron pilots meant. It felt as if I had just finished a hard game of rugby football!

During these trials close attention was given to reducing engine- and propeller-vibration levels, and in due course quality control improvements in propeller manufacture and balancing did reduce the roughness to some extent. It was then decided that the main cause of discomfort still affecting the pilot was through his seat, so this was spring-mounted with spring-rates calculated to 'de-tune' or mask the heaviest vibrations. This measure was partly successful and after ten more of these 'vibration' tests a standard was reached considered 'barely acceptable for Service use'. The Typhoon would always be a rough and noisy aircraft, characteristics which were not liked but which were offset by its advantages of speed, manoeuvrability, and steadiness and accuracy in ground-attack operations.

But the two more serious problems remained to be dealt with; the Sabre engine failures, and an increasing number of incidents of structural failures and loss of life.

The main engine problem was found to be a fundamental flaw in the design of the sleeve valves which with use became prone to seizing up, whereupon the engine stopped abruptly. The cure was to chrome-plate the sleeves thus reducing friction, and this modification was seen to be a success in the squadrons by the last quarter of 1942.

The third major problem, structural failure, was harder to resolve. By August 1942 three Typhoons had crashed in mysterious circumstances and in each case the tail or pieces of it had been found some distance from the main wreckage. Investigations showed that in each case the aircraft had been in a high-speed dive prior to the incident, and one of these had been a scheduled dive test from Langley in the hands of their skilled and very experienced experimental test pilot Kenneth Seth-Smith. Neither he nor the others had had a chance to escape by parachute.

Re-equipment of squadrons with Typhoons continued throughout the winter of 1942–43, and more fatal accidents occurred with the same symptoms. Finding a solution became the major task at Langley.

My second 'tour' at Hawker, this time as an experimental test pilot, had begun in the summer of 1943. After a stimulating introduction to the new Tempest series, performance testing the Mk I and V prototypes, the hopefully final trials in the Typhoon tail-failure investigation became one of my priority tasks. It proved to be cutting-edge test flying in a big way!

For more than a year since the first tail failure an intensive programme of recalculation in stressing and aerodynamics, followed by flight trials comprised mainly of eliminating any flight conditions that could have a possible bearing on these structural failures, had together produced nothing definite. Yet the accidents were still happening and there were now fifteen known cases of Typhoon tail failure. My detailed briefing in the Langley experimental department before taking over these tests was given mainly by flight test engineer Charlie Dunn and deputy chief test pilot Philip Lucas, with inputs from Freddy Page from the design office.

The especially instrumented Typhoon IB EK152, which had been re-exploring the flight envelope at all practical combinations of speed, G, rolling pull-outs and excess yawing at low and medium altitudes, was now to take these combinations to high altitude where the Mach number effects could introduce additional stresses.

This was the period in 1942–43 when fighter manufacturers and the Royal Aircraft Establishment (RAE) at Farnborough were still in the early stages of exploring the phenomenon of total loss of control in compressibility. The term 'sound barrier' had not yet been invented but it had been established at Langley by Bulman, Lucas and Seth-Smith that if a Typhoon was dived steeply from 30,000 ft or above at full power the smooth airflow over wings and tail would begin to break down into local shock-wave patterns at above 400 m.p.h. IAS and 20,000 ft, and that the higher the altitude at which these speeds were reached the more violent the 'compressibility' effects. Control had been lost in some of these dives but had been regained as the aircraft reached lower altitude and denser air where the Mach number (the aircraft speed expressed as a percentage of the speed of sound) fell below the critical level.

As an aircraft approaches the speed of sound the air ahead of it begins to compress, and locally over wings and tail the speed of the airflow increases and breaks down into shock-waves. The aircraft is then 'transonic' and if it is not a supersonic design the shock-waves move erratically over wings and control surfaces, causing violent trim changes, heavy buffeting and finally loss of control in pitch and roll leading into an ever-steepening dive.

Among the first pilots to experience and report on these phenomena had been George Bulman of Hawker during his early investigations in 1941–42 of the prototype Typhoons and Tornados. In Germany Mano Zeigler with the Messerschmitt Me 262 jet fighter and Heinrich Beauvais of the Rechlin test centre with the Bf 109 and Fw 190, had encountered similar problems in the same period.

George Bulman was probably the first pilot among the Allied nations to describe these events clearly and professionally, and he concluded in a memorandum to his pilots at Langley in 1943: ". . . and whatever you do don't trim it out of the (uncontrollable) dive, because it will recover below about 15,000 ft as the Mach number reduces, and when it does, if you've trimmed against the nose-heaviness it will pitch-up violently and probably break something". This was good advice which was supported by the aerodynamic specialists of the Aero Flight at RAE Farnborough.

I had already flown into the initial buffeting and roaring noise-level increase of compressibility in the recent dive tests, and I now felt well-briefed for this next stage. These were the beginnings of the understanding of what was fast becoming a serious limitation on fighter capability. It was thought that no matter how much more engine power became available, fighter design would not be able to penetrate this new barrier. But there was also the clear possibility that the Typhoon structural failures could have occurred in 'compressibility'.

My task now was to take the most extreme combinations of misuse of controls that had been tested successfully at low levels up to high altitude and repeat them at the highest achievable Mach number. I listened to this briefing with interest. It had been presented so clearly and professionally, as with everything else at Langley, that it sounded almost straightforward.

In the next few days I flew some scheduled preliminary tests in EK152 to conditions of maximum rudder-load yawing at 400 m.p.h. IAS/Mach 0.7, and then to higher Mach numbers, and it was impressive to stand on the right rudder pedal at maximum force and feel and see the slip-ball go off the clock in port yaw, with thankfully no untoward effects.

Then came the 'corner-point'. We were to try to reach the 'worst case' fin-load by diving to reach 500 m.p.h. IAS at as high an altitude as possible, and, with the aircraft trimmed in the dive at full throttle and fine pitch, take the feet off the rudder pedals and knock off both ignition switches in order to impart the maximum yawing stress to the fin and rear fuselage which could result from a sudden engine failure. That is, the maximum design load case for the fin.

This caused some thought! It was apparent, but not mentioned in the briefing, that we were actually looking for the last and most severe point at which the tail might break off! In the professional and dedicated atmosphere of the Langley experimental flight test office I thought it unwise to mention this, as everyone knew what we were doing and at this point it was my job. But I did for a moment (and later in the cockpit of EK152) wonder if going back to a front-line squadron might not be a safer occupation!

But this was the ultimate point. None of the fatal accidents in the RAF had been resolved, and more lives would be lost if Langley did not find the answer. I knew that a probable cause had by that time been established — failure of the elevator mass-balance bracket leading to catastrophic elevator flutter if it broke at high speed. I also knew that EK152 had the modified and strengthened brackets, but still no-one knew if an extreme combination of yawing and high Mach number in compressibility could also cause a failure. Now we were going to find out.

For this critical test it was necessary to wait for favourable weather and this occurred on 16 October 1943 with only broken fair-weather cumulus layers at low altitude and some cirrus at altitude. In the climb to altitude I found that the layered cloud was more extensive than expected, and it was necessary to search for an area clear enough for the dive. While doing this there was time to consider again the nature of this flight.

At the top of the climb and if the conditions were exactly right I was scheduled to push over into a steep dive at full throttle and hold the dive and then, in the roughness and control deterioration of compressibility, take my feet off the rudder pedals, switch off the ignition switches and in the resulting violent yaw just sit there while the Typhoon lurched sideways at 500 m.p.h., possibly overloading the fin to the point of structural failure. This would be the result of a conscious decision of a type which very few pilots would have to take in the whole of their flying careers, yet it was one which the experimental test pilot must often accept as part of his normal work.

This rather negative thought was soon replaced by the feeling that this was an exciting 'first-time' test and, in a small way, exploration of the unknown and as such a significant contribution to making this powerful fighter a better and safer aeroplane, and it was well worth doing — so let's get on with it.

At 30,000 ft, above the highest cirrus layer, there was no sign of clearance below, and I turned towards the south until suddenly the ground appeared ahead at the bottom of a shaft in the clouds. I recognised a bend in the Thames near Windsor, turned tighter and rolled down into the gap at full power. A final trimmer adjustment as the altimeter wound quickly through 400 m.p.h. and 24,000 ft, and then it began.

Heavy buffeting and increasing general roughness was accompanied by a roaring step-change in noise level. The port wing began to roll down against my strong right-stick correction, and then the nose dropped suddenly into an increasing dive angle which I could not hold even with maximum back-stick. The Typhoon was now out of control and diving nearly vertically and rolling left and there was no way I could hit the ignition switches, and I only just managed to pull back the throttle before resuming a full-strength two-handed pull on the stick estimated later at 40–50 lb. But it was to no avail.

The Typhoon, which now felt right out of my control, continued rolling left in a steepening dive to what seemed to be over the vertical. At 500 m.p.h.-plus the ground was coming up very quickly indeed, but this was hardly considered. Training, briefing and instant reaction concentrated on the altitude now passing 15,000 ft. There was not much time left; when was the elevator control going to recover? Then it began to and the nose, slowly at first, began to rise out of the vertical spiral dive and then the ailerons regained effectiveness. The noise and buffeting reduced, and then EK152 was pulled out into level flight at about 8,000 ft.

It had been an impressive experience but it had not achieved the planned test point. It would have to be done again!

In the debriefing meeting it was decided that there would be no point in trying to repeat these flight conditions and that we would have to settle for the 'engine-cut' maximum yaw at 500 m.p.h. at the highest Mach number we could achieve without loss of elevator control. This was calculated to be at about 12,000 ft/Mach 0.7, so this was planned for the first day of suitable weather.

This occurred on 8 November, a clear anti-cyclonic day with a north-westerly wind and with few clouds and endless visibility. Perfect for the job. This time I climbed EK152 out of Langley to 20,000 ft on a westerly heading and pushed straight over into the dive, bringing the power up smoothly and trimming the rudder into the dive at about 450 m.p.h. passing 15,000 ft. Then with the ASI steady on 500 m.p.h., and in noise and roughness with the port wing beginning to drop and the elevator still effective but becoming heavy, I lifted my feet from the vibrating rudder pedals, bent forward against the harness and, still with full throttle and 3,700 r.p.m., knocked off the ignition switches.

Though expecting it, I was still surprised at the momentary violence of the motion that followed the abrupt cessation of engine roar. The Typhoon yawed left with a jerk that threw me hard against my right shoulder harness, and the already loud wind-roar rose with a very loud click apparently from the area of the starboard cockpit window. This was the moment, but nothing worse happened. The tail had apparently stayed in one piece, and I throttled back, reduced r.p.m., trimmed out the yaw and eased the Typhoon back into level flight and, when the ASI was dropping down through 400 m.p.h., leant forward and switched the ignition switches back to ON. Even at this moderate speed the Sabre caught with a throaty rumble and shudder, and then we were back in conventional and calm flight.

After a number of further fill-in test flights to complete this thorough investigation (including a repeat of the 500 m.p.h., engine cut dive but this time under negative G!) it was concluded that there were no conceivable combinations of adverse flight conditions that could have caused the tail failures, that the Typhoon's structural integrity was sound, and that the most probable cause of the failures had been fatigue failures of the elevator mass-balance brackets. These were all replaced with strengthened brackets in the aircraft in service and of course on the production line, and although there were some more unexplained accidents in the 400-strong Typhoon force which went on to major successes in the coming battles for Europe, none were attributed to the original cause.

Typhoon Trial operations

Between the first flight of a new type and its entry into full military service it had to complete four separate and essential phases of testing: experimental and development to identify defects or shortfalls in design, construction and conformity to specification; acceptance trials by A&AEE Boscombe Down to confirm the manufacturer's claims; production standard testing to ensure quality control of the whole production run; and finally 'Service' operational trials.

In the latter phase the new aircraft is introduced into active operations progressively and any shortcomings are identified for urgent rectification prior to full 'operational release'. It was in this phase that I was privileged to take part in the introduction of two new British fighters in the Second World War, the Hawker Typhoon in 1942 and its much improved development the Hawker Tempest in 1944.

After the technical and operating difficulties encountered during its first year of service as high-altitude air combat fighter, an alternative application of the Typhoon to low-level ground-attack began in November 1942 from Manston in the form of short-range 'Rhubarb' sorties in daylight, operating in pairs against rail, road, and barge traffic, and singly in night attacks against similar targets in the moon period of each month. This all happened against a background of scepticism at headquarters, where strong doubts were being expressed as to whether these heavy, cumbersome-looking fighters which did not look at all like Spitfires and had a bad technical record could be used more effectively at low level than in the high-level fighter role in which they had already failed comprehensively.

The unit given what many thought the dubious honour of undertaking the first of these operations was No. 609 (West Riding) Squadron, RAuxAF which had had a distinguished record in the recent Battle of Britain (and saw no good reason why they should not still be on their beloved Spitfires). Many pilots and ground personnel in the squadron regarded with some suspicion the announcement by their CO (the author) that day and night 'ground-attack' against transport, airfields and other military targets was now to be added on an experimental basis to their current and already demanding role of standing patrols from Ramsgate to Dungeness throughout the hours of daylight against low-level Bf 109 and Fw 190 raiders.

The author's Typhoon Ib, 'PR-G' when he was CO of 609 Squadron, Manston 1943. (Zeigler)

Initially these sorties were carried out by the CO, flight commanders, and senior pilots in order to gain direct experience which could, if it proved practical, be extended to all the pilots in due course. The first sorties were mounted in November 1942 with bad-weather daylight attacks in pairs on trains before the end of the month, and solo sorties by moonlight. These were an immediate success with five trains attacked and no aircraft damaged. The Typhoon was confirmed to be suitable for low-level penetration in quite extreme weather conditions and for finding and attacking targets to very close range with accuracy and good effect with its heavy armament of four 20 mm Hispano high-velocity cannon; but some operating defects were revealed.

As had already been established in 'fighter sweeps' at altitude, the thick windscreen and 'car-door' type side window frames were an uncomfortable limitation on search vision and reduced the pilot's confidence. He just could not see as well all-round in a hostile environment as he wished to. But the control qualities, stability and general ease of flying low and fast and when necessary in bad weather, and of recovery and landing often in atrocious weather when other fighter squadrons were grounded, were all positive bonuses. The Typhoon could be well used by day and night against pin-point ground targets, but it could be improved.

Its forward vision proved adequate though rather restricted in good visibility, but in mist, rain, and low light conditions finding targets and holding them while turning in to the fast diving attacks needed to reduce the risk from Flak often proved difficult. When this type of operation was extended to night attacks by moonlight there was often a not-unexpected difficulty in identifying targets against the varying shades of dark outlines of trees, hedgerows or small buildings seen only dimly against a misty pearl-grey moonlit background. In these conditions it was only the white trail of steam from a locomotive or the brief glow from an open firebox that revealed a train, and these signs could easily then be lost if they disappeared behind the thick windscreen frames or the gunsight reflector bracket when turning in to attack.

Repeated experiences in these conditions also showed that the light-loss through the armour glass and 'dry-air sandwich' glass behind it, and also through the gunsight reflector itself, all downgraded vision in the critical run-in. Then the final problem, the bright orange range bars and graticule images reflected in the gunsight itself, all severely downgraded vision of already indistinct targets.

These aspects could be improved, but following indifferent dismissal from headquarters staff whose attitude when approached was merely 'use the equipment you've got', experiments were initiated 'in the field' at Manston by 609 Sqn. Nothing could be done about the windscreen frames of course, but the 'dry-air sandwich' glass

The cockpit of Typhoon 'PR-G' with gunsight directly reflected in the windscreen.   (Zeigler)

Great squadron, great pilots! No. 609 (WR) Squadron RAuxAF at Manston in 1943. The author (CC) is second from left in the doorway.   (Zeigler)

The author hands over 609 Squadron to Alec Ingle in May 1943. They were to meet again as POWs in StalagLuft III five months later! (Zeigler)

was removed experimentally from the author's aircraft 'PR-G', a glycol-soaked rag being carried to wipe away internal misting or frosting. The squadron armourers then removed the gunsight reflector glass and adjusted the sight to reflect directly into the windscreen (these two measures removed four separate light-reflecting surfaces between the pilot and the outside world). Finally and with major effect a special blanking slide was fitted into the barrel of the gunsight which eliminated the range bars and graticules (which were not necessary for ground attack) and left only the aiming spot (pippa) reflecting in the windscreen itself.

This configuration was tested first in a night attack on two trains on 22 December and next day in further train attacks. The results were impressive. There was now no noticeable relative light-loss between the single-glass panels and the centre armour glass panel, and with only the gunsight spot in the way the final attacks were made with much improved visibility and significantly reduced risk of losing sight of the target.

These methods had significantly improved attack vision in the worst conditions, and as no support was apparent from headquarters 609 continued on its own initiative throughout the winter to fly with these improvements in a large number of attacks against transport targets, attacking over 100 trains in a two-month period, mostly by moonlight. In the process the squadron began to change opinion on the capabilities of the Typhoon and to shape the course towards establishing the formidable battle-winning Typhoon ground-attack force operations from Normandy to the Baltic in 1944/45.

Many of the Typhoons in that battle were still the early unmodified versions with restricted vision properties, but the force re-equipped during the summer of 1944 with Series 2 aircraft with the vastly improved 'Tempest style' refined forward windscreen and all-round rear visibility sliding canopy, and from then on Typhoon pilots no longer suffered restricted vision. The perseverance of the early Typhoon pioneers had paid off.

Chapter Four

Tempest

Following a further spell of operations commanding 609 Typhoon Squadron from September 1943 I was posted back to the Hawker factory at Langley in May 1942, this time specifically to join a high-priority programme of testing the newest Typhoon developments, the Tempests, and completing the company trials in time for the aircraft to be issued to squadrons in early 1944 for the coming invasion of Europe.

Tempest development flying

In the summer of 1943 the Hawker factory at Langley was a scene of great activity with continued mass production of Hurricanes Mk IIA and IIC, mainly for the Middle and Far East theatres, and with the Typhoon's development problems still far from solved and calling for intensive experimental flying.

The first production Tempest V, used for the high-speed dive tests at Langley in 1943. (British Aerospace)

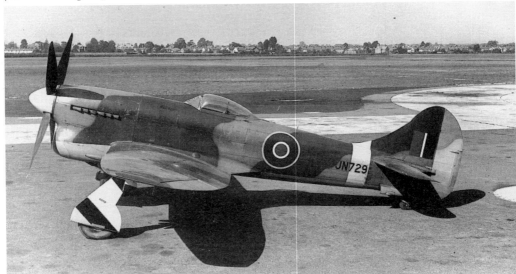

Another view of JN729 at the Langley factory. The tarmac is crowded with Typhoons and Hurricanes on test. (British Aerospace)

In addition, and of especial interest to the experimental test pilots, Philip Lucas, Bill Humble and I, the new Typhoon II developments were in flight test status with the first prototypes, HM585 the technology demonstrator for the Tempest's new thin, elliptical wing; HM599, the Tempest I with Napier Sabre IV engine and wing-mounted low-drag radiators, and the first production Tempest V JN729.

After initial tests had shown the new wing to have excellent handling qualities, the emphasis moved quickly on to performance. Tempest I HM599, was soon shown to have at least a 50 m.p.h. increase on the Typhoon, and Tempest V JN729 a lesser but still useful increase to about 430 m.p.h. But the most valuable change of potential performance was the design Vne (never-exceed limit) of 545 m.p.h./IAS, and the test programme soon concentrated on clearing this area.

I was involved from the beginning in both these aspects, and some absorbing flying resulted. For example on 22 October when flying the Tempest I on 'full throttle level performance' I saw a higher indicated speed at 10,000 ft than I had ever seen before in level flight. This was subsequently calculated in the flight test department and corrected to a true airspeed of 467 m.p.h. — higher than the existing world speed record held by the Germans in a specially prepared Messerschmitt pre-war. At this speed the Tempest proved smooth and crisp in control and it was clearly the fastest propeller-driven fighter in the world at that time. In subsequent tests it exceeded 470 m.p.h. at its maximum power altitude around 18,000 ft.

But performance was only one aspect. The handling round the whole new flight envelope had to be proved, and here a problem was found. A vital design target was to provide the Tempest with fast and practical rate of roll up to its limit speeds both in level and diving flight. This was an area in which the current Spitfires and Bf 109s in service were limited severely by stiffening ailerons beyond about 450 m.p.h. IAS, and a Tempest with full rolling ability to beyond 500 m.p.h. would have a major combat advantage.

Initially the Tempest prototypes were built with interim geared-tab ailerons before

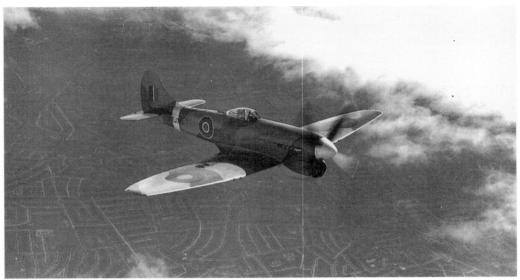

A Series 2 Hawker Tempest V on test from Langley.   (British Aerospace)

The 'new' Tempest wing often led to the aircraft being mistaken for a Spitfire.   (British Aerospace)

fitting the new 'spring tab' ailerons designed by F. W. Page at the Hawker drawing office, which were expected to introduce a break-through in the design of controls for high speed flight. Progressive dive testing, first with geared tabs and then fully repeated with spring-tabs, was carried out from September 1943 onwards on the first production standard Tempest V, JN729, and I was charged with most of this interesting work in 26 flights in September and October.

The method was to apply 'partial rolls' with 'half stick' and 'full stick' deflections in full-throttle dives at careful increments, from 400 m.p.h. until reaching Vne 545, or until a problem was found. In the event these trials progressed smoothly with the geared tabs and no problems were found, other than heavying stick forces (hinge-moments), up to about 480 m.p.h. IAS.

The next test schedule called for partial rolling repeats at 490, 500 and 510 m.p.h., and the sortie took place on 21 September. It was a grey day with light rain and layered cloud up to about 7,000 ft but clear above, so I took JN729 up to 15,000 ft aiming to dive to reach the highest test point below 10,000 in order to keep out of compressibility and then recover with adequate clearance above the cloud tops.

With full throttle and fine pitch the Tempest accelerated in its usual smooth and confident way in a 45° dive and I cleared the 490 m.p.h. half and full-stick points, noting that the stick forces were too heavy for agile combat but still smooth and linear; then on to 500 m.p.h.

The half-stick roll to the right through 90° was normal, and also the reversal to wings level.

Passing through 10,000 ft and noting the approaching cloud tops, I rolled right with full stick and abruptly, after about 30° of bank, the stick leaped over to full throw, the roll rate increased with a violent jerk and the Tempest was diving upside down! Here it was, aileron 'over-balance', and what had seconds before been a calm, progressive test had suddenly become a critical emergency. In an inverted dive at 500 m.p.h. with the cloud tops rushing up below there were only two options — either to try to continue the roll through the remaining 180° to wings-level and then pull out of the dive before reaching the clouds, or risk over-balance in the opposite direction when trying to roll back to wings level.

In far less time than it takes to read this I had slammed the throttle closed and continued the roll round. Then, as the wings neared level, I attempted to pull off the over-balanced stick. It would not move with one hand, but with a two-handed wrench it moved back and at about half-throw and with another jerk the stick-force returned to normal. By then JN729 had rolled right round again into a left bank and was responding to back-stick with the ASI dropping back towards 450. Then we flew out of this brief embarrassment into controlled flight just above the cloud layer at 6,500 ft.

It had been an interesting moment, and from the violence of the aileron snatch I felt that there was a possibility of damage somewhere in the aileron control circuit. I flew JN729 rather gingerly back to Langley and, after landing safely, called for a safety check of the controls for damage or circuit-stretch. None was found, but this sortie determined that this had been the limit for this gearing setting for the aileron balance tabs, and as the forces were already too heavy at these speeds for combat manoeuvre there was no chance of increasing the tab gearing to clear the 545 m.p.h. requirement. Freddy Page's spring-tab ailerons were going to have to work.

With Philip Lucas and Bill Humble now concentrating on the Bristol Centaurus engined Tempest II, in 20 further flights by the author in JN729 the aileron tab gearings were tuned to give optimum rate of roll up to 450 m.p.h. IAS, and then the spring-tab ailerons were introduced and retested vigorously throughout the flight envelope to 545 m.p.h. IAS and Mach 0.76. They were completely successful and achieved the highest roll-rate at the highest indicated airspeed of any of the fighters on either side in 1944/45.

On 2 February 1944 I made the final flight in this spring-tab programme in JN729 and pronounced it fit for Service Trials. Then on 5 February I completed the dive clearance of the production series Tempest V with underwing drop tanks in JN730.

By the end of 1944 at Langley the Tempest had become the fastest propeller-driven fighter in the world; the Tempest V had achieved a high standard for delivery to the RAF, and the third in the series, the Tempest 2 with Centaurus radial engine, was well into its manufacturer's trials and showing great promise.

As a background to all of this, the main Typhoon problems had been cured and the RAF now had a formidable force of these powerful ground-attack fighters already in action, flown by highly trained and motivated pilots for the coming 'invasion' across the channel.

Hawker still had much important work to do, but the company could feel with justification that 1944 had been a good year at Langley.

Tempest trial operations (1)

I left Hawker in February 1944 on posting to form and command the first operational wing of Tempests with headquarters initially at Castle Camps. Our Tempest V operations began in May at the RAF Newchurch advanced landing ground (ALG) in Kent, and it seemed like turning the clock back to the many Typhoon-experienced pilots in the squadrons.

Numbers 3 and 486 Sqns of No. 150 Wing, 85 Group, 2nd Tactical Air Force (TAF), had just completed re-equipment with the brand new Hawker Tempest V fighters which had begun to be delivered from the Langley factory to the MUs at Kemble and Aston Down in February, and these new fighters were now about to be assessed in trial operations.

The situation was very different from the troublesome introduction period which

Number 486 (NZ) Squadron was the first to equip with Tempest Vs.   (Imperial War Museum)

had been experienced with the Typhoons in 1942. We knew that the Tempest was a significant improvement over its predecessor, incorporating many of the changes which the pilots had called for, and we believed that the structural weakness of the Typhoon had been eliminated and its controllability at high speed much improved. We also hoped that the Sabre engine reliability had been improved to a point where we should no longer have to worry about frequent failures and fast, hard forced landings.

In the past month of working-up training the squadrons had covered low-level formation in pairs and 'finger-fours', full squadron formations, wing formations with two squadrons (the third squadron, No. 56 having yet to replace its Typhoons with Tempests) and then attended armament practice camp at Ayr where high 20 mm-gun scores had been obtained against ground and air (towed) targets. Finally they had practised night flying — first solo, then in pairs and finally in squadron formations by moonlight.

This training had gone well, and with rapidly growing enthusiasm for their new task the Tempest squadrons were anxious to get started and operationally experienced 'before the balloon went up'. The 'Invasion' day was thought to be less than a month away.

The first Tempest operations began on 7 May and soon confirmed that the precise controls, high cruising speed, fine gun-aiming stability (and reliable guns which fired 'full-shoots' virtually every time without stoppages and with encouraging accuracy), together with immensely improved forward and all-round cockpit vision, all added up to an exciting prospect. Our Tempests were ready for the great battles to come, we were faster in level flight and much faster in the dive than the opposition, and we felt immensely privileged to be the first to take Tempests into action.

Furthermore, whatever the battle for Europe should bring we had, we strongly believed, the finest, fastest fighter most suited to the varied roles expected of us. At the low and medium altitudes in which the coming air battles supporting the invasion and the subsequent armoured drive through Europe were expected to take place, the Tempest would be superior to all of the enemy's aircraft and in many ways to all other Allied fighters. Throughout May rapidly mounting ground-attack successes of the Tempests against rail, road and airfield targets, significantly without losses, boosted the already high morale in the Wing.

In these first operations there was no longer concern about the sleeve-valve failures in the Sabre engines and the tail structural failures which had bedevilled the introduction of Typhoons, but there was one new worry with the Tempest. In factory testing and more recently with the squadrons there had been a mounting number of cases of 'runaway' propellers. When this happened, always without warning, the r.p.m. suddenly surged violently 'off the clock' and unless the pilot reacted extremely swiftly in slamming the throttle closed, the out-of-control propeller allowed the engine to over-rev violently. This immediately resulted in failure of the engine and in all probability catastrophic failure of the reduction gear and complete loss of the propeller.

A number of these incidents had occurred, including one to my Tempest just after take-off from the Langley factory, leading to a hurried and, according to onlookers, a rather 'hairy' immediate forced-landing back at Langley. The cause had been identified, after much dissension between the airframe manufacturer and the propeller firm as to which was responsible, as a leak in a hydraulic seal in the propeller which, when it occurred, lost the vital oil pressure controlling the propeller constant-speed unit and the propeller 'ran-away'.

A modification was in hand to strengthen the seal with a copper band, but this had not yet reached the squadrons, and runaways remained a problem for some weeks before all the Tempests could be modified. So this for a time was an added worry for the Tempest pilots setting off across the Channel for low-level attacks. Enemy Flak was quite enough to face without the prospect of engine failure as well!

But all the rest was a bonus. To the new wing, spring-tab ailerons, a new fin and rudder, strengthened elevator mass-balance brackets (the cure for the Typhoon tail failures) and increased performance had been added the completely redesigned and refined windscreen and sliding canopy giving the fighter pilot the best all-round vision of any fighter at that time and setting a new standard which was followed in the later marks of the Typhoon, and the American P-51 Mustang and P-47 Thunderbolt, and in Spitfires from the Mk XIV onwards. The Allies were at last catching up in this respect with the enemy, whose Fw 190 had set a new standard of fighter cockpit vision in 1942.

In a final and valuable development the Tempest Vs also had their gunsights modified to reflect directly into especially selected 'Grade A' armour glass windscreen panels (a productionised and official version of the 609 Squadron 'local mod'), thus eliminating the troublesome obstruction to night or bad-weather vision previously caused by sight reflector glasses and surrounding metal brackets. The pilot could now line up on his target air-to-air or air-to-ground with completely clear vision ahead except for the orange-coloured gunsight reflected references.

From the first experiences of ground-attack with Tempests in daylight in may 1944 these improvements were outstanding. Once the pilot had manoeuvred his target into view through the front windscreen he was no longer conscious of any obstruction to his vision of it in the final critical seconds of attack.

This became even more apparent during the Tempest's first air–air combat on 8 June when three Bf 109G-6s were shot down at about 450 m.p.h. in the swirling manoeuvres of a dog-fight, and when a '109 more than filled the centre windscreen panel of my Tempest gunsight references were exactly as required and caused no distraction from or interference with vision of the target.

This valuable facility was appreciated even more from 16 June when the Tempests with their superior speed became the spearhead of the air defences of London against the V1 flying bombs. These very small, fast targets were, except in ideal weather conditions which seldom happened, nearly always difficult to see and line up with into

The author's first 150 Wing Tempest at Castle Camps, March 1944. The modified gunsight directly reflected in the windscreen is clearly visible. (Imperial War Museum)

an effective firing position. The Tempest's unobstructed forward vision was of great value throughout these critical day and night operations.

So, in the relatively short time of six weeks since first firing their guns in anger, the Tempests of 3 and 486 Sqns had 'worked up' very effectively in all their initially planned roles. The manufacturer's efforts in improving the basic Typhoon design had been highly successful, and the expectations that had developed strongly during introduction of the Tempests were now being fully justified in action.

Tempest trial operations (2)

The defence of London against the Fieseler F1.103, or V1.

Preparation for the expected attack by the V1 flying bomb began in early 1944 with planning for the concentration of heavy and light anti-aircraft artillery from Hastings to North Foreland, across Kent and Sussex to south London, the main area of the expected threat; and with the selection of squadrons of the fighters considered most suitable for interception of these high speed pilotless aircraft, and advanced airfields from which they could make the quickest intercepts as far away as possible from the main target area, London — close to their launch site or, failing that, at least over the Channel.

Little was known of the capabilities of the V1 other than its dimensions (from good reconnaissance photographs by Photographic Reconnaissance Unit (PRU) Spitfires, expertly interpreted by Constance Babington Smith and others, of the Peenemunde rocket testing establishment on the Baltic coast), and that it would probably operate at medium to low altitude and at speeds which would present problems for our fighters. Accordingly the defence task was allotted to the fastest available fighters, the Spitfire XIV, P-51B Mustang and the new Tempest V, potentially the fastest of them all.

By March 1944 the squadrons had been notified of their forthcoming deployment to ALGs in Sussex and Kent, and many Mosquito night-fighter squadrons were alerted to be prepared to add V1 interception to their existing night home defence task. Pending the V1 attack all of these squadrons would continue with their current tasks in preparation for the forthcoming invasion of Europe, but would revert immediately to V1 defence upon receipt of the code-words Divert Alert. There was no briefing on tactics of methods of attack. So little was known of the weapon's capabilities that methods for interception were left to the unit commanders to work out at station level. It was therefore with mixed feelings that the signal Divert Alert was received at the fighter stations on the night of 15 June 1944.

At Newchurch our new Tempests had proved excellent in ground-attack operations in the run-up to D-Day and, just recently on 8 June, in combat against Bf 109-G6s; and 3 and 486 Sqns did not exude enthusiasm at the thought of changing their active role to, as they saw it, the passive one of defending these shores against a small pilotless aircraft which was in fact a bomb! How were they supposed to attack it, and would it even be possible to shoot one down without our powerful 20 mm shells exploding the 1,800 lb amatol warhead? Then what would happen? How close in could one come in the attack without the explosion damaging or destroying the Tempest?

The questions could not be answered and it was a real case of 'suck it and see'. I told the assembled pilots in the briefing tent at Newchurch that we would treat the initial attacks as a normal radar-controlled intercept on an incoming raid; that I would ask the radar controllers, if they had height information, to position the fighters with about 1,000 ft height advantage at the point of intercept so that we could gain overtaking speed in the final diving attack; and that once we had gained actual experience we would modify tactics accordingly. For a start I suggested that we should not go in closer than about 300 yd when firing. Finally I said that any V1 we saw was going to kill people in

London if we let it through, and we would do our damnedest not to let that happen.

During the night of 15 June the night sky over Newchurch reverberated with a staccato roar which sounded like wave after wave of unsilenced motorcycles, and occasionally from about 3 a.m. onwards brilliant orange lights could be seen fleetingly, tearing overhead in occasional gaps in the low cloud sheet. With no sleep that night we were at Readiness at dispersal before daylight, and my 'operations' phone confirmed that a heavy 'Diver' attack was in progress on London and that Mosquito squadrons were intercepting. Their first success was reported at about 4.30 a.m. and then, with the first streaks of dawn light showing through rain clouds, two sections of Tempests were ordered off at 4.45 a.m.

Leading the first with Bob Cole of No. 3 Sqn I took off down the Newchurch flarepath, indistinct through the rain-spotted windscreen, and retracted the undercarriage. Keeping navigation lights on to help Bob Cole I checked in with radar control, who immediately said: 'Target for you 20 miles south of Folkestone heading north-west, height probably 2,000 ft. Buster.' I acknowledged and set maximum continuous power which soon had the Tempest indicating 385 m.p.h. in a slight climb.

In continuous rain this was now an 'instrument' sortie as I could see nothing below and only a broken cloud base rushing by overhead until at the radar controller's next call I increased to 3,000 ft in and out of broken cloud. Concentrating on the controller's steers I briefly realized that he was aiming us for a near head-on intercept, and at a probable closing speed around 800 m.p.h. the chance of sighting a small target in the prevailing murk was small indeed. There was also the possibility of colliding with it without seeing it in time to avoid it.

Then the controller again: 'Target straight ahead, port side, Blips merging.'

Coming off instruments as the grey dawn light spread between broken layered cloud I called 'Turning Port' to Bob in case he might not be in contact and quite suddenly there was a small dark object apparently shimmering and streaking past low on our port side. I called 'Tally Ho!' and pulled into a hard diving turn towards the object, which seemed to be a dark grey shining tube with now, as we turned behind it, a pulsing yellow flame at its back. Then it flew into a pearly-grey cloud-bank and disappeared.

Calling 'Opening up' to Bob Cole, I set full throttle and fine pitch again and with its throaty roar the Tempest was soon indicating over 400 m.p.h., and I asked the controller for further steers as I had lost sight of the V1. He confirmed my heading and said: 'Your target is just ahead of you, and you are crossing in at Folkestone'.

A few more seconds blind then a break in the cloud and there, a few hundred yards ahead, a slim thin-winged aircraft with a brilliant pulsing flame from, it seemed, near the top of its fin and rudder. My Tempest was slowly overhauling it and, intent on catching it before it reached cloud again, I maintained full power. From directly astern and a little below this small and very fast aircraft, now clearly seen despite the rain, I centred the gunsight aiming spot on its glaring athodyde (ramjet) flame and opened fire. The cannon shells could be seen bursting on its port side and wing and then after about 2 sec firing the ramjet flame went out.

The V1 remained steady, wings level and began to nose down. Open country was faintly visible between patchy cloud below, but I knew the town of Ashford must be somewhere ahead so I called in Bob Cole to finish it off, and pulled away to port. Bob, whom I had not seen since the interception began, had been there all along and he slid up alongside and opened fire. A few more visible strikes and the lethal-looking flying bomb rolled over, dived straight down and immediately a shimmering white globe of visible shock-wave rose up from where it had hit in a field, mercifully we noted with no apparent habitations nearby.

This was the first V1 destroyed in daytime; the second was brought down by the other 3 Sqn section a few minutes later, and a total of 11 by the Newchurch squadrons, 3 and 486, before the end of the day.

Much was learnt from this experience and over the next week in which the Newchurch Tempests and some Spitfire and P-51 units flew continuous over-lapping sorties from dawn to dusk while the Mosquitos covered the night hours. With this new knowledge plans and tactics were soon improved along the following guidelines.

The flying bombs were mainly aimed at London, and as their launching sites were mostly known the probable flight paths were predictable and could be patrolled. They were flying generally between 1,500 and 3,000 ft and were therefore frequently in and out of any low and medium cloud. Their speeds normally varied between 370 and 400 m.p.h. and the fastest could only be caught in level astern chases by Tempests, all other types of fighters having to dive to catch them, and this brought problems in radar positioning.

Mosquitos could only catch them from a fairly steep dive, but this difficulty was often offset by their much greater visibility on a clear night when the ramjet flame could be seen for 20 miles or more.

Head-on ground controlled radar intercepts with a relative closing speed of approximately 800 m.p.h. reduced the chances of making visual contact in any but good visibility conditions, so the controllers were told to aim for offset or beam intercepts whenever practical, and always when possible to try to put the fighter 1,000 ft or more above the plotted height of the V1. The range for opening fire on these small targets (20 ft wingspan and 3 ft fuselage diameter from dead astern) was critical — too far back and the fighter missed, too close in and the fighter could be brought down when the V1 exploded.

Trial and error led to the conclusion that 300 yd was the best compromise and this could be judged with the fighter's range-setting gunsight. Night interception was a greater difficulty as at the necessary close range the ramjet flame dazzled the pilot, destroying depth-perception. This was cleverly resolved by the RAE which quickly designed a simple night-sight which showed the target flame as a double image when closing in until at the correct 300 yd the images became one and the Mosquito could open fire.

The Tempest's gunnery with its four 20 mm cannon eventually proved highly accurate, but this accuracy also had the effect of frequently exploding the V1s. When this happened the fighter pilot could not avoid the explosion and at 400 m.p.h. the Tempest flew straight into the fireball after brief sight in fractions of a second of the flash of ignition, then a heavy thump of shock-wave and momentary searing heat. Then through into the clear air beyond the explosion, generally with pieces of debris still flying past.

Sometimes the fighters suffered debris damage and less frequently were brought down. Almost always there was fire damage to the fuselage and the fabric-covered rudder and elevators. In the first few days pilots returned with burnt jacket sleeves or, if they were flying in the hot weather with rolled-up shirt sleeves, their left arms were blistered or burned by flame entering the cockpit cooling air vents under the left side cockpit coaming. This difficulty was soon eliminated by shutting the vents!

There was a sharp learning curve in this operation and the success rate improved markedly after the first week, in which many V1s intercepted had slipped through and reached London with devastating effect.

Newchurch was required to report with recommendations to HQ No. 11 Group which controlled the battle over Kent and London and was responsible to HQs Air Defence of Great Britain (ADGB), and we submitted an urgent request that all the 'freelancing' RAF and Americans fighters, which had begun to swarm into the battle zone and seriously confuse and interfere with the vital radar controlled intercepts, should be banned from Kent, Sussex and Greater London which should be declared a 'no-fly zone' for all non-authorised aircraft.

We also asked for the Royal Observer Corps (ROC) to be deployed at close intervals along the coast from Hastings to Dover with signal (smoke) rockets, which should be fired towards V1s crossing the coast by any two ROC posts seeing them to provide pursuing fighters with a position indicated by converging rockets. We also recommended that AA Command should refrain from shooting at V1s which were obviously being pursued by fighters. All of these recommendations were implemented quickly except one.

The AA/fighter interface quickly became a subject of inter-Service rivalry and obduracy instead of the immediate co-operation which is so often vital if chaos is to be avoided in combined military operations. Eventually, with an increasingly bad national press and questions in parliament, Sir Roderick Hill of ADGB and General Sir Frederick Pile of AA Command finally reached an accommodation whereby vast numbers of heavy and light AA guns were moved into concentration in a narrow belt around the South coast, and the fighters were restricted to breaking off their chases at the coast. Other fighters could then patrol inland between the 'gun belt' and London. Though it was a major achievement by AA Command, this all took four weeks to set up, and meantime the enemy did not reduce the pressure but stepped up their attack, which continued to be dealt with mainly by the fighters.

With pilots flying four or more interceptions each day and some at night as well, when serviceability permitted, their skills increased dramatically. Most Tempest sorties resulted in their guns being fired and often there were further sightings of V1s when on the way back to base with no ammunition left. This presented a challenge. How else to stop this flying bomb reaching London?

Pilot initiatives varied from the Gung Ho 'fly in and ram' to more sophisticated and generally more successful methods. We found that the V1 giro stabilising mechanism (with lateral authority of only ±20°) could be toppled by the slipstream of a fighter crossing close in front of it, but this was a rather difficult thing to do as it involved losing sight of the bomb when it was directly behind the fighter! Some V1s were brought down in this way, but another technique proved more practical, if a trifle hair raising.

If a Tempest (with its advantage of surplus speed) was brought into close formation with the V1 such that the Tempest's wingtip was edged in under that of the V1, then by gently raising his wingtip the Tempest pilot could, with the boundary airflow over his wing, lift the V1's wing until its giro toppled without the fighter ever colliding with the missile. It was an unusual experience to formate at 400 m.p.h. within 6 in of a ton of high explosive, especially on the first occasion when we did not knew whether or not the cunning Germans had fitted detonators in the V1's wingtips!

This was 'experimental flying' in every sense, but in the event the precision control of the Tempest allowed the manoeuvre to be completed smoothly and with no contact, and the V1 rolled over to port and dived into the ground.

With massed raids arriving every day, sometimes in a continuous stream and sometimes in concentrations of 30 to 40 crossing the coast on a broad front in only a few minutes, this strained the radar stations' controlling of the fighters to the limit. But they seldom got through without at least being fired on by fighters or guns, and often by both at the same time. Pilots benefited from this multiplicity of targets and soon acquired the new techniques necessary for attacking this then totally new phenonemon, the cruise missile.

Though crude and dependent on navigation solely by steering with giro compass-coupled autopilot on a preset heading, the V1 quickly demonstrated its ability to penetrate defences, especially in the frequent bad weather which did not affect it at all.

The fighters found that new standards of accuracy were necessary, both in their own flying and in the information from ground radar control, who found it difficult enough to bring the fighters into visual contact with these small, fast targets in good visibility, and often impossible when visibility was less than a half mile. Pilots had to develop a sixth sense of which way and how much to turn when told 'target ½ mile ahead, crossing right to left' when still unsighted and continuing at full throttle, very conscious that the first sighting might be on a collision course with no time for avoiding action.

Often the fighter would be brought in behind for a long stern chase (and only Tempests could catch the fastest V1s in level flight). At dawn, dusk or at night the flaming exhaust of the V1 would be seen many miles ahead in good visibility; but in any light conditions when in cloud, rain or mist making contact would depend on accurate instrument flying and determination to press on at full power, accepting the risk element of collision when overtaking 'blind'. The night mosquitos who could 'see' the V1s on their A1 radar did not have this problem, but they did have the problem of having to dive to catch their targets.

By the end of June the fighters' success rate had increased to over 50 per cent of sightings but it was apparent that still far too many successful intercepts were failing to destroy their targets. The fighters were firing off all their ammunition often without causing lethal damage, and there was a clear reason for this. Throughout the war the guns of fighters had been harmonized, not on a point for optimum concentration at a given range, but on the basis of mathematical calculations by gunnery experts in the Air Ministry Armaments Branch known as 'Fighter Command Standard Spread Harmonization'.

When guns and gunsight were harmonized to this against the 'pattern' boards provided, it seemed that each of the eight machine guns (of a Hurricane, for example) were pointing in different directions and none at a central aiming point or target! The reasoned explanation for this was that the calculated 'dispersion' pattern would ensure that the maximum percentage of bullets would hit the target from any one burst of fire.

With experience many pilots had doubted this, and now at Newchurch, with daily instances of good pilots in good attacking conditions failing to destroy their targets, we took matters into our own hands. I felt that the 'standard harmonization' was theoretical and academic and did not take enough account of the major cause of inaccuracy in fighter gunfire, namely the pilot's 'stirring' effect when trying to hold the gunsight aiming spot on a fast-moving target in rough air, wake turbulence, sunglare dazzle and other disturbing factors.

We knew that the Tempest was exceptionally steady directionally and in pitch, and that the four 20 mm cannon were high-velocity weapons of high accuracy over what was then the long range of 1,000 yd. But the V1 was also an exceptionally difficult target, especially from dead astern, where its 8 in-thick wing and 3 ft-diameter fuselage were often difficult even to see in poor light from the 300–400 yd of the optimum attacking position. We believed that by point-harmonizing our guns and gunsights at 300 yd the cannon shells would be concentrated to a far better degree which would tend to balance our pilot 'stirring'.

The boffins pointed out that if you put all your shells through one small area of sky they would all miss if you were not aiming straight! So, failing to obtain a sympathetic response on the subject from 11 Group Armament Branch, I had the guns of my Tempest (JN751) point-harmonized. The results were spectacular. On the next sortie I exploded a V1 with one burst and shot down another with the remaining ammunition before landing back at Newchurch. A heavy raid was in progress and I shot down two more that day, again with only short bursts.

I ordered all of the Wing's guns to be point-harmonized after our day operations ended, and this was completed over the next two nights without interfering with the day actions, by a remarkable sustained effort by Wing Armaments Officer Tubby Cottingham and his enthusiastic armourers supported by the fully extended servicing wing. The results were twofold and immediate; the first was a dramatic improvement in success rate and a reduction in 'ones that got away', and the second was a predictable and irate instruction from 11 Group to restore 'standard' harmonization to all aircraft.

With the continuing heavy pressures on Newchurch I felt that my service career was of less importance than the vital job in hand, and in any case I had long since ceased to entertain thoughts of a personal long-term future. So Newchurch continued to apply its illegal 'point-harmonization' with increasing success which was further emphasised when we eventually returned to ground-attack activities on the Continent later that summer.

Then a new factor became evident. It was noticeable that, with all pilots operating in the same conditions of weather and target opportunities, a few emerged as very much more successful than the others. In the first eight weeks of sustained battle the squadron pilots on average each destroyed eight to ten V1s, but in this period the three most successful pilots shot down 130 V1s between them (all on Tempests). The most outstanding feature was the experience of 501 Sqn, especially deployed from the Night Fighter Development Unit at Ford to operate with Tempests, first at Newchurch where they had some early casualties, and finally at Manston. This squadron scored 88 V1s at night, but no fewer than 60 of these were by their CO and only 28 by the rest of the squadron in the same period and with the same opportunities.

It became clear that a few particularly talented pilots had quickly developed an unusual ability to use all the information available on every sortie and to co-ordinate it with exceptional flying skill and anticipation, persevering with great tenacity in conditions of adverse weather. This would often entail taking off in 'unflyable' weather with the knowledge that after the usual full-throttle, high-speed chase a landing would have to be made short of fuel at some unplanned diversionary base where the weather would probably be almost as bad. The qualities needed for this ability were not easy to define, although at the end of the campaign it could be seen that all of the most successful pilots had been rated 'above average' fighter pilots before this.

There was also something else. These pilots developed and maintained an exceptional 'situational awareness' which even in the most stressful circumstances enabled them to resolve instinctively the problems in time and space inevitably remaining at the crucial point of the intercept if the target was still not in sight when the ground radar controller could help no more. This was emphasised when two senior and distinguished pilots, one from headquarters and one an experimental test pilot from the Hawker Tempest factory, visited Newchurch to gain personal experience of the overall operating problems.

Flying with our squadrons on intercept sorties on a number of occasions, neither managed to bring their guns to bear even though their leaders finally shot down their targets. Much chagrin and frustration ensued, but they need not have felt embarrassed because by then we all knew that only daily concentration on these special operations in all conditions could bring a pilot up to the level of efficiency achieved by the leading squadrons at that time.

In the final outcome, at the end of the main (June–September) period of the battle the fighters' total of 1,744 V1s destroyed was nearly matched by the AA guns with much-improved accuracy in the last month, with 1,460. Of all the fighters the Tempests of Newchurch and Manston were the most effective, with 726 destroyed.

VJ Day 50. Not only in the UK, but throughout the community of the Allies of the Second World War, we have recently celebrated the end of that tragic global conflict, a war which had affected dozens of nations. Inevitably that resulted in many millions of casualties, so we also commemorated those who died then, that we might live as we do today. Actually, how we live today is almost certainly not what they had in mind; but it is we who have fouled things up since.

No. 3(F)Sqn Newsletter September 1995

Last command

My war ended, rather prematurely I felt, in a German prison camp after being shot down by ground fire near Bocholt in Germany while leading the Volkel Tempests in a ground-attack in October 1944. After being held prisoner by the Russians for nearly a month after the end of hostilities, in May 1945 I eventually rejoined the Service for some interesting test flying at the Central Fighter Establishment (CFE).

This was followed by posting to form the first Wing of the new Centaurus-engined Hawker Tempest IIs at Chilbolton in August, and finally by a posting back to CFE, now at West Raynham, to command the Air Fighting Development Unit (AFDU).

The AFDU was my last command in the RAF before I rejoined the aircraft industry in 1946. When I took over the unit in October 1945 its current task was comparative assessment of the gun-aiming qualities of all current in-service fighters. These included the very new Gloster Meteor III and de Havilland Vampire jets, the Griffon-engined Spitfires Mk 14, 21 and contra-prop 22 and the Tempest V and II.

This provided some interesting flying and the 15 ft² targets on the Wainfleet range in the Wash quickly separated the good from the less good in terms of ease of target acquisition, steadiness and accuracy in the firing pass, and of course the direct comparisons of hits scored with each type under (as far as possible) similar attack conditions of light, visibility and wind.

At that time the Air Fighting Development Squadron (AFDS) had a large percentage of pilots with some previous test flying experience at Boscombe Down or at the MUs, and all had one or more distinguished operational tours behind them. So there was much experience there and at least five of the pilots went on to serve as chief experimental test pilots in industry, including 'Fifi' Fifield (Martin-Baker), Bob Moore (SAAB), Bill Waterton (Glosters), 'Wimpy' Wade (Hawker) and the author (English Electric, BAC, and British Aerospace).

The outcome of these trials was not surprising to us, though it apparently was to many at staff level! The new jets both proved to have such low directional damping that their 20 mm gun scores by all pilots were relatively low and unsatisfactory. The Griffon Spitfires were all better in this respect, especially the Mk 22 with contra-rotating propellers (and zero propeller torque); but the most consistently higher scorers were the Tempests V and II and of these the Tempest V's dead-beat directional damping even in high turbulence made it the most accurate gun platform of all.

None of this was unexpected to those of us who had expended thousands of 20 mm shells against enemy targets with Tempests and Spitfires during the recent Normandy to Germany campaign, but somehow these experiences had not filtered back to headquarters where with the coming of 'peace' the general view seemed to be that the 'jets were the best' in everything. But in AFDS at that time we had to show that this was not so in the important aspect of gun-aiming.

Another feature of these trials was the first Service assessment of the brand new and revolutionary Giro gunsight, the GGS Mk 1. It was perhaps unfortunate that the powers had selected a Spitfire XIV for the first installation, as the bulky new gunsight virtually filled the Spitfire's windscreen and seriously reduced forward vision. Its mounting also brought the back of the sight giro mechanism into such close proximity with the pilot's face as to create an obvious hazard in a 'hard' landing. Obvious, that is, to us at AFDU but apparently not to the Armament Branch specialists who described as 'rubbish' my suggestion that almost any other fighter cockpit would be more suitable for these tests.

However, only a few weeks later the GGS aircraft had a forced-landing following engine failure and the unfortunate pilot was produced, with a face somewhat modified by hard contact with the GGS, as confirmatory evidence at our next CFE armament meeting! The chairman, the Group Captain/Armaments, Branch was not amused!

The GGS principle was of course a certain success as it introduced a control and an improved standard in gunnery which very soon raised the average fighter pilot capability to score hits, especially on a turning target. But at AFDU we maintained a conservative view that a 'good shot' would still be able to do better with the standard 'fixed' gunsight than when endeavouring to follow a wandering giro-stabilised pippa even though it gave the correct lead-angle.

This period at AFDU was valuable in providing unique opportunity for an overview on the capabilities of fighters at that time and, 50 years later, it is interesting to reflect that being both battle-experienced and also objective in following the strong policy of CFE in assessment, we did not go along entirely with the current 1945 wave of over-enthusiasm about 'the jets' even though they were fast, interesting and in the case of the Vampire only, fun to fly.

The Vampire and Meteor had the great advance of this new, smooth and quiet turbine power and were 50 m.p.h. or so faster than the fastest piston engined fighters of the period, but the Meteor was cumbersome and could not match Spitfires, Tempests or P-51s in manoeuvrability, while the Vampire though very agile and aerobatic had comparatively poor gun-aiming stability and very short fuel endurance. Neither the Meteor III, operationally Mach limited at 0.78, or the Vampire at 0.74, demonstrated a significant improvement in compressibility limits compared with the 0.76 of the Tempests and rather less for the Griffon Spitfires, and both were altitude-limited for practical operational purposes to 37–40,000 ft.

So we concluded at CFE that for that period the balance, against the known threat, of the later Griffon Spitfire for 20–30,000 ft and the Tempest Vs and IIs for combat air patrol (CAP) below 20,000 ft, together with the Tempests capably replacing Typhoons in the low-level tactical strike role, was very adequate for the time, and that P-51 Mustangs were still the only practical (and very effective) long-range fighters. However, with the arrival of the second-generation jets within a few years with improved aerodynamics and the new, powerful axial-flow engines, we expected that the piston-engined fighters would become outdated as maximum speeds rose from their 450+ m.p.h. to the 500–600 m.p.h. and more of the jets. But we foresaw at the end of 1945 that this new generation of fighters would need a drastic improvement in Mach capability to approach or hopefully exceed the speed of sound. These thoughts were indeed soon seen to have been prophetic.

Chapter Five

Testing the World's first propeller-turbine aircraft

I left West Raynham in January 1946 and, deciding against accepting a permanent commission in the RAF in favour of joining the aircraft industry at this fascinating period of the new jet era, I served with Gloster Aircraft, testing the new Meteor IVs and then de Havilland with the Vampires until finally joining English Electric in May 1947 as chief test pilot. Before this an intriguing experience occurred at Gloster.

In 1945 the aircraft industry of the West was preoccupied with the new and exciting evolution of the gas turbine engine and of a second generation of jet fighters and bombers to take advantage of them.

In addition to its Derwent centrifugal-flow engines and the newly-developed Avon series axial-flow jets with greatly increased power, Rolls-Royce had initiated the world's first investigation into the practicability of a major order of improvement in fuel economy with a propeller-turbine. The programme involved driving a five-bladed Rotol propeller through a spur reduction gear designed by Lionel Howarth and mounted on the front of a basic Welland centrifugal-flow jet engine.

Ground testing had been satisfactory in the test cells at Hucknall, and Gloster Meteor Mk.1 EE227, provided by the Ministry of Supply, was modified to 'turbo-prop' configuration with two of these propeller turbines, now named Trents, in place of the original Welland jets. The world's first turbo-prop flight test took place on 20 September 1945 at Church Broughton flown by Eric Greenwood, chief test pilot of the Gloster Aircraft Company, and some major problems were encountered.

Greenwood reported that the engines functioned correctly though with much propeller-order vibration, but that the Meteor's aircraft handling qualities had deteriorated severely and that, not unexpectedly with the engines each only giving 1,400 lb of static thrust, performance was much reduced from the jet standard. The increased side area forward caused by the propellers, together with propeller torque, had resulted in directional instability causing handling difficulties; and then a major problem arose at the end of the first flight.

When, on flaring to land, Greenwood closed the throttles on the conventional two-lever control system (per engine), one for power and the other for propeller r.p.m., this not only closed engine power to idling but at the same time 'disced' the propellers to the maximum drag, and the aircraft hit the runway at a high rate of descent, luckily without causing serious damage.

The Trent Meteor at Moreton Valence. (Imperial War Museum)

For the next few flights, mine included, the briefing was changed to ensure that a high throttle setting was maintained until touchdown and that fine speed control was adjusted with the propeller pitch levers. It was a cumbersome system and tended to be confusing, and later for the main part of the Trent test programme the control system was modified to one 'power' lever per engine with interconnected throttle and propeller r.p.m. It was never a fully satisfactory system for operational flying but it was safer for the test programme!

Before flight No 2, twin additional fins were added to the tailplane to improve directional stability and then the aircraft was flown in February 1946 to Gloster's experimental base at Moreton Valence for further evaluation, first by Greenwood and then, on 14 May, by the author. The engine controls, still in their twin-lever form, were significantly different from those of the Welland and Derwent jets in which one power lever controlled engine speed limited only by r.p.m. and jet pipe temperature set limits. With the Trents the pilot set maximum throttle on each engine for take-off and the propeller pitch levers at Full Fine, and he then monitored jet pipe temperature and r.p.m. relative to red-line limits.

Take-off was prolonged by sluggish acceleration, and above the normal turbine whine a thrashing roughness indicated the presence of the propellers. Rotating at about 110 kt, the aircraft entered only a flat climb and was obviously severely underpowered. Levelling at 10,000 ft after a slow climb, cruise power was selected by reducing power with the throttle levers and with the pitch levers remaining at maximum.

In turbulence through broken cloud the 'snaking' typical of all Meteors in that period was even more pronounced and directional damping was in fact found to be marginal throughout the flight envelope although acceptable for test purposes. The

The Trent Meteor with one propeller 'feathered'. It could not maintain height in this condition with undercarriage and flaps down.

'thrashing' roughness from the propellers was present in all flight conditions and was a marked deterioration on the characteristic smoothness of the pure jets.

With this restricted performance there was no point in making an operational assessment in this aircraft, which could be outperformed by piston-engined fighters like the Tempest, so the rest of the sortie concentrated on safety aspects for its role as a test-bed for the turbo-prop principle. Here a major problem (alerted in the briefing) was confirmed. In simulated single-engine flight with one engine at maximum torque and the other at a power setting simulating a feathered propeller there was adequate single-engine controllability in the 'clean' aircraft configuration below 10,000 ft, but with undercarriage down even at 2,000 ft the aircraft would not maintain height on one engine, and with flaps down as well it entered a steep rate of descent! This inadequacy did not preclude its limited use for testing the Trents, but all flying with this low thrust would have to be planned to allow 'energy management' recovery in the event of an engine emergency.

With little else to commend it I brought EE227 rather gingerly down the final approach at Moreton Valence, controlling speed with the pitch levers, and noted that although it was still vaguely like a Meteor in response to controls it felt generally 'soggy', especially directionally, and only in the flare and gentle touchdown on the soft action levered suspension' undercarriage was it unchanged from the Meteor I jet.

Soon after this the aircraft was returned to Rolls-Royce for the engine controls modification, and it eventually went to RAE Farnborough for further turbo-prop investigation. I did not have to fly it again, and felt no disappointment at all!

Chapter Six

Vampire production testing

The years immediately following the Second World War were times of contrast in the aviation world. Mass production for war was cancelled abruptly with consequent disruption and unemployment in the industry, while at the same time this was the beginning of the jet era and some fortunate factories were contracted to design and, if successful, build the new jet fighters and bombers.

After a last task in the RAF evaluating Meteor IIs and IIIs at the CFE I took this experience into the industry, first testing Meteors and then Vampires prior to beginning the trials of the RAF's first jet bomber, the Canberra.

An incident during a production test on a Vampire at English Electric's Samlesbury production plant was unexpected.

Following the Second World War there was a natural and widespread cutback in military aircraft procurement, and the main aircraft companies faced major reorganization. The war years of mass production and high employment were over it seemed and unlikely to return; but there were some exceptions.

This was the beginning of the jet era. In Germany the Messerschmitt Me 262 had already shown much promise in operations in the last year of the war, though limited by the direct and misconceived orders of Hitler to use it mainly on fighter-bomber attacks for which it was much less suited than air defence. At the eleventh hour small numbers of Me 262s were eventually employed in the fighter role against allied bomber formations over Bavaria with significant success.

The Allies had followed the German lead with the development of two British jet fighter designs, the Gloster Meteor and the de Havilland Vampire, and the Americans had flown prototypes of the Bell XP-59 Airacomet, but none of these were developed sufficiently to become effective before the war ended. One squadron of Meteors (616 Sqn RAuxAF) began operations from Manston against the V1 flying bomb attacks on London in which they had little success, scoring only 13 V1s out of the more than 1,700 hundred destroyed by the RAF in the summer of 1944. Later the Meteors were moved to the Continent to take part in the final battles for Germany, but were again only able to achieve limited successes against the multiplicity of targets, air and ground, available at that time.

But the Me 262 was showing the way, and both in the UK and America it was seen that evolution of airframe design to take full advantage of the greatly increased power of the soon-to-be-available second-generation jet engines would be essential if the

The author demonstrating a Vampire I at the 1947 SBAC Display at Radlett. (British Aerospace)

West was to be able to match the clearly emerging threat of strong jet-equipped forces from the Iron Curtain countries. So jet development and production was not slowed down after 1945 for a number of years, and the companies involved continued to work at full pressure. One of these, English Electric in Lancashire in the north-west of England, was heavily involved. As a wartime subcontractor to Handley Page, English Electric had built many hundreds of Hampden and Halifax bombers so successfully and of such good quality that the company had been selected as early as 1943 to become one of the first in the new jet field.

Design and in some cases production contracts were put out for jet fighters at this stage to de Havilland for the Vampire, Gloster for the Meteor, Supermarine for a jet development of their Spiteful piston-engined fighter, the Attacker, and to English Electric for a subcontracted production run of over 1,000 Vampires because de Havilland had insufficient capacity at that time owing to mass production of its highly successful Mosquito.

Then came an unwelcome surprise to the rest of the industry. The 'newcomer' English Electric was also granted a development contract, with potential for large-scale follow-on production for the B.3/45, destined to be Britain's first jet bomber. In 1947 this breakthrough in aviation technology, soon to become famous as the Canberra, was well on the way in design and prototype build had begun.

As the designated test pilot for the B.3/45 I had been involved with its design for over a year by the summer of 1948, and had been able to keep in jet practice at Warton in a programme of high Mach number 'compressibility' investigation with a Meteor IV in direct research for the new bomber's coming trials, and in any spare moments testing the Vampires coming at high rate off the company's Samlesbury production lines.

A Vampire I at the English Electric factory, Samlesbury, in 1947. The author flew 567 Vampires on production test and demonstrations during 1946–49. (British Aerospace/ NW Heritage Group)

This flying was enjoyable in the light, manoeuvrable Vampire, and uncomplicated with one exception. There were at that time no aids to navigation whatsoever at Samlesbury, nor at the newly developing experimental airfield at Warton. This was not unusual as factory testing had continued to be conducted traditionally throughout the war years without radio, but now at Samlesbury the English Electric Company did have VHF radio for local airfield control. Accordingly all test flying was carried out by pilot-navigation which was simple in visual flight conditions, but this seldom occurred, particularly in the Lancashire winter months.

English Electric Vampire production at Samlesbury in 1947. (British Aerospace/NW Heritage Group)

The production test schedule for the Vampire, though straightforward, was quite demanding in bad weather. It consisted of take-off and maximum-power climb to 30,000 ft, then a maximum-power level flight for 2 min to record ASI and engine figures, particularly jet-pipe temperature which with the Goblin engine could sometimes over-run its limits. Pulling up from the 'level' the Vampire would be climbed to 40,000 ft, oxygen and controls checked and then came preparation for a dive to Mach 0.74, the compressibility buffet onset and test limit.

The airspace over Lancashire was free for testing at that time, before the onset of controlled airspace and the establishment of the first UK airway, Amber 1, which was soon to run north-west over the Pennines just east of Samlesbury. Accordingly in good weather the test flights could take place anywhere over Lancashire, Yorkshire or Cumberland, limited only by the Vampire's short range and fuel endurance.

Cloudy, overcast, rain or fog conditions were another matter, however, and the test flights were controlled to a close pattern. The climb was made to the west from Samlesbury, and then continued to the west for the high speed run. On completion of this the Vampire would be off the coast at Blackpool and would be turned through 180° on to due east at 40,000 ft, and then dived to the Mach limit providing this could be reached above or out of cloud. Then followed an instrument descent if necessary through cloud to the cloud-base which would be reached in the general area of Preston, followed by slow-speed handling and stalling below cloud in the Samlesbury area. At this point the fuel state would be low and the landing was made at Samlesbury.

With experience and continuous practice it became possible to fly these patterns without any sight of ground from entering the cloud-base until descending back through the cloud after 40–45 min, and always be sure of breaking out within a few miles of Samlesbury; but because of the high ground of the Pennines a few miles to the east (Winter Hill was the high point) these operating limits had to be strictly observed.

Exceptions were when the cloud base was lower in rain, smoke or sometimes snow, and the Vampire would be flown out below cloud towards the coast where often the cloud-base would be higher or broken, and then a shorter climb schedule would be flown for a subsequent descent for a cloud-break over the coast heading out to sea. But this had to be done with precise calculation by the pilot.

These apparently restrictive circumstances did not interfere unduly with English Electric's successful production of Vampires, 1,369 of which were delivered from Samlesbury between 1946 and 1949.

My log records 471 Vampire test flights at Samlesbury, the total work-load being shared with long-serving test pilot Johnny Squier. One of these flights on 30 July 1948, was of unexpected interest.

One of the latest series production Vampires, Mk V, VV453, was ready for its first flight. This mark incorporated a number of improvements on the earlier series including the uprated Goblin 2 engine and cockpit pressurisation, and consequently the production test schedule had been revised to extend the climb to 43,000 ft (the required service operating ceiling being 42,800 ft) to check engine performance and cabin pressurisation performance and integrity.

At this period test pilots were receiving training at the Institute of Aviation Medicine (IAM) at Farnborough in its 'high altitude and decompression chamber' in anticipation of the testing at increasing altitudes which would soon be required with the new second-generation jets. The safe limit with oxygen breathing only was officially regarded as 40,000 ft, and flight above this altitude would need cockpit pressurisation and, to cover the emergency loss of pressure case, assisted breathing by 'pressure-breathing' waistcoats and later by 'partial pressure suits and pressure helmets'; but these items were under development at that time, and I had taken part in this work with the IAM specialists.

For the pressurised production Vampire Mk V, however, we were extending the tests above the 'safe' 40,000 ft limit because we had faith in the integrity of the pressurisation system and because as yet 'the authorities' had not got around to telling us not to! In the ponderous way of officialdom this situation was to be repeated identically some years later with the much higher altitude performance testing requirements of the Canberra.

Vampire VV453 climbed steeply away from Samlesbury directly into an 8/8ths cloud base prevailing over Lancashire at about 2,000 ft, and broke into brilliant sunshine above a dazzling white cloud sheet at 5,000 ft. I steadied on a heading of 280° and carried out the routine checks on controls, trims and engine conditions, and then the maximum performance 'level' at 30,000 ft.

Pulling up from this, still on 280° heading, I checked pressurisation and engine figures again passing 40,000 ft, and decided to top the climb on the same heading before turning eastbound for the descent and Mach limit dive. The aircraft was still climbing well with everything relaxed and normal and the altimeter winding up to 43,000 ft when — bang! What felt like a very clear explosion was followed by debris flying into my face and a continuous roaring noise and a violent drop in temperature. I knew at once that this was a pressure cabin failure and the 'explosive decompression' for which we had been trained at Farnborough.

I knew also that I had only about 2 min to retain consciousness before I 'blacked out' with anoxia, and that I had better get the emergency drill right! Holding my breath to delay the effects of anoxia, I throttled back to idling at once, opened the airbrakes and eased the stick forward to enter a shallow descent, rolling left onto an easterly heading. I then trimmed this in the hope that the Vampire would not nose down into a steep compressibility dive and, with a last view of the altimeter passing about 39,000 ft, I must have lost consciousness briefly for I next noted it unwinding quickly through 34,000 ft, and was aware that conditions were very rough, noisy and cold.

Gradually realising that the Vampire was now in a steep dive and buffeting heavily, I pulled back hard on the stick and the aircraft responded slowly, the airbrakes having prevented the dive reaching full compressibility. I levelled out at about 33,000 ft, the Mach no. dropped, the noise subsided a little and I was able to take stock of the situation. Above and to the right of my head there was a plate-sized hole in the Perspex canopy — that was where the pressure had gone!

After this disorientating experience I had no sure knowledge of position above the continuous white cloud sheet. Remembering that the cloud base had been little higher than the Pennines to the east of Samlesbury, it would not be wise to continue descending on an easterly heading until breaking cloud, and assuming that I was somewhere over the Lancashire coastal area I began a cautious spiral descent to the cloud tops at around 6,000 ft, and then straightened out on to north-westerly heading in cloud.

With the suddenness which was always a surprise the cloud broke below at about 2,000 ft, and immediately I recognized the Wyre at Fleetwood and turned south-east for Samlesbury,

The incident had resulted in no further damage. The canopy failure was traced to a crack in the Perspex which had spread back from the canopy forward frame, and after a new canopy had been fitted the aircraft was soon ready again for a repeat flight test.

But I had a severe headache which lasted for some days, though luckily undamaged eardrums. It had been valuable experience for the much higher altitude testing still to come in the trials of the Canberra and Lightning throughout the 1950s.

Chapter Seven

Canberra

1949 was a year of great expectations in British aviation. Our first jet bomber (B.3/45) and first swept-wing jet fighter (Hunter), and the world's first jet airliner (Comet) were all under development in this country. I was in charge from the beginning of the trials of the English Electric B.3/45 Canberra jet bomber, which included an early unexpected incident and some later complications in the subsequent supply of Canberras to the United States Air Force.

One of the factors which a test pilot needs to keep well in mind is human error — and not just his own! For example, one day in 1943 at the great Hawker Aircraft production factory and experimental test centre, Langley, I was taxying across the bumpy grass airfield to begin an experimental test flight on one of the new Tempest V fighters which were in the final stages of contractor's tests prior to Boscombe Down service trials, when I noticed something different. The elevator circuit seemed strange.

E. W. 'Teddy' Petter, chief engineer, English Electric Co. Preston. (British Aerospace)

Don Crowe, chief production engineer. (British Aerospace)

David 'Dai' Ellis, flight development and wind tunnel expert. (British Aerospace)

Ray Creasey, the genius behind Warton's aerodynamic success. (British Aerospace)

Turning to line up at the boundary I exercised the controls in the normal way and again found a difference in the elevator, which seemed heavier to move statically than normal. Moving the stick to full travel forward and back and releasing it each time caused it to stay where it was. There was some increased friction somewhere. I thought of ice in the hinges — it was a frosty morning — and momentarily considered taking off to see if the rough ride would shake it free, but decided against it.

Slightly frustrated at not being able to fly this interesting sortie, I taxied back in and told the ground staff to look for an obstruction in the elevator circuit. They found one rather quickly! This was one of the first programmes to involve in-flight recording of data, and Hawker had installed a pack in the rear fuselage containing basic instruments and a recording cine camera. In this instance the webbing straps holding the instrumentation pack to its tray had been tied round the elevator control runs which ran just beneath it. A little more movement of the stick by the pilot could have jammed the elevator entirely!

With the arrogance of youth I then took the view that I could never make a stupid mistake like that, but that in future I would need to be suspicious of the work of all those involved in preparing 'my' aircraft. It did not take long for disillusion to set in when my own mistakes made it clear that it is human to err in any sphere of human activity, and that in the air the results of human error can be more drastic more quickly than they generally are on the ground.

Nevertheless over-confidence again eroded caution before long, and after five years of interesting test flying of the new-era jets following the Second World War, leading to the fascinating first flight programme at Warton on the English Electric B.3/45, Canberra, Britain's first jet bomber, I had become fairly convinced of my own infallibility!

Then came the second prototype B.3/45, VN813, this time engined with Rolls-Royce Nenes as an insurance against delayed development of the RA2 Avon axial-flow engine specified for, and actually already in the first prototype, VN799.

Britain's first jet bomber prototype, the English Electric B.1, before flight, at Warton in 1949. Serial VN799. (British Aerospace)

With larger nacelles to accommodate the centrifugal-flow engines the aerodynamics were adversely affected, especially at the high speed end where a loss of Mach 0.04 was apparent. Otherwise the aircraft handled well and the trials proceeded without difficulty until on one day in early 1950, when I was flying it on aft CG handling assessment.

All went well as I worked through the schedule noting lighter stick force-per-G at the lower speeds in relation to those of the first, Avon engined, prototype. During the flight the CG had been progressively moved back by scheduled fuel balancing between the three fuselage tanks, and only during the last test points had I noted 'lightening off' in pitch to near neutral — pilot-induced-oscillation (PIO) was not far away!

Static stability was still positive however at 200 kt IAS or above and it was not until

The B.1 airborne! May 1949. (British Aerospace)

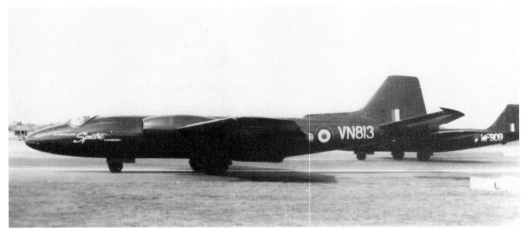

The second B.1 prototype, with large Nene engine nacelles and original long dorsal fin. Seen here with the D. H. 'Spectre' rocket engine for trials. (British Aerospace)

I reduced speed for letting down towards Warton that the stick force gradient virtually disappeared below 150 kt IAS. It felt to be at or very close to the 'neutral point', and this was not supposed to happen!

With the fuel remaining it would have been simple to balance the CG further forward for landing, but I still did not feel this necessary and continued on the approach with the longitudinal stick forces at virtually zero as speed fell below 110 kt IAS. The aircraft was still flyable with care, so I continued to the runway, flared and very nearly over-flared with little or no 'feel' about the elevator, and then we were down.

I closed the throttles and then it happened! As speed dropped the nosewheel began to rise when it should have remained firmly on the ground. Full forward wheel put it back momentarily, and then it rose firmly into the air once more! Progressive wheel braking then returned the nosewheel into contact until as forward rolling speed reduced to standstill the ultimate embarrassment occurred! The nose rose again firmly and quickly until with a 'clunk' from the rear the tail bumper hit the runway and we had finally arrived with VN813 sitting on its tail with the cockpit about 20 ft above the runway. There was no way I could taxy in or even get out of the cockpit until help arrived!

The aircraft had clearly landed with its CG aft of the aft limit (and behind the main wheels!) which said a lot for the basic controllability of the aircraft, and even more about the competence of the pilot who had thought it unnecessary to check the fuel balancing requirements in the flight test schedule on the assumption that the engineers could not have got it wrong. A dangerous assumption and an object lesson for the future!

In November 1949 I delivered the first prototype Canberra to Boscombe Down for its initial 'preview trial' and, being potentially the RAF's first jet bomber and a radical departure for the time, it was arranged that I would give conversion training to the Boscombe test pilots and then remain at Boscombe to monitor the trial and provide manufacturer's assistance where needed. This unusual procedure was seen to work well with benefit to both sides, and my final report on the trials is reproduced here in its original form.

(English Electric Company internal report)
FINAL REPORT ON PRELIMINARY HANDLING TRIALS OF CANBERRA PROTOTYPE VN.799. AT BOSCOMBE DOWN. 15.11.49
(declassified 30-year rule)

Upon arrival at Boscombe on Saturday the 12th of November it was encouraging to learn that no major difficulties had been discovered or severe criticism produced during the intensive trials of the second week.

A considerable amount of flying had been carried out at full forward and full aft loading, and the pilots were unanimous in saying that the aircraft was stable at these conditions at all speeds and altitudes within the limits recommended by the Company.

Control handling to 45,500', to .8M at various heights, to 460 kts IAS at 7,400' and to 4½G, had been carried out during the 24 flights totalling 30 hours flying time which had been completed in the 18 days of the trials.

Much emphasis was placed on rudder investigation and asymmetric flying, and it was confirmed that the machine could be climbed away from 110 kts on one engine with wheels and flaps down at the landing weight.

Full load handling had been carried out up to 40,000', and had been entirely satisfactory.

During the final phase investigation was carried out of the buffet boundary, and the results were apparently regarded with satisfaction.

A meeting was held with the three pilots concerned on the 13th of November, and at that meeting W/C Davies gave the following as the major criticisms which would be forthcoming as a result of these preliminary trials, from the pilot's viewpoint:

1) The rudder would be criticised as being out of harmony with the elevator and aileron, in that it is light about neutral, and that this lightness becomes more marked with increase in altitude and Mach No. Careful investigation of the rudder had not revealed a tendency to lighten off with full rudder application and there was no longer suspicion that the rudder is ineffective or overbalanced, as there were no conditions of flight in which it failed to give satisfactory control. The feel would be however criticised strongly by one pilot and to a lesser degree by the other two, though this criticism was not reflected by the opinion of W/C Keynes, C.F.I. of C.F.S. This latter officer flew the machine on the 13th of November to assess it from the training aspect and reported that he thought the controls perfect; but when asked about the rudder he said that it was slightly lighter about neutral than the other two controls but that he would not criticise this severely.
It is clear however that this condition should be improved.

2) The slight tendency to buffet of the flaps at the full flap speed was criticised as a "feel" criticism and not as a "control" criticism and there was agreement that this buffet did not persist below 110 kts, and that it was in no way severe.

3) There were many criticisms of the vision properties of the perspex canopy, but subsequent experience at high altitude showing that the canopy does not mist or ice appreciably had changed their views quite considerably. The matter would need careful consideration, especially with reference to the "waving" or distortion reported at high altitude.

4) The nose up pitching moment produced by flap operation at the maximum flap speed, and the lack of sufficient tailplane range to trim this was criticised

severely from the night and instrument flying aspect. Further tailplane range would be called for.

5) The buffet produced by operation of the bomb doors might affect bomb aiming and this would have to be investigated. There was no criticism of this operation from the point of view of trim changes up to the speeds which they had been permitted to investigate.

6) Trials at full forward CG had produced evidence that full "up" elevator travel was required for the landing. On a number of occasions the pilots had found the wheel fouling their harness locks however carefully these had been adjusted previously. This was considered unsatisfactory, and an alteration would be called for in elevator to stick gearing, or in reduction of the width of the brake operating mechanism. A rider was added that the neutral position of the stick is now regarded as perfect, and should on no account be altered. It was also suggested that there may be a question of whether there is sufficient "up" elevator for the full forward landing case at the lowest approach speed possible.

7) Free play in the pilot's Martin-Baker seat was criticised severely. This should be rigid.

8) Criticism was made of the high control forces encountered when taxying down or across strong winds. Internal control locks would be called for.

9) The oxygen regulator was regarded as too far out of reach, and should be repositioned within easy reach of the tightly strapped pilot.

10) Assuming the retention of engine oil temperature gauges, these should be grouped with the jet pipe temperature gauges.

11) The R.P.M. indicators were regarded as very confusing and recommendations would be made for improvement.

12) The P.12 Compass was regarded as totally unsatisfactory in its present position.

13) The suitability of the G3 Compass was queried.

14) A request would be made for the press-to-speak button to be moved to the top of the starboard spectacle above the standard position for the tailplane trim switch.

15) Severe criticism was made of the arrangements for pilot ejection, and it would be suggested that the Malcolm seat principle would be preferred, where two pulls on the blind complete the whole operation.

16) W/C Davies (Commanding Officer 'B' Squadron) still criticised the flat approach, though this criticism was not confirmed by other pilots. He would regard the development of effective dive brakes at low speed as of the greatest importance.

17) The removal of the aileron trim wheel to the port side of the cockpit would be required, and the possibility of aileron trim by electric actuator would be suggested.

18) The flap control switch is disliked and there would be a request for its operation by the "standard cockpit" type lever.

19) The comfort factor of the pilot's seating position was criticised in varying degree, but the general opinion was that it was quite impracticable for periods of longer than two hours with the present equipment.

From the above list it will be seen that there are likely to be no criticisms involving major structural alterations, and that the majority of the more serious questions are already under consideration.

In general, there appears to be a feeling of considerable surprise and gratification that a prototype should behave so extremely well over so great a range of speed and altitude. This good impression has been enhanced by the unusually high standard of serviceability which has been maintained to produce a daily average of 1,2/3 hours flying time for eighteen consecutive days.

Seven different pilots flew the machine and they were unanimous in their praises of it, all stating that it was one of the finest machines they had ever flown.

To wind up the trials Gr/Cpt. Broad arranged for comparative manoeuvre tests to be carried out at altitude between the Canberra and the latest operational type of service fighter, namely — the Mk 8. Meteor. The first of these tests on the 12th of November was not completed owing to the fact that the Meteor, while climbing at full power was unable to keep pace with the Canberra which was climbing at full load (39,500 lbs) and climbing power.

The Meteor pilot returned to base to check his machine for open wheel doors etc. and when no defects were discovered, the following day was occupied in timing the Meteor on the climb at operational load. The best time produced was 17½ minutes to 40,000', and it was quite clear therefore that the Canberra was superior in this respect.

However on the morning of the 14th of November a further test was carried out with the Canberra at 34,000 lbs. and the Meteor at operational weight, and the two machines took off together from the main runway. When the Canberra reached 40,000' at climbing power the Meteor was 1,500' below it climbing at full power.

An attempt was then made at 40,000' by the Meteor to line its sights on the Canberra which was carrying out a 2G weave. This resulted in the Meteor stalling at 1.6G and the test was discontinued.

Height was lost to 30,000' where the same test was carried out, and at this height the Canberra was still able to prevent the Meteor from closing by its superior manoeuvrability. After landing, the pilot commented on the superiority of the Canberra over the Meteor 8 under all the conditions of the flight and pointed out that where the maximum speed of the Meteor in level flight was apparently .73M at 40,000', the Canberra could manoeuvre adequately at .78M and could reach .8M in level flight comfortably.

After this test the trials were declared to be complete. The machine was therefore refuelled and returned to Warton.

R. P. Beamont
CHIEF TEST PILOT.

Distribution: Mr. Petter
                  Mr. Ellis
                  Mr. Smith
                  Mr. Page
                  Mr. Harrison
                  Mr. Crowe
                  Mr. Ellison
                  Mr. Creasey
                  R.T.O.
                  Flight Observer
                  File

Copy to: Mr. Sheffield
RPB/LL.

The prototype English Electric B.1. Canberra. Smooth lines show in the first air photographic sortie, June 1949. (British Aerospace)

Canberra ceiling climb

English Electric's early confidence in the high-altitude performance and systems integrity of the Canberra B.Mk 2 had stemmed from rapid success in the first year of experimental testing since flight 1 on the B.Mk 1 prototype VN799, in 1949. The first flight had been made on the inauspicious-sounding date of Friday 13 May, and 40,000 ft had been exceeded (to 42,000 ft) only 12 weeks later. With rapidly increasing confidence, exploration was soon being made of engine and airframe handling, fuel system and cabin pressurisation performance, and stability and control response above

The first Canberra B. Mk 2 prototype, which carried out the initial high-altitude exploration above 50,000 ft in 1950. (British Aerospace)

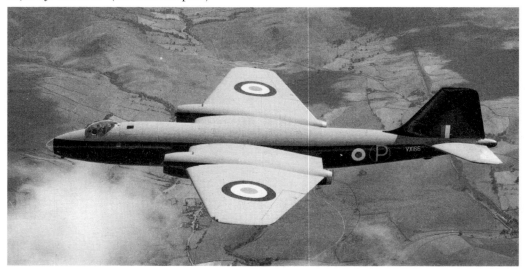

The B.1. Canberra on its first public display. Farnborough Air Show, September 1949. (British Aerospace)

45,000 ft, and 50,000 ft was reached in VX165 on 16 January 1951. This was already some 10,000 ft above the practical capability of any other jet bomber developments at that time, and also comfortably above the interception height of the jet fighters in service anywhere in the world.

English Electric directors and the Warton support party at the Farnborough Display of 1949. Teddy Petter and Sir George Nelson in centre. (British Aerospace)

The Canberra had in fact proved so tractable, controllable and reliable that Warton had decided to continue to 'expand the flight envelope' beyond the RAF specification requirement of 48,000 ft. This led not to technical but to administrative problems!

In the Air Ministry rules for testing, limitations were imposed by various factors associated reasonably enough with crew survival. The IAM had established that for crews trained in its Farnborough pressure-chamber, 41,000 ft was the permitted limit for an unpressurised aircraft with oxygen breathing only, but that in an unproved pressure-cabin aircraft with the initial risk of 'explosive decompression' a maximum 'safe' height would be no more than 37,000 ft until full integrity had been established by many hours' testing at that height.

However with a 'pressure-breathing' waistcoat and later a full partial pressure system (PPS) with specially fitted mask, this 'explosive decompression' risk height was progressively extended to 47,000 ft. Flying at 50,000 ft and above would have to wait, the authorities said, until a full pressure suit (first experimented with in the 1930s and still under development for Service use) would be needed. This was all quite clear, but for the Canberra programme at Warton there was one small detail; not even the interim pressure waistcoat was available and the prototype Canberras had been flown regularly into the 'unsafe' region above 45,000 ft in order to maintain momentum in this exceptionally successful programme.

So, flight testing continued and when 50,000 ft was reached in VX165 on 1 October 1950 no limiting factors or systems problems were experienced. The Canberra continued to handle completely normally at that, for the period, great height, and there was excess performance in hand. I believed another 3,000 to 4,000 ft was possible.

There now arose a quandary. Partial-pressure waistcoats and masks had at last become available but the Ministry would not raise their operating limit above 47,000 ft. The Warton flying at this height and above without this equipment for many weeks had produced confidence at the manufacturer in the integrity of the cabin pressurisation system on which the crews' lives did indeed depend at these heights. So, knowing that further requests to authority to extend the 47,000 ft formal limit would be fruitless, and also that the full aircrew partial pressure suit and helmet would not be available, perhaps for years, Warton went ahead.

In these flights all engineering aspects continued to be satisfactory, and although at the climbing Mach number 0.72 the margins of usable speed range were narrowing, the Canberra was still easy and undemanding to fly and of course smooth and eerily quiet at the low indicated speed near its ceiling. After thorough engineering checks had confirmed no abnormal signs in airframe or systems it was decided to establish the last unknown extreme point in the Canberra's already exceptional flight envelope.

Canberra VX165 was next prepared with a low fuel load and Warton's flight test engineer, Dave Walker, who had flown on all the previous high-altitude series was, to his chagrin, offloaded to save weight. Although this low-weight flight would not represent a practical operational case for the B.Mk 2, it would help to establish the practicability of flight at these altitudes when more power became available in subsequent developments.

The aircraft climbed through an 8/8ths cloud sheet on north-westerly heading, reaching 40,000 ft in 10 min at this light weight and 50,000 ft 15 min later. With all systems normal and fuel balancing at regular intervals with the fuselage tank pumps to maintain the required CG, I continued the climb under easy control in trimmed flight maintaining the steady course for minimum disturbance to accurate flight.

At approximately 150 n.m. from Warton and approaching the Western Isles although, still over cloud, I could not see them, 54,000 ft was reached with cabin pressure altitude rising at the correct rate (from its normal indicated 10,000 ft at lower level), the engine jet pipe temperatures, oil pressures and temperatures were still comfortably within limits, and at Mach 0.72 and climb power there was still a 400 ft/min indicated rate of climb.

Indicated speed was now below 200 kt IAS and as I eased the throttles to maximum power for the 5-min limit, I also eased VX165 into a steeper climb, steadying at Mach 0.7. The rate of climb increased slightly, steadied and then began to drop away as the IAS dropped below 150 kt. At 54,800 ft there was 150 ft/min left and the indicated speed was down to 140kt IAS. I held this for a few more minutes and the rate-of-climb indicator showed zero, and a very slight aft movement of the wheel resulted in slowly dropping IAS and altimeter. This was the absolute ceiling for this weight; the Canberra had reached 55,000 ft.

With the aircraft still delicately balanced, as entering a slightly too-steep dive would soon have the Canberra into compressibility, the characteristics of which had been well-charted below 45,000 ft but as yet no higher, I maintained full power, eased the nose down and as the Mach number recovered to 0.74 smoothly reduced power and began a gentle turn through 180° on an estimated heading for Warton, being well out of VHF/DF range at this point (these early Canberra years being without benefit of radar surveillance). This was another milestone for the Canberra. No other military aircraft in the world at that time could reach 55,000 ft which was, I reflected, 10,000 ft above

The author poses the new-shape PR.9 for the photographic aircraft. (British Aerospace)

the absolute maximum theoretical intercept capability of the RAF's current Meteors.

This experimental flight was no demonstration of operational capability, but it did show clearly that the Canberra B.Mk 2 in standard form could be operated easily to 50,000 ft and that higher altitudes should indeed prove practical in the future with increased engine power.

With the successful entry of Canberras of various marks into RAF service from 1951 and later into many overseas air forces including the USAF, Royal Australian Air Force and Indian Air Force, a new era had arrived. These airforces now had a light bomber which could not be reached by their own jet fighters or those of their potential enemies, if any.

In the RAF the high-altitude-role Canberras, which had played havoc with the defence interception exercises in 1952 and 1953, were soon replaced with the introduction of the V-bomber series with capable radar bombing systems (which, owing to delayed development of the radar, Canberras did not have). The Canberras, showing their remarkable design flexibility, were concentrated on photographic reconnaissance with the PR.3, and in their new roles in NATO, the Mk 6 and 8 low-level strike and nuclear deterrent force.

The value of the PR.3 and the improved PR.7 was soon established in vital 'cold war' operations over the Soviet Union, but even their missions at 50,000 ft plus soon came at risk from the rapidly developing threat of surface-to-air missiles (SAMs), and priority was put on the ultimate Canberra development, the PR.9. This aircraft, with Rolls-Royce Avon RA24 engines giving nearly twice the thrust of the original RA2s of the prototype Canberra, had a redesigned wing with increased area and span to reduce wing loading and hopefully to provide a major increase in operating altitude. The wing was redesigned to increase substantially the chord between the nacelles and the fuselage, thereby reducing thickness/chord ratio to reduce drag, and further increasing wing area hopefully to delay the effects of compressibility and permit a higher operating Mach limit. Things did not work out quite like that.

An interim prototype, WH793, based on a PR.7 airframe, was converted for English Electric by the Napier company at Luton and had the new wing and engines, but not the newly designed nose which would feature on the production aircraft, with a single-seat pilot's cockpit aft and a forward navigator's position with a Martin-Baker ejection

Author wearing pressure-breathing helmet and jerkin in the Canberra PR.9. (British Aerospace)

seat, and a new 'clamshell' opening canopy at the pilot's station. New power-controlled ailerons and rudder were also fitted on WH793.

Initial flight trials showed the expected very high take-off and climb performance (now similar to that of the Lightning supersonic fighter!) and otherwise generally similar handling to its predecessors. The excess thrust did, however, necessitate limiting the power used at take-off to the amount which could be contained with the new power-rudder asymmetrically in the event of an engine failure on take-off. This was quite critical and we found that 90/90 per cent was adequate for full load take-off and also for the immediate single-engine emergency in which, after gaining safety height in a shallow climb, full power on the 'good' engine could then be used from 160 kt IAS upwards.

After shakedown testing at Luton by Mike Randrup, Walter Shirley and I, WH793 was flown to Warton for its main test programme which included investigation of the power-controlled ailerons and rudder. In the early part of this phase the new performance proved to be spectacular, 30,000 ft from take-off in 2½ min again being similar to the performance of a Lightning in reheat, and things looked promising for the planned 60,000 ft operating height.

Investigation of the high-speed envelope at the tropopause was less encouraging. Mach number limits and buffeting were similar to all the earlier Canberras with vibration beginning at 0.82, heavy buffet at 0.84 and nose-down trim change occurring at around 0.85. But this was of less importance than maximum practical altitude and, by now fitted up with full partial-pressure equipment including a 'pressure helmet' which was exceedingly uncomfortable to use, I explored this last 'corner-point' on WH793 on 23 November 1956.

Rate of climb was sustained well to 50,000 ft and here handling was satisfactory and indistinguishable from the earlier marks except for the increased power remaining. Continuing the climb to 54,000 ft showed none of the drop-off in performance of the Mk 2 and the PR.9 felt comfortably in its element, climbing at maximum continuous power at Mach 0.72 and at about 800 ft/min.

We were now climbing on a southerly heading from Warton into unexplored territory and the midday sunglare gave dazzling reflections in the already severely restricted vision area of the pressure helmet visor. From now on there was an increasingly 'unknown' factor and a cabin pressure failure (or canopy failure) could drastically alter the priorities! It was becoming difficult to maintain the cockpit instrument scan and the vital checks of engine instruments in these 'first-time' conditions, so I initiated a gentle turn to port downsun, still climbing.

There was a momentary change in flight conditions and on levelling wings on the new heading with the sun behind I could see that we had dropped a few knots and were not climbing. Lowering the nose a little produced recovery to Mach 0.72 and a 600 ft/min climb rate was resumed.

There had been some speculation about the installed thrust of these RA24s, as to whether they might not sustain their design power at high altitude, and this sudden performance loss could possibly be a sign. But there had been no progressive indication of decreasing thrust on the climb so, once more in steady conditions and on a southerly heading, I increased angle of attack (AoA) with a small back movement of the wheel, the nose rose a few degrees and simultaneously ASI and Mach number began to drop and the rate of climb reduced to zero — all without touching the throttles. Forward wheel to lower the nose to the horizon again gave immediate increase in ASI and Mach number and a resumed rate of climb. Repeating the sequence produced the same results. This was positive indication that at this weight and height induced drag from the new long-chord wing centre section was high and becoming critical.

Gentle turns each way produced the same symptoms and it was becoming clear that although there was still positive climb performance in straight climb — we were now at 56,000 ft and climbing — in operational manoeuvring flight there would be little flexibility at this height.

So now to establish the absolute ceiling for this flight condition and, continuing a gentle turn onto a southerly heading again, I eased WH793 back into a climb and at 57,000 ft the indicated rate of climb was still 600 ft/min. Each throttle was cycled slowly and smoothly to flight-idling and back with no surge-line problems and normal gauge readings well within limits. This again checked the climb, which was resumed after a loss of 500 ft, when maximum power was reset for the final five minutes while again closely monitoring jet-pipe temperatures and cabin pressure.

At 58,000 ft the rate of climb was down to 250 ft/min and falling, and holding the climb angle I allowed the Mach number to drop slowly to 0.7. There was no climb left. The PR.9 seemed motionless in smooth, almost silent (in my new noise-attenuating pressure helmet) suspension under the very dark blue sky above and the brilliant dazzling sun-glare ahead. Far away below was broken cloud cover with the Welsh mountains small, flat and almost plateau-like to starboard. The smoky smudges of Wolverhampton and Birmingham were to port and the silver Severn river wound ahead to its estuary reaching from Avonmouth towards the south-west, and was that Lundy just a shadow on the far horizon?

The altimeter showed 59,900 ft, so close to 60,000 that correction for instrument and position error might well confirm the target figure, and all systems and the cabin pressure level were performing satisfactorily. But the PR.9 was not going any higher than that. Still at maximum throttle a small increase in AoA with back-wheel produced the sensation of a descending lift, and with 500 ft/min rate of descent soon showing I reduced AoA into a positive descent at Mach 0.75, throttled the engines to flight-idle, called Warton for a QDM (magnetic heading) and started the long drift-down through 60,000 ft of altitude to our sea-level base on the banks of the river Ribble estuary, 100 miles away to the north.

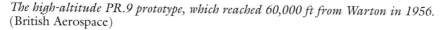

The high-altitude PR.9 prototype, which reached 60,000 ft from Warton in 1956.
(British Aerospace)

The prototype had flown faultlessly to design operating level with all systems functioning correctly and handling qualities not significantly changed from those of its excellent and docile predecessors at lower altitudes, but there had been no adequate margin of performance at the peak, and it was becoming clear that we would be unable to recommend an operational clearance higher than 55,000 ft.

It was with a sense of anticlimax that I guided this powerful, docile and likeable new prototype in its smooth, near-silent glide back to Warton, hoping with not much confidence that some other technical explanation might be forthcoming for this performance shortfall — an unusual phenomenon at Warton. But there was no practical solution; the induced drag of the new wing was excessive.

The production version of the PR.9 with revised nose and crew stations proved to be a successful reconnaissance aircraft, much enjoyed by its pilots in over 30 plus years of service in the RAF in which its high altitude short-fall was compensated for by the ever-flexible RAF, who used it very effectively in low-level reconnaissance and continue to do so at the time of writing in 1995!

In later years the superiority of the basic Canberra B.2 design with the 'old' wing was re-emphasised when Mike Randrup reached 70,310 ft in the Scorpion rocket-powered WK183, and Walter Gibb achieved 65,890 ft in WD952 with prototype Bristol Olympus engines.

American Canberra

During the week before Christmas 1952 a shock-wave went through the English Electric Company's establishment at Warton and their head offices in Stafford and London. On 21 December Canberra B. Mk 2 WD932 had crashed in America killing one of its USAF evaluation crew, the other having escaped by ejection seat.

In a spectacularly successful programme of testing and also world-wide demonstration flights since the prototype's first flight in 1949, the Canberra had become famed for its performance, manoeuvrability and reliability as Britain's first jet bomber, and it had already entered service with the RAF and been demonstrated by them with international acclaim in a 'showing the flag' tour of South America by 12 Sqn led by AVM Dermot Boyle (later Sir Dermot, Chief of the Air Staff and, after retirement, chairman of the British Aircraft Corporation).

The Canberra's strong export potential had already been clearly established when, in 1952, the USAF had also confirmed a requirement for over 400 Canberras. They were to be adapted to meet a defined 'night intruder' role, and all the aircraft were to be built under licence in America. This was a major surprise to all concerned in this country. The official British reaction had been predictably reserved. Too little, it was said, was known about this new and advanced aircraft and it would be premature to allow the Americans to commit themselves to this relatively untried product!

The Americans brushed these arguments aside, however, and two production B. Mk 2s, WD932 and WD940, had been delivered for evaluation earlier in the year to the factory airfield of the Glenn L. Martin Company at Middle River, Baltimore, both flights establishing Atlantic crossing records on the way. At once these two aircraft were subjected to intensive testing and evaluation by USAF crews from the Wright-Patterson Air Force Base test centre at Dayton, Ohio, and the programme appeared to be proceeding without problems. It was seen as the latest event in the exceptional success story of the RAF's new world-beating jet bomber from this hitherto little-known factory in the north west of England, English Electric. Then disaster! WD932 had crashed near Baltimore.

With only days to go before the Christmas holiday, chief engineer Freddy Page announced his intention to fly out to Baltimore, and chief aerodynamicist Ray Creasey and I were notified to go with him; this despite messages coming in from Baltimore to the effect that 'the investigation will not get properly under way until after the holiday'. Freddy Page's flight on Christmas Eve was delayed and he spent the following Christmas Day uncomfortably in the temporary hutted buildings of the newly developing Heathrow Airport awaiting a Stratocruiser that could take him to America.

Meanwhile I had a virus infection and my wife, Pat, explained in the clearest terms that I was unfit to travel. I started my journey not feeling much better on Boxing Day and eventually arrived, with Ray Creasey, at Baltimore on the 27th. It was snowing and very cold, and everyone was on holiday!

The morning of the 28th found 'the Brits', Page, Creasey and myself, in the freezing cold on Martin's flying boat slipway alongside Chesapeake Bay together with a small group of Martin engineers who clearly did not want to be there, receiving pieces of Canberra wreckage as they were brought in by a salvage lighter, crunching through the ice, from the crash site on the coast of the bay about 20 miles away.

It soon became apparent that the port wing had failed outboard of the engine under excessive 'G' loads, which should not have happened if the test conditions had been within the safety factored margins clearly set down in the flight limitations manual prepared by the English Electric Company for this USAF programme and approved by the British ministry authorities.

In a detailed discussion with Martin's flight test staff headed by their chief test pilot, E. O. 'Pat' Tibbs, Ray Creasey and I reviewed the circumstances of the USAF test programme and its required test points, and we found these in order. But as the analysis continued, our attention became focused on one particular aspect. If the aircraft had been subjected to excessive G loading by the pilot, how had this come about?

The pilot was not available to us. This matter, we were told, was 'subject to USAF investigation procedures'. But Tibbs said that the USAF pilot had stated that after clearing the earlier test points successfully, he had 'as scheduled pulled 4.6G at 420 kt IAS at the aft CG limit, and the aircraft just blew apart'. It had not done this of course during the earlier Warton trials involving more severe conditions before clearance into RAF service, testing so there had to be another factor. Was it possible that the pilot could have pulled excessive 'G'? Urgent transatlantic telephoning soon confirmed that for the type of structural failure we were seeing in the wreckage, at least 7G would have been needed and possibly more.

Could the pilot have misread the 'G' reading on his accelerometer? I knew that the stick forces required to pull 5G from trimmed flight at 450 kt IAS were very high, and that to inadvertently pull on to 6+G would have required very considerable pilot effort which he could not have ignored! There had to be some other cause, and Ray and I came to the same possible solution. Where was the CG at the fatal test point?

If the CG, as controlled by the pilot with fuel distribution between the main fuselage tanks, had been within the approved range of forward/aft limits, the test should have been completely safe. But if the actual CG had been allowed to drift aft of the aft limit by a relatively small amount through failure to balance the fuel distribution correctly before these tests, the aircraft would remain controllable in level flight but on pulling 'up' elevator it could theoretically have become violently unstable and pitched up to excessive G values before the pilot could take remedial action with forward stick.

It began to seem likely that this was the cause of the accident, but it soon became clear that we were not to be permitted access to the Wright Field test pilot or to the USAF official papers on the subject. These were in fact never revealed to us as, it had to be assumed, the subject was regarded as too sensitive by the USAF.

Meanwhile the fierce winter conditions had not improved my health, and neither did a prolonged three-day wintry journey back to the UK, delayed by an engine change in our Stratocruiser at Gander and by severe blizzard conditions at Rekyavik.

The following morning, in reviewing the situation with Ray Creasey in Freddy Page's office it seemed that we were agreed on 'pilot error' as the most likely solution, but Page said that he had called for a thorough investigation on the stressing case for the known scheduled conditions for the test, and also for a hypothetical overshoot to the theoretical case for structural failure. 'But all of this will take some time', he said.

I had a good idea of what was coming, having thought it through many times in the long flight back, and I said; 'We'll need to inject a note of confidence before then?' 'Yes we will' said Freddy Page. 'So we had better set up a repeat "structural demonstration" at a fully representative flight condition as soon as possible?' I said. Page said he thought so too, and did we see any problems?

On paper there were none, but now that it came to the point there had to be a possibility of some 'build' defect having occurred in the production line since the structural flight test clearance of the B. Mk 2 for the RAF in early 1952 and not of course re-tested in this respect since because the fault, if any, would have been unknown. I looked at Ray Creasey, who in turn looked worried, and then I said to Freddy Page: 'Only one problem. I'd like to get rid of this bronchitis before we fly that test again'.

On 7 February 1953, a dull, cold day in broken low cloud and rain, with Canberra B. Mk 2 WD958 off the production line and prepared and loaded to represent the Baltimore crash test condition but with a slightly further aft CG (i.e. a more severe case), I pulled 5.2G at 450 kt IAS. The aircraft did not pitch up and the wing did not come off.

The Martin B-57 Canberra went on into successful production for the USAF, and was soon acclaimed as their most effective night intruder in the Vietnam war.

High over New York

The cockpit 'greenhouse' of Canberra B. Mk 2 WD940 was comfortably warm in the sunglare at 38,000 ft with the Avon engines humming smoothly, all systems serviceable and our destination, Baltimore, still 2 hr away. Behind lay the white cloud sheet of a frontal system I had just climbed through with Dennis Watson and Bob Rylands from a 300 ft base in rain at Gander, Newfoundland, and we had cleared the tops south of St John's according to navigator, Watty Watson. The sharp edge of the front spread out behind to the horizon in each direction, east and west; and now ahead stretched the coastline of Nova Scotia, bathed in the morning sun with inland myriad lakes among rolling pine-clad hills.

This was the second English Electric jet bomber for the USA on delivery to the Martin Company for testing prior to the start of a massive contract for the supply of Canberras to the USAF — the first export programme for a British military aircraft to the United States since the de Havilland D.H.4 in the early 1920s. The first Canberra for the USA, WD932, had been delivered earlier in the year by the RAF (Sqn Ldr Arthur Callard).

The year was 1951, only two years since the Canberra's first flight and many faint hearts in government and industry in Britain were still voicing reservations about selling (licence building) to a foreign power as being 'premature and ill-advised' at such an early stage in development of this very advanced new design. The manufacturers, however, were confident and the test aircrew particularly so. The prototypes and early production aircraft had shown great potential in testing and had met or exceeded all targets set for them.

As the chief test pilot responsible for introducing the Canberra to the Martin company I had flown WD940 across the Atlantic in record time from Aldergrove to Gander, and it was now on its final leg to Baltimore, Middle River, the factory and test base of the famous Glenn L. Martin Company which had been selected to develop and build a 'production' run of over 400 Canberras, modified to meet the specific requirements of the USAF. So this flight was, for a Canberra, a pleasantly normal operation with no critical tests to perform and only the routine tasks of navigation and the progressive observation of systems performance and of actual fuel consumption against estimates to ensure that there were no discrepancies. The Gander–Baltimore leg would be flown in little more than 3 hr, and with more than 5 hr cruising fuel on board there were no critical aspects to be watched. There were, however, some points of more than usual interest.

We were now passing 40,000 ft, the cruise-climb technique in use having only recently been established as the most fuel-efficient method of long-range cruising with the new jets. The technique was simple and beneficial to the pilot flying manually for long periods (no autopilot was fitted to early Canberras), and it consisted of setting the engines at maximum cruise r.p.m. and then stabilising the planned optimum cruise indicated Mach number (IMN), in this case 0.74. This would be held constant for the rest of the flight until throttling back for the descent and let-down to destination.

By holding constant speed at constant power setting, the aircraft would continue to climb slowly as the fuel burn reduced aircraft weight, and this 'cruise-climb' technique resulted, with the Canberra, in the quite new phenomenon of topping the initial max climb-power climb on, for example, a 2,000-mile flight, at around 41,000–42,000 ft,

Canberra WD940 arrives at Martin Airport, Baltimore, March 1951. Left to right, Rylands, radio operator, pilot Roland Beamont and Watson, the navigator. (Glenn L. Martin Co.)

and then cruise-climbing to reach 48,000–50,000 ft at the point of starting the final descent some 1,800 miles later. At first it had been suggested that non-steady-state altitude would be difficult for the pilot, and would add complications to air traffic control height separations. But in the event 'flying the Mach meter' proved actually less demanding than holding both ASI and altitude constant for long periods, and at Canberra altitudes there was not going to be any other traffic!

So this flight progressed in brilliant and unlimited visibility down the eastern seaboard of the American continent, and in accordance with our flight clearance from Gander I called (on VHF) the first reporting point, Halifax Nova Scotia. A clear reply confirmed good weather in the New York area and cleared us on to Cape Cod, but then said 'state your altitude'. By this time we were at 44,000 ft and, as it was a British security matter, I said: 'That's classified information — please confirm any conflicting traffic'.

The voice said 'negative' to this and then at a distinctly higher note demanded 'state your altitude!' I regretted the impossibility of this and, with the voice receding into the distance as we passed beyond his sector, cruising at Mach 0.74, Watty Watson and I had discussed the possibility of our becoming a defence exercise as we approached the New York metropolitan defence zone. This seemed highly likely to me!

Meanwhile the Canadian coastline passed astern and far ahead, shimmering in the midday glare the coast of Maine and then, on the port beam, appeared the unmistakeable landmark, Cape Cod. Bangor, Maine was our next reporting point and my call was responded to immediately by an urgent voice demanding that 'you state your altitood'.

Again regretting that this was not possible for security reasons, we continued on our serene way with the voice saying: 'The height is a mandatory requirement for Traffic Control!'. And I replied: 'But there isn't going to be any other traffic up here is there?'. Then we were out of his range and I decided to make a point which I was sure would not be lost on our new American friends.

Navigator Watson confirmed that our fuel position was 'fat' with large reserves for the final 300 miles, and I could now see vapour trails criss-crossing our path ahead and

Meeting Glenn L. Martin, president of the Martin Company, with Chet Pearson, Martin MD, behind. Bob Rylands is on the right. (Glenn L. Martin Co.)

Demonstrating WD932 for the Martin factory work force at Middle River, Baltimore, in March 1951.   (Glenn L. Martin Co.)

The Canberra B(I)8 prototype.   (British Aerospace)

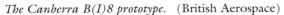

below. So I opened up to climb power for the permitted period, steepening the climb, and finally set maximum r.p.m. for the five minutes allowed in any one hour. Cape Cod was now behind us and Long Island stretched out ahead with the sprawling concrete and shining waterways of greater New York on the horizon.

Vapour trails were much in evidence ahead but far below as we approached 48,000 ft, and with the New York area controller also now sounding off about our 'altitood' we slipped smoothly over the greatest city in the world at comfortably above 50,000 ft. This we knew was at least 5,000 ft above the theoretical intercept height of any fighter in the world at that time, including the USAF's North American F-86 Sabre swept-wing fighters, and very probably much nearer 10,000 ft above practical interception.

With New York now astern, a smudge to starboard showed the mass of Philadelphia, with Pennsylvania stretching to the western horizon, and soon straight ahead the glinting waters of Chesapeake Bay, our destination. Now from 51,000 ft the green forests of Virginia and Maryland far ahead were dotted with small cotton-wool puffs of fair weather cumulus cloud, and with visibility unlimited the remaining 200 miles required only simple visual navigation.

With power down to flight-idling the gliding descent began at Mach 0.74 in almost unreal quiet. No radio assistance was needed as the Chesapeake Bay bridge came into sight from 50 miles, and soon Baltimore City and the white runway of Middle River Airport with the Martin Company's flying boat slipway on the edge of the Bay.

Air Traffic confirmed clearance to land and then WD940 was coming smoothly down towards the final approach over the yacht-studded inlets fringing Chesapeake Bay.

The Canberra flared with its usual smooth precision, and its wheels rumbled on its new home territory. From now on Canberras would become an increasingly frequent sight in American skies as they served in the USAF in many roles for over the next 20 years.

This was a satisfactory way to introduce our new British bomber to the American military aviation scene, and it was with no great surprise that about 30 min after arriving at the Middle River flight operations centre we were told 'You are wanted at the Pentagon a.m. tomorrow!' After a quick turnround servicing by our English Electric ground crew who had been flown over to assist in the introduction to Martin, I flew a requested demonstration over the Martin factory and Middle River Airport which was again received with acclamation. No-one on that side of the Atlantic had seen a jet bomber flown like a fighter before the Canberra.

Early next day I was ushered through tight security at the Pentagon at Washington into a room full of general officers impressively bedecked with stars and medal ribbons. After courteous and obviously interested discussion about the capabilities of the Canberra, one of the generals said: 'There appeared to be some communications problem on your flight, Beamont?'. I said: 'No sir, no problem', and the general replied: 'Well, you weren't able to report your height when requested repeatedly'. I replied: 'This is a British military aircraft and its performance is classified secret'. 'But the air traffic controllers needed information for safe height separation', they said. 'General', I said, 'from Halifax to overhead New York I was flying at an altitude well above the capabilities of any other aircraft, military or civil, in the world at this time. There weren't going to be any other aircraft there.'

'Well,' said one of the generals, 'just what height were you over New York?' 'Fifty-one thousand feet,' I said, 'and we were not at the Canberra's ceiling either.' 'Gee Wizz!', said the room with one voice, and it became immediately clear that this conversation would reverberate round the USAF establishment in the months to come.

Engine fire
Following first flight on Friday 13 May 1949 the English Electric B.3/45 Canberra test programme had made such rapid progress that the prototype was sent to Boscombe Down for 'preview' trials only five months later, and it passed these with flying colours.

Over the next ten years eight variants of the basic design were tested with great success and of these types seven were issued to squadrons. The eighth was the B. Mk 5 target marker variant for which the Air Ministry finally decided there was in fact no requirement so it did not go into production. But the prototype successfully launched the uprated Avon RA7 engine installation and the increased fuel tankage ('wet wing') which became standard in the Canberra B(I)8 variants.

During these trials the Mk 5 VX185 became the first-ever aircraft to fly the Atlantic in both directions in one day, crewed by the author, Peter Hillwood and Dennis Watson, taking 10 hr 3 min for the round trip Belfast–Gander (Newfoundland)–Belfast and averaging over 600 m.p.h. for much of the return leg which took 3 hr 24 min with the benefit of a following 'jet stream' at 40,000 ft most of the way.

From 1949 to 1979 I had accumulated over 1,000 hr of Canberra testing without serious incident, and then one day in 1967 when one of the last Mk 8 series was due for production test at Samlesbury I decided to take time off from my priority Lightnings to fly it. It was always pleasurable to fly at Samlesbury whose over 400 Canberras had all been produced with their own brand of enthusiasm, quality workmanship and Lancashire hard-headed resolution, and this flight seemed to be no exception.

Though not in strict 'currency' on the Mk 8 I was in practice on the B. Mk 2 'development' aircraft WD937 which we still kept at Warton for photographic 'chase' and occasional 'continuation training', so I soon felt comfortable with this Mk 8 as I ran through the production test schedule and then started the engines.

It was a fine clear day with no weather problems and the hills of the Trough of Bowland to the north sharply outlined against a brilliant sky, heralding rain to come later.

I had always liked the offset fighter-style clear view canopy of the Mk 8. There were some less satisfactory features in the cockpit, such as inadequate view of and inconvenient positioning of the VHF controls, and also the pedal-operated wheel brakes insisted on by the Air Ministry Operational Research Branch apparently because they conformed to American practice. In my view they were less efficient and easy to operate than the control wheel-mounted lever brakes of all the previous variants.

Taking off from Samlesbury's short main runway into a strong north-westerly crosswind, and at light load took less than half the distance available and I worked through the production test schedule in the climb to 40,000 ft and then dived to the clearance compressibility limit of Mach 0.84 at 35,000 ft over the Solway Firth. Next, a maximum power 'level' for 2 min at the Tropopause (32,000 ft on that day), and then down on reciprocal heading to check Mach limits at 20,000, 10,000, and, at 5,000 ft, the 500 kt IAS limit. Here buffet was limiting at 490 kt IAS, which was acceptable, the required service limit being 450 kt IAS.

This had brought us back towards Barrow and the rest of the flight was a gentle, pleasant cruise at near idle power back over the Fylde to Samlesbury airfield nestling in its wooded valley between the shining River Ribble and the industrial smoke of Blackburn and Accrington. The B8 whistled gently across the red and black Canberra assembly hangars with throttles closed, then I opened up into a left-hand climbing wing-over into the downwind leg. The enjoyable Canberra sortie was almost over when — bang! The aircraft shuddered, there was a distinct yaw suggesting thrust loss on the starboard side — and there on the engine panel the starboard fire warning red!

Although r.p.m. and oil pressure were normal there was no starboard jet pipe temperature (JPT), so automatically throttling back the starboard engine I also closed its high-pressure (HP) cock, and the red light went out. Here at the serene end of a normal sortie was technical trouble which needed some correct decisions and procedures to ensure a safe outcome. It was a long time since I had done a single-engine landing in a Canberra, but I remembered that it was no problem provided the single engine safety speed was closely observed.

I called a 'precautionary' on the RT and then, remembering the strong crosswind, asked the Tower for wind strength. They confirmed gusting 15–20 kt at 320°, and the 'dead' engine was on the 'wrong' side for Runway 27 with that crosswind!

Samlesbury's second runway, 320, was into wind but was only 850 yd — not practical for jets in normal circumstances, and I could always divert to Warton's 2,500 yd; but after my last 13 years of 180 kt approaches and 150 kt landings on P.1s, Lightnings and the TSR.2, the Canberra's gentle docility did not seem in any way dramatic or demanding in these circumstances and I confirmed a 'single-engine' landing on the very short Runway 32.

Downwind lowering undercarriage at 190 m.p.h., turning in over the hill sloping down to the 320 approach. Now the critical part, speed held above 160 m.p.h. to finals at 100 ft. Flaps down, retrim and bleed off airspeed without touching the 'good' engine. Port throttle closed at 50 ft and 300 yd short of the runway threshold, glide in to a gentle touchdown at 100 kt on the 'numbers', wheel forward, nosewheel rumbling, brakes on for full Maxaret automatic braking system (ABS) and slowing down nicely to turn off after 850 yd on to the perimeter road leading into the main factory tarmac. Then port engine shut down and, after a short cooling period, brakes ON.

Vehicles appeared. The cockpit door opened, and a voice said: 'Why've you stopped the bloody thing here!' I said: 'Try taxying a Canberra in on one engine with no nosewheel steering', and the voice agreed that it might be difficult, and then said: 'Take a look at this!'

'This' turned out to be the starboard jet pipe protruding about 6 in back from the engine nacelle (where it should have been only about 1 in proud). The engine/jet pipe joint had blown apart, allowing hot turbine gases to flow through a 4 in gap into the wing and surrounding structure. It had been just as well to close that HP cock very quickly to shut off the fuel!

Wg Cdr Harcourt of the RAF's Canberra OCU with the author celebrating the Canberra's 20th Anniversary, Warton 1969. (British Aerospace)

Chapter Eight

The P.1

While the Canberra trials were making famous progress at Warton in the early 1950s, a new major breakthrough in technology was emerging from English Electric in the form of the P.1, Britain's first truly supersonic fighter prototype. I was in charge of the test programme which, though very successful, was not without incident.

Supersonic over Britain

At 40,000 ft over the Solent on a fine August day the visibility seemed to go on for ever. The Isle of Wight spread out below on the starboard side of the cockpit like an atlas map, and beyond to the south the sunpath glinted across the Channel too remote to show individual waves. In the far distance a thin line showed where the coast of France near Dieppe merged into the horizon mists.

Eastward, England's white chalk cliffs were visible to Cuckmere, Friston and just possibly Beachy Head, while in the north the reservoirs of Staines showed at the edge of the west-wind driven smoke haze of Greater London.

The author prepares for first flight of the English Electric P.1, WG760, at Boscombe Down, August 1954. (British Aerospace)

The P.1's 60° wing sweepback was very advanced for its time and it proved highly manoeuvrable and fast. (British Aerospace)

The upper air was turbulence-free and totally smooth, and the aircraft seemed suspended in almost motionless quiet under the blazing sun, its engines humming smoothly and little wind roar from around the smooth lines of the windscreen. The aircraft was not on autopilot and was being flown manually with delicate, precise finger-tip control, and in perfect trim such that when the stick was released briefly the aircraft remained steady and undeviating in course and height. This could have been the thousandth flight of a well proven subsonic jet fighter, yet there was something different.

The coastline 40,000 ft below was disappearing behind at a breathtaking rate and in the cockpit there was a phenonemon that had never before been seen over England — The Mach meter was steady at 1.02, and the aircraft, the English Electric P.1, was in level flight at supersonic speed under full and pleasant control, and this was only its fourth test flight!

This was a moment to savour for it was the very pinnacle of achievement in an

WG760 in very close formation with the camera aircraft. This was the aircraft involved in the undercarriage incident described. (British Aerospace)

engineering campaign which had commenced six years earlier in the temporary design offices of the English Electric Company, first at Preston and then at Warton aerodrome, a run-down air base of the USAF deserted since the end of the Second World War.

In 1947 the Government in its wisdom had suddenly cancelled its own sole research programme for a transonic aircraft which was already in build by the Miles Aircraft Company, on the spurious grounds that supersonic flight would be too costly for the British taxpayer and too dangerous for the test pilots. This decision left Britain isolated in relation to the intense efforts at that time of the American aircraft industry and also of the newly-emerging French industry, both of which had recognised that a race for supersonic flight technology would become inevitable, and that those left out of it would not only suffer from falling behind in this vital discipline, but would also put their national security at risk. There would be no defence against a supersonic air striking force by one with only subsonic capability.

While preparing for the flight trials of their exciting new B.1 jet bomber prototype to Air Ministry Specification B.3/45, English Electric had become very conscious that only a fully supersonic fighter would be able to intercept the new-era jet bombers. Despite government discouragement, the company had succeeded by 1948 in achieving a turn-round of opinion in Whitehall and a go-ahead for a design study for a fully supersonic fighter technology demonstrator.

This, the P.1, was evolved in 1949–53 against a background of hazardous research flying at Hatfield with the D.H.108, at Langley with the Hawker P1052 and Hunter developments, and at Vickers Supermarine with the 510 and Swift developments, all of which were aircraft of subsonic level performance which could with varying degrees of control deterioration in compressibility approach, and in some cases reach, transonic speed, but only in steep and barely controlled dives.

This dangerous phase took the lives, in this country alone, of test pilots Geoffrey de Havilland and 'Wimpy' Wade, and it had become clear that this era of 45° wing-sweep fighters with relatively thick wings and high tailplanes would not produce a truly supersonic fighter. The Hunter was developed into the best of the series with a maximum level performance of approx Mach 0.94 and it began to enter RAF service in 1954, replacing North American F-86 Sabres of similar performance which had been on loan (to NATO) from the USAF since 1951.

Taking into account all relevant experience from wartime Germany and post-war America and France, English Electric had evolved its P.1. It had a slim, low-drag fuselage with a simple 'pitot' nose air intake for twin, totally enclosed, Armstrong-Siddeley Sapphire axial-flow engines, a radical shoulder mounted wing with 60° leading-edge sweep angle and thickness/chord ratio reduced to 14 per cent at the root and 10 per cent at the ailerons. The configuration was completed with a thin all-moving tailplane mounted at the bottom of the rear fuselage to eliminate any destabilizing effects of wing down-wash at high angles of attack.

This latter philosophy was pursued staunchly by English Electric despite powerful official opposition by RAE Farnborough. It was ultimately shown to be the key to the aerodynamic success of the Lightning series, and set the standard of design fashion for the tailplane position for supersonic fighters right up to the present day.

But there was time only for this briefest thought — now Britain has a supersonic aircraft! Then down to the essential tests and observations in the few moments left before reaching the minimum fuel for safe recovery to base.

Engine power responsive to throttles up and down while still supersonic, and engine figures noted within limits. Cabin pressure and temperature controlling normally. Then response to three-axis control pulses, crisp, responsive and well-damped.

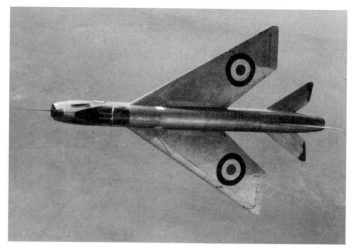

The second P.1A prototype, WG763, was used primarily for supersonic gun firing trials. (British Aerospace)

Rolling smoothly into a port turn with 30° bank, still supersonic and then pulling smoothly to 2G on the accelerometer, gave what seemed to be ideal control forces harmony and smooth, stable manoeuvrability such that it was practical to continue the supersonic turn through 180° on to the reciprocal heading back towards base, while watching closely for the effect of increased transonic drag rise in the turn. As expected a sudden small-amplitude pitch-up trim change occurred, and the Mach meter dropped sharply from 1.0 to 0.98 as the P.1 became subsonic and the transonic shock-wave cone moved forward again over the ASI pitot-static sources.

It was now necessary to reduce power quickly to conserve fuel for the 100-mile return to base, the P.1 was handling so well that some combat-rate control inputs were tried at Mach 0.95 in the descent, and these showed superb controllability. This was only flight No 4, yet the P.1 was already showing all the hallmarks of classic fighter agility.

With Portsmouth Harbour and the shining Solent abeam again to port, the long, white Boscombe Down runway came into view dead ahead, and aiming directly at it from 30,000 ft I momentarily increased to maximum power and watched the Mach meter wind up from 0.95, hesitate at 0.98 and then jump to Mach 1.02 again with no vibration or trim change. Those on the ground at Boscombe would hear the sonic boom and would be in no doubt that we had a supersonic P.1!

Four years later in 1958, following many hundreds of test flights exploring the supersonic performance and manoeuvre capabilities of the first two P.1 prototypes WG760 and WG763, and of the full fighter development P.1B Lightning XA847, the latter aircraft was in a similar situation on 25 November, but with two significant differences.

The Lightning prototype was climbing in full reheat and already supersonic in a steep climbing turn over the North Wales coastline at Great Orme's Head, prior to heading North for a schedule of tests over the Irish Sea. This flight was to be the culmination of a series of major test successes which in the year past had proved this new fighter throughout its 'Service Limit' flight envelope to speeds in excess of Mach 1.7 (1,100 m.p.h.) at altitude and Mach 1.1 at low level. Now, if conditions were right, we were going to take the Lightning to twice the speed of sound, Mach 2.0, for the first time.

In the previous week stability and control, engine performance and intake stability (freedom from surge-line problems) had been established by progressive testing and analysis of the results from Mach 1.75 to 1.9, and now the technical office was confident that there remained only three unknowns which might or might not prevent the aircraft reaching Mach 2, or cause problems at or beyond that speed.

The earlier tests had demonstrated a clear performance margin. The thrust-over-drag would be sufficient for speeds beyond Mach 2.0, although this would be temperature sensitive and dependent on a high Tropopause and a low outside air temperature (OAT). Excessive skin temperature might affect the canopy with thermal stress, and the engine intakes might encounter 'buzz' and 'surge' which could be serious. Most importantly, directional stability might prove inadequate at these speeds with possibly dire consequences. With two test schedules, the high-speed case and a lower-speed stability one, the decision would be made by the pilot during the climb.

Now XA847 was climbing in its usual brilliant fashion in perfect finger-tip control, the Mach meter at 1.1 and all systems functioning normally. At 35,000 ft, 3 min after take-off, the sky to the north along Warton's supersonic 'Test Run Alpha' was clear to the Isle of Man and beyond to Galloway with only broken cumulus clouds at 5,000 ft or lower. Warton radio confirmed the Met Temperature as –67°C at 40,000 ft.

This was what was needed and I confirmed 'high-speed schedule' and levelled out at 41,000 ft on 340° heading. Here it was again, the decision point to fly into the unknown with an aircraft which had never before been there. But now I had to work very quickly on continuous observations of engine conditions and control responses.

Mach 1.5, 1.6, 1.7 — the speed was increasing prodigiously as the engine reheat efficiency increased with high-speed 'ram effect'. There was scarcely time to note down the vital observations as each new point was reached, while at the same time maintaining 'head-up' safety checks of the flight path ahead and on either side for signs of conflicting traffic, such as vapour trails or sunlight glinting on aircraft. Recent experience had concentrated the minds of all concerned on the definite technical limitations at that period of the radar surveillance in this respect, and there was of course no on-board radar in this test-instrumentation-packed aircraft.

With Douglas already passing to port at a sensational rate, and St Bee's Head close down to starboard, the Mach meter wound on unchecked, 1.85–1.9, and now into the unknown.

Gentle control inputs with normal responses. A slight nose-down trim change corrected with the stick-mounted trim switch. Engine panels all normal with jet-pipe temperatures still within limits. The specially fitted ram-air (outside air) temperature gauge showing +95°C and rising — the set never-exceed safety limit being 115°C.

At Mach 1.95 there was a sudden small increase in high-frequency vibration — intake buzz onset? But this did not increase as speed continued to rise.

Mach 1.99 and still increasing. Left rudder input and release the stick for the vitally important 'Dutch Roll' stability test — damping cycle and yawing moment normal and acceptable — and then Mach 2.0 (approximately 1,250 m.p.h.) — the first time in a British fighter!

But this could be a critical moment. At twice the speed of sound the Lightning was fast running out of the supersonic run sea-space and it flew on over Dumfriesshire directly away from the Warton base with the fuel gauge of this prototype showing, already, a potential fuel crisis! But there were more critical tests to complete in seconds before cutting the power.

XA847 was rolled gently to starboard at Mach 2+ and pulled into a 2½G turn with smooth and satisfactory controllability. Now for the critical engine intake tests. Reheat power was cut carefully to avoid sudden reduction of 'dry' thrust r.p.m. in the intake-fuzzy risk zone; and then at Mach 1.98 and slowing the throttles were inched down,

98 per cent, 95 per cent, until, with no change in engine note or vibration levels, the throttles were slammed closed passing Mach 1.9 still in the 2½G turning descent — the potential critical condition for 'buzz' and possible compressor surge.

Nothing dramatic occurred and the engines wound smoothly down to flight-idling while the sudden thrust loss and great increase in drag effect threw the pilot hard forward against the harness.

Meanwhile this sweeping turn, initially at twice the speed of sound and at this point still above Mach 1.7, had encompassed most of East Dumfriesshire and Westmoreland. I steadied on course for Warton and became subsonic again when passing over Windermere at 20,000 ft and completing the final checks on engines and systems, all of which were normal. Only then was it possible to think of what had just happened.

Seven minutes after take-off from Warton we had reached twice the speed of sound for the first time over Britain. It had been done without problems and with the predicted smoothness and controllability which was to become the hallmark of the future Lightnings of the RAF. Now on this still beautiful, clear day over the lakes and mountains of the Lake District with Morecambe Bay shining ahead and Blackpool Tower already visible above the coastline of the Irish Sea, this tremendous British fighter was gently descending at merely 90 per cent of the speed of sound with engines at idling in serene and, it seemed, total security.

This was a milestone which re-established British aviation among the world leaders after ten years in the void following the government's inexplicable and scandalous opt-out in 1947. From this day it could be seen that on top of all the previous testing experience with this remarkable fighter, the scene must surely now be set for 20 years or more of progressive development to take full advantage of constantly improving weapons systems so as to exploit the Lightning's full potential and keep the RAF abreast of world fighter technology or even in the lead. But with yet another brilliant stroke of negative policy making, succeeding governments (and Ministry departments) failed to take this patently obvious route and the Lightning, after being actually threatened with early retirement in the mid-1960s, in the event served out 27 years with the RAF, acclaimed as the finest all-weather supersonic fighter of its time, but never with the advanced weapons capability which was more than its due.

But this was all in the future. I curved XA847 gently back into the Warton circuit with the last of the fuel, settled on Finals at 175 kt IAS and let this aeroplane, the finest-ever fighter in my experience, slide down 'short finals' characteristically as if on rails, to flare with smooth, positive back-stick over the runway threshold marks for its gentle nose-high touchdown at 155 kt IAS. I felt that this had been a good day and that the Lightning was on its way to repeat the fame and fortune of its famous Warton predecessor, the Canberra.

P.1 Supersonic testing at Warton

By March 1955 the P.1 prototype WG760 was well into its intensive experimental programme at Warton following its exceptionally successful initial company trials at Boscombe Down from August to October 1954 during which handling and performance out to Mach 1.2 had been explored for the first time in a British aircraft in level flight.

Back at Warton the programme had settled into the routine of system proving, flight envelope expansion following flutter clearance, landing and take-off performance measurements and the vital specific fuel consumption/cruise air mile per gallons/drag measurements. After over 100 flights, most of them supersonic, this very advanced aeroplane was becoming acceptably routine in operation and a very pleasant experience.

The test pilot is not of course keyed up in anticipation of drama in every moment of every flight as is customarily implied by much of the media, but he must remain aware at all times of the need to watch for inconsistencies in systems performance or any sudden changes in flight conditions. This is the normal professional approach essential in all flying operations, with perhaps slightly more emphasis owing to the untried and unproven nature of the aeroplane on test.

It was with no more than the usual enthusiastic anticipation that I climbed into WG760 one morning in early March 1955. 'Flutter' (flight resonance) clearance to 650 kt IAS was scheduled with excitation by wingtip mounted explosive exciters. Known as 'bonking', this was a very different activity to that in the modern usage of the word and a lot less fun! The weather was clear over the Irish Sea supersonic run, and another of our most enjoyable P.1 flights was on its way.

The test point was achieved and Vibrograph recorded, and then with its customary low fuel state remaining the P.1 was headed back towards Blackpool and thence into the Warton circuit. All systems were serviceable and there was the chance of another sortie, possibly two more, before the end of the day.

With a prevailing anticyclone to the north there was a light easterly wind at Warton where Runway 08 was in use. A leisurely 45° climbing roll over the airfield into the downwind leg and then I selected undercarriage down on the base leg of a tight curved left-hand circuit to join Finals over the Ribble estuary at about 2000 yds from the 08 threshold — then starboard green and port red undercarriage lights! Here was our first P.1 undercarriage asymmetry, and with no more than two circuits fuel left this changed the priorities into 'Precautionary', but not for long!

Overshooting low past the Tower I called for their assessment which was 'Port leg half down'. Assuming there was air in the hydraulic system it was possible that reduced air loads or yawing air loads might help the hydraulics to complete the cycle; so I slowed to 190 kt IAS — no change; then yawed sharply to port with a bootful of rudder as much as could be contained with aileron to hold the resultant powerful rolling moment due to yaw — still no change!

An UP cycle was then successful but the following DOWN cycle produced port red, starboard green as before.

With fuel now down to 400 lb per side, sufficient for only one more tight circuit and approach, here was the moment of decision — use the fuel to climb for ejection over the Ribble estuary, or try a landing?

It had always been agreed that with the P.1's 60° leading edge sweep 'shoulder' wing a landing with asymmetric undercarriage could prove fatal in the likely event of the aircraft turning over. In any case the digging-in port wing tip would cause a violent swing to the left, and in this case landing on 08, it would head straight towards the cluttered tarmac and buildings.

This prototype was being so successful and was so vital to Warton's programme and to the RAF that I did not give it a second thought but declared an emergency landing and lined up on 08 again with the last of the fuel, the port undercarriage still red and the other green.

At short Finals ATC called 'Port undercarriage still hung up'. I doubt if I acknowledged this, but at about 200 ft with 800 yd to go and at about 168 kt IAS I gave it as much port yaw (right rudder) as I could hold laterally with aileron. There was a clunk, the port green came ON, I throttled back, flared and landed.

I have never been able to understand why I dismissed the 'safe' option of ejection and just went ahead to try the landing — but it turned out to be a fortunate though not necessarily 'the right' decision!

Chapter Nine

Lightning

Following the success of the P.1 trials, the major fighter development for the RAF, the P.1B Lightning, began its flight test programme in 1957 and by 1958 it had become the first British aircraft to achieve Mach 2.0, twice the speed of sound. An incident in the early testing is described in this chapter.

During the first critical years of flight development of the P1.B prototype and Lightning 'DB' (development batch) series, the Rolls-Royce Avon RA24 engines had given excellent service with few major problems, although hot gas leaks had caused concern with repetitive fire warnings and some localised hydraulic fires, and reheat unreliability had resulted in delays to the test programme and embarrassment in some aerobatic manoeuvres (particularly at Farnborough displays).

But in the main, throughout the extensive flight envelope of this new Mach 2-plus fighter, the RA24's performance had been excellent with a total absence of surge-line problems or other restrictions in handling, and it was becoming what is today known as a 'user-friendly' engine.

Then one day in 1958 (the first flight had been in May 1957), the final exploration of the flight envelope to supersonic speeds at low level was scheduled to 700 kt IAS.

It was a sparkling day in late afternoon sunlight over the Irish Sea as I turned XA847 on climb out from Warton's runway 27 on to a north-westerly heading on 'Test Run Alpha' to accelerate midway between the Lancashire coast and Douglas, Isle of Man, to limit risk of sonic booming either coastline.

At 500 kt IAS and 500 ft I set the throttles at 'Max Dry' and then forward into full reheat. With its usual exhilarating thump in the back the Lightning leapt forward with the ASI spinning quickly round to 600 as I glanced at it briefly and then concentrated on the sea ahead which, with white topped waves, seemed sufficiently visible for safe height judgement at low level at this and faster speeds. But by now the sea was racing by and height judgement was rendered more difficult progressively by altimeter error increasing with speed.

The Mach meter hesitated and then slipped on to 1.05. Supersonic and with no tremor from the airframe or change in the controls or flight conditions except for increasing airflow noise level as the ASI continued unchecked, 650–660–670 kt.

All was flashing speed and thunderous noise and the vital need to hold the Lightning at a safe clearance from the water which was now only a blur from below onward to about a mile ahead, where the white caps could still be distinguished. The engine and

XA847, the first P.1B Lightning and the aircraft involved in the engine-surge incident described.
(British Aerospace)

systems gauges gave normal readings, and even at these high 'ram' temperature
conditions the cockpit auto-conditioning remained comfortable.

So this remarkable prototype continued towards its first-time 700 kt IAS, and then
without warning Bang, Bang, Bang — and a lot more, just like continued very close
cannon fire or hits by explosive shells.

There was another cause of concern. With every explosion the airframe shuddered
and shook and a halo of yellow fire flashed round the top of the intake just ahead of
the windscreen, or so it seemed.

I instinctively eased back stick and throttles together to gain safety height and reduce
speed, and as the ASI dropped below 650 kt or so the banging and general commotion
ceased and we were once more in serene and smooth supersonic flight, still below
1,000 ft. Never before had I experienced anything like this. It seemed almost certain
to have been intake surge but the engine panel showed normal values as I carefully
slowed through transition to subsonic. Even so there seemed to be a strong possibility
of turbine-blade or duct damage from such a violent incident.

So a gentle return to base was appropriate and with Point of Ayre on the Isle of Man
now in sight to port I turned starboard, climbing to 10,000 ft for a Mach 0.9 cruise
back to Warton, exercising the throttles carefully and individually on the way to look
for signs of engine damage, but there was none.

During the return leg I puzzled about the intake 'flames' — in a compressor surge this
should not happen unless there was some severe internal damage, yet the engines were
still handling quite normally. But before landing at Warton the thought had occurred
that compressor surge could produce shockwaves round the intake and that these could
become visible in humid air and then be illuminated by the golden evening sunlight!

It was an interesting theory anyway, and after an uneventful landing when discussing the
event with an attentive group of engineers and engine company representatives the general
opinion was that this had indeed been our first encounter with the 'surge-line' on the RA24,
and that the 'flames' effect could well have been sunlight on shockwaves. Nevertheless,
thorough duct and engine health inspection would now be needed before the next flight.

Good progress in first-time flight envelope expansion tests can never be permitted

XA853, one of the early development testing Lightnings. (British Aerospace)

to introduce over-confidence in the test team until all the ultimate test points have been reached and firmly established with safety margins and reliable test results.

Lightning ceiling climb

In the late 1950s the P.1B Lightning trials were also entering the high-altitude phase at Warton and had proved very successful up to 60,000 ft at supersonic speed in every aspect of stability and control, engine and systems suitability and cabin pressurisation. Only one area, engine and jet pipe hot gas leaks, gave rise to frequent fire warnings and sometimes the hazard of localised fires had caused problems, but by the early 1960s most of these had been resolved and now we needed to investigate and demonstrate the highest practical altitude capability for Service use.

Firstly, practical flight with weapons system capability (short of firing weapons, which would be done in later trials) had been demonstrated up to 60,000 ft. The next phase was to investigate controllability and, particularly, engine and reheat modulation and combustion stability to the highest practical altitude. At these extreme heights the Lightning remained comfortably controllable with care not to achieve excess AoA and a pro-spin situation. For although the spinning programme (led by Jimmy Dell) had been entirely successful and the Lightning had proved non-critical in recovery, 'departures' (disturbances from stable flight) had not yet been assessed above 45,000 ft and nothing could be taken for granted in relation to possible changes at extreme altitudes.

It is characteristic of supersonic aircraft that the ceiling in 'dry' thrust (without reheat) is limited by power and the sharp transonic drag-rise to substantially lower altitude than the supersonic ceiling with reheat at its maximum efficiency.

Accordingly in this phase of the Lightning trials the final climbs were started at Mach 2 after acceleration up the Irish Sea at the tropapause of the day under radar control, first under Warton's surveillance and then handing over to Ulster radar (Northern Ireland RAF network). The Lightning was pulled up hard into a 30° climb at maximum energy and power through 40,000, 50,000 and 60,000 ft, and into a 'ballistic trajectory' which would top out (with full back-stick) at around 70,000 ft at Mach 1.1, depending on the variables of tropopause height and temperature on the day.

The fame and performance of the Lightning brought many VIP visits to Warton in the late 1950s. Here the Commander-in-Chief of Fighter Command, Sir Thomas Pike, flies a T.4 with the author. (British Aerospace)

In these 'ballistic' climbs on every occasion the reheats would flame out in the region of 65,000 ft, but the engines maintained stable combustion in 'dry' thrust to the highest altitudes and it was a relief that there were no cases of flame-out or, especially, double flame-out which could have led to critical dependence on the uncomfortable and restrictive partial-pressure suits and helmets.

Many successful flights were made to 65–70,000 ft without drama and then on one

Julian Amery, Air Minister, with the author in 1959 to fly a T.4 at Warton. (British Aerospace)

Sir Hector Macgregor, C-in-C. Fighter Command, with the author in 1959. (British Aerospace)

sortie in 1961 Desmond (Dizzy) de Villiers was scheduled to do a repeat reheat stability check to 65,000 ft — his first at that height. All went well on his run up Test Run Alpha, Warton's own supersonic test run over the Irish Sea from the North Wales coast, and on reaching Mach 2.0 he called 'climbing'. There was the normal silence for a minute or two and then his voice: 'Mayday! Mayday! I am in an uncontrolled dive with full back stick at 60,000 ft and I can't get the nose up — I'll have to eject!'.

By this time I was on the Warton ATC line and told them: 'Tell him to check his flaps!'. But before they could do this de Villiers came back on the air saying: 'It has just pitched up and I think I have control again!'. But he did not sound confident.

I was fairly sure what had happened, and the subsequent debriefing confirmed that there was no technical failure. All Lightnings had protection against overstressing the flaps after take-off in the subsequent very fast acceleration after undercarriage retraction,

The author, Lord Caldecote (MD), Freddy Page (Chief Engineer) and ACM Sir Thomas Pike at Warton in 1959. (British Aerospace)

Lightning! The world's most manoeuvrable Mach 2+ fighter in the 1960s. This is XG308, the second of 20 development aircraft. (British Aerospace)

in the form of a 'blow-up' valve which automatically selected Flaps Up when the speed exceeded 250 kt IAS. This was accompanied by only a small trim change which could be missed by a pilot who thought he had already selected his flaps up; and this is what de Villiers had done. He had then flown the rest of the very fast and steep climb profile, concentrating on accuracy and observation of scheduled test points and unaware that his flaps, though up, were in fact still selected down but held up by the blow-up switch!

All went well as he rocketed up through 60,000 ft, then at around 65,000 ft in the

Roll-out of the first Lightning T.4 at Warton, April 1959; XL628. (British Aerospace)

The author preparing for the first flight of the Lightning T.4 prototype, XL629, on 6 May 1959.
(British Aerospace)

steep climb as his ASI fell below 250 kt — the flaps came down! This produced a strong pitch-down which he could not hold with full back stick, and the Lightning went into an ever-steepening dive. De Villiers, quite reasonably and under great pressure felt that he was having a power control failure of some kind and then, although he cut the throttles to idling power in the dive, IAS increased quickly and as it exceeded 250 kt the flaps automatically retracted and the aircraft pitched up and back into control!

This was in a sense a design fault, for if a system can be misused by pilot error it inevitably will be at some time. But it was also an example of the complexities of designing a protective system against pilot error which could in fact lead to another sort of error!

After much debate the authorities accepted that there was no need for change, and that this possible pilot error would in future be covered by greater emphasis in briefing. But de Villiers never made that mistake again!

'Ballistic' energy climbs continued from Warton until full knowledge had been amassed of engine and airframe behaviour and systems performance at these great altitudes, and in the process the highest flight recorded was by Jimmy Dell, who reached 75,000 ft in Lightning Mk 3 XN734 starting from a high, cold tropopause on 7 March 1964. Thirty years were to pass before Warton began flight trials of a new supersonic fighter capable of exceeding that height, the Eurofighter 2000.

Lightning T.4 display flying
During the development of the Lightning it became famous for impressive displays at Farnborough in the late 1950s. But there was one display which was not quite the success it might have been.

Farnborough air displays are not events in which technical defects are a normal occurrence. Immense effort is put in to preparing demonstration aircraft to the highest possible standard, but of course there is always the newness factor and many participants are in the earliest stages of their test programmes with as yet unproven reliability.

Nevertheless in over ten consecutive years of demonstrating at Farnborough, apart from reheat ignition unreliability in the early years with the P.1B Lightning, I

The author delivers XL628 to the Farnborough Display, September 1959. This aircraft was lost in a structural failure in October, the pilot Johnny Squier ejecting safely. (RAF Museum/Charles Brown collection)

Left and below: The author brings the new T.4, XL628 in to tight formation with the camera Meteor on its first flight. (British Aerospace)

Landing the T.4 on Flight 1. Note the drag 'chute, which fell off at the Farnborough Display! (British Aerospace)

The new-shape two-seater nose is clear in this fine shot of the T.4 on Flight 1. (British Aerospace)

encountered only two embarrassing events. The first occurred on the first public showing of the English Electric B.3/45 Canberra when an under-stressed flight test instrumentation crate fell out of the bomb bay when the doors were opened at the top of a half-loop, and took the starboard engine panel instrument readings with it.

The second was even more exciting! On 7 September 1959 the Lightning T.4 prototype, XL628, was shown at Farnborough for the first time, and as this was the third 'Lightning year' at the Society of British Aircraft Constructors (SBAC) Display we felt confident in our knowledge of how to present the aircraft in relation to the conditions and environment at Farnborough.

One of the factors always to be considered at that time was the smooth runway surface which, with heavy tyre rubber deposit in dry weather, could become very slippery when the rain came — which it generally did some time during the display week. Accordingly during recent weeks at Warton I had explored with the engineers the practicability of air-streaming the drag 'chute before touchdown and had proved in practice (on the P.1 WG760) that with careful judgement it could be streamed short of the runway threshold at about 50 ft resulting in a smooth nose-up trim change and flare for touchdown. It worked like a charm and saved about 200 yd on the landing run, but one had to be careful that the streaming speed was not in excess of the 'weak-link' safety speed which would result in the drag 'chute being cast off!

So, after a good practice on the Sunday I put the trainer through its planned routine on the Monday opening day and then, on short Finals in a light drizzle of rain, passing the Black Sheds and the Pilots' Tent I pulled the drag 'chute handle at 50 ft and 155 kt IAS. There was a jerk, the nose began to pitch up into the flare, the main wheels touched down and then — nothing! The 'chute had either self-jettisoned or candled I thought, and I was left with a 'chute-less T.4 now well past the President's Tent and still at around 140 kt IAS on the slippery runway.

The remaining runway ahead looked very short and here the Dunlop Maxaret ABS wheel brakes had to do their best. This they did, but as we rapidly approached the perimeter track turn-off at the Laffan's Plain end we were still doing about 40 kt and were quite clearly not going to turn off or stop before the end of the runway!

This now became a damage limitation exercise. I did not know just how rough the overshoot area was, but I could see only too clearly the maze of approach-lighting poles that we were now running straight into. So with the last of the steering energy from the hot brakes I tried to steer the Lightning between the first set of poles, and then in a cloud of dust and dirt from the rough ground and missing all the poles we eventually made it back on to the firm perimeter road, thankfully out of sight of the enthralled crowd.

Though somewhat embarrassed at this display of incompetence I was relieved to find at dispersal that no damage had resulted from our 'off road' excursion other than stone-cut tyres, and that the drag 'chute failure had been caused by 'pinching' of the cable between the tail bumper and the runway — I had cut it too fine with the AoA! All in all not a satisfactory day I felt, although the T.4 display had apparently been well received. But the event was well summarised later when the C-in-C Fighter Command, who had been watching his new Lightning supersonic trainer from the President's Tent observed, 'I wondered if T.4s always land like that!'

Chapter Ten

TSR.2

The British Aircraft Corporation TSR.2 supersonic bomber/reconnaissance aircraft of 1964 was more famed for its widely publicised political cancellation than for its undoubted technical success. One incident in its short and successful test flying period might well have had more serious consequences.

TSR.2 — Flight No. 2 at Boscombe Down

On 27 September 1964 the first flight of the BAC TSR.2 had been limited by severely de-rated engines which were still in early development, and by the undercarriage which had not been cleared for retraction. Within these restrictions the flight had been very successful with all test objectives achieved and much valuable data gathered. A qualitative assessment showed that this was an impressively precise and controllable aeroplane right from the start.

But the optimism generated by this first experience was then frustrated by a lengthy delay for fitment of modified engines and design clearance for undercarriage retraction. In the event the undercarriage was the longest delaying factor and XR219 was not cleared for flight again until 31 December, three months after Flight 1.

At the year's end it was unlikely that weather conditions favourable for a critical test flight would occur just when needed, and in the morning of the 31st a low cloud base caused postponement until the afternoon. Then the short winter day became a major

The TSR.2 prototype on preparation for flight, Boscombe Down, August 1964.   (British Aerospace)

The author in the cockpit of TSR.2 XR219. (British Aerospace)

consideration as there would be insufficient light after about 4.30, but by 2.30 p.m. conditions improved and preparations for Flight 2 began.

During the installation test runs of the two modified engines a high-frequency vibration had been noted by the Bristol Engine Company engineers who had expressed a wish for 'the pilot's' opinion on whether it was acceptable for flight. I had carried out a check-run and a taxi-run and had agreed that we could try it. Possibly the change of mass as the wing took the load off the undercarriage on take-off might change the characteristics of the vibration; and so in the event it did!

Preparation for Flight 2 was no less intensive than for the first flight, the purpose of which had been, as always on these occasions, mainly to demonstrate to the Ministry customer and indeed to the mass media that the thing which represents so much taxpayer's investment flies and flies well.

But now on Flight 2 it was the intention to start the test programme proper, get the undercarriage up and away, and begin to find out the qualities of this complex new aeroplane.

After completing the pre-flight checks, lengthy at this early experimental stage in the

The first flight of TSR.2, 27 September 1964, at Boscombe Down. (British Aerospace)

programme, XR219 was taxied slowly out to the threshold of Boscombe's runway 24 with the sky now clearing and the winter sun low on the western horizon and in fact shining directly down the runway, and this showed up a new problem. The optical qualities of the centre armour glass windscreen panel were now badly affected by the low-angle sun-glare which caused a mottling effect and interfered with the vital forward vision of the runway.

Nevertheless I decided that this could if necessary be an instrument-reference take-off, and that after the planned flying time of 45 min the setting sun would have moved further round to the north-west and would no longer be dazzling for the landing. This proved to be over-optimistic and, in retrospect, an unwise decision.

But we needed, very badly in view of continuing adverse political and media comment, to get TSR.2's testing under way, and at 2.40 with only one hour's practical daylight left in this last day of 1964 I checked that Don Bowen was ready with the recording instrumentation and the fuel system and power controls monitoring in the back cockpit. Then with Don's cheerful 'affirmative' I opened up power to 'Max Dry'. As r.p.m. stabilised heavy high frequency vibration was again noticeable, but it did not increase as I moved the throttles into 'Intermediate' and then Maximum Reheat and released the brakes.

The aircraft accelerated smoothly down the centre-line with little necessary steering input, and then came the unexpectedly early nosewheel lift (which we had established in the taxy trials and Flight 1) on easing back the stick from 130 kt IAS.

This aircraft was again remarkably docile on take-off and flew itself off with pilot actions limited to achieving and maintaining climb-out incidence, and then reducing power to avoid reaching the undercarriage placard speed until we were ready to investigate undercarriage retraction. Forward vision at this point was virtually nil through the sunglare-mottled windscreen.

But on throttling back the situation changed from straightforward and easy control to sudden, unexpected emergency.

With what, on calm reflection, was at the time a very strange sensation, the images in the outside world, which were difficult enough to see through the windscreen 'mottling' and even through the clearer side panels when climbing straight into the glaring sun, suddenly blurred and became almost indistinguishable; so did the instruments and switch controls in the cockpit. I knew where they were, but accurate readings of, for example, the vital ASI, altimeter and artificial horizon were now impossible. For a few brief seconds this was disorientating but then reasoning took over as I felt greatly increased vibration through all parts of the cockpit and seat, and then the sensation of vibration in my head and yes, in my eyes themselves! This had to be an escalation of the 'engine' vibration problem and it had resulted from reducing power, so now to open up to Max Dry and see what happened. Immediately the vibration level reduced and I began to see clearly again.

I made an R/T call that I was abandoning the test schedule and had an emergency, and then logic suggested that as the ground tests had indicated No. 1 engine to be the main vibration source, with No. 2 still at Max Dry I closed the port engine down gently and briefly saw the r.p.m. at 97 per cent and dropping as my vision literally 'greyed out' again in the resulting high vibration level. Throttling right back to flight-idle on No. 1 immediately reduced the vibration level and clear vision came back.

We were now, on only the second flight, in our first experience of asymmetric flight (one engine) and still with undercarriage and flaps down this could now become critical quite quickly with only the currently derated power on the 'good' engine.

I levelled out at 2,000 ft, retracted the flaps and continued in a gradual descent to reduce drag and maintain an adequate safety speed while I started the next logical step — to bring up the No 1 engine power to the point at which the vibration/vision level became critical again. This occurred at 87 per cent N_h (r.p.m. of HP stage of turbine) and established that there was a band of engine speed from 87 to 96 per cent N_h in which this aircraft could not be flown safely because of deteriorated pilot vision! There was certainly no way it could be landed in this condition.

Two alternatives appeared to be either to use both engines at above 96 per cent N_h, which would be excessive for the final approach, or to control the approach in asymmetric power keeping No. 1 below the critical r.p.m. range.

Telling Don Bowen and Jimmy Dell why I was cancelling the schedule and what I proposed to do, I turned XR219 back towards the downwind leg of the Boscombe circuit, and then set up what I hoped would be a practical way of controlling an approach. At 2,000 ft and now with undercarriage and flaps down, control with asymmetric throttle to less than 87 per cent on No. 1 and No. 2 up to 99 per cent as required was adequate to maintain level flight without incurring vision loss, and this was rechecked satisfactorily at 95.5 per cent on No. 1 and 90 per cent on No. 2. These settings would give reasonable margins for controlling an approach, but in the event of any need to overshoot, No. 1 engine would need to be accelerated quickly through the vibration range to give the necessary thrust margin for climb performance.

This would have to do although the vibration levels still demanded an urgent landing. But only 4 min after take-off we were well over planned landing weight, so while positioning for approach, I checked reheats at 200 kt IAS and both lit satisfactorily, burnt off more fuel, and then were cancelled.

Then sharp bank inputs were checked at 200 kt IAS, giving good response and roll-rates.

Setting up and maintaining the final approach was complicated by the need for asymmetric throttle adjustments, and then at 190 kt IAS the sunset glare again increased the mottling effect in the windscreen and reduced visual contact with the runway to virtually nil. Sideways vision through the quarter panels remained good and the flare was judged only by sideways reference on the runway lights, having maintained approach power at 190 kt IAS until over the threshold marks.

After completing the flare with no direct vision ahead, power was cut and a smooth touchdown occurred on the centre-line immediately followed by a massive lateral oscillation at the cockpit which seemed to fling my helmeted head from side to side hard against the canopy and to cause momentary total disorientation. This was a repeat of the undercarriage 'lateral' oscillation incident experienced on Flight 1, but after recovery of vision of the runway as the oscillation died away the drag 'chute was streamed effectively and the second flight of TSR.2 was concluded, not successfully but certainly with never a dull moment (see original experimental flight test report on page 129).

At de-briefing there were some raised eyebrows when a few of the engineers apparently found it difficult to accept that excessive engine vibration had caused the pilot loss of vision, but when the frequency of the vibration was identified from the trace recorders a call to the IAM at Farnborough confirmed that the natural frequency of the human eyeball exactly matched the measured cockpit vibration frequency. TSR.2 had also again succeeded in blurring the pilot's vision to the point of incapacity at the critical point of touchdown, luckily only briefly! These were certainly new experiences!

Earnest investigations over the next few days failed to find the cause of the engine problem and I was invited to 'try it again'. I declined and suggested again that as I had reported in debriefing I had also felt a possible thrust 'shunting' and this could have been associated with the fuel or engine combustion systems which should also be investigated. This was done and revealed an out-of-tolerance fuel pump in No 1 engine. This was changed and a test-run showed that the vibration had been eliminated.

From Flight 3 onwards that problem was cured, but serious undercarriage sequencing failures then demonstrated the correctness of the decision not to try a 'first-time' undercarriage retraction during the vibration difficulties on Flight 2!

The severe undercarriage lateral vibration remained throughout the test programme until Flight 22, when it was cured by a damper-strut modification.

So the path to progress in the early testing of TSR.2 was certainly paved with frustrations, but undercarriage cycling was not finally functioned properly until Flight 10. From then on progress was rapid and impressive.

BRITISH AIRCRAFT CORPORATION (OPERATING) LIMITED
PRESTON DIVISION

Total Flight Time: 00.13   Flight No.: 2
Take off: 15.44   Landing: 15.57   Date 31st December, 1964
(Start-up – shut-down: 00.51 mins.)

EXPERIMENTAL FLIGHT REPORT

Aircraft Type: TSR2   Pilot: Mr. R. P. Beamont
Serial No.: XR.219   Navigator: Mr. D. J. Bowen

OBJECT OF TEST: Schedule No.: 2B
Undercarriage operation and general handling.

TEST CONFIGURATION:

START-UP LOADING:

Fuel: Indicated contents:		Tare Weight and Equipment 58371 lbs	
Forward group	10500 lbs.		
No. 2. tank	3700 lbs.	Crew	340 lbs.
Aft group	8050 lbs.	Stores	lbs.
No. 4 tank	2750 lbs.	Water	lbs.
Total ind. fuel	18600 lbs.	LOX	24
Usable fuel	19151 lbs.	Fuel	20838 lbs.
Unusable fuel	1687 lbs.		
Total Fuel	20938 lbs.	Total Weight	79573 lbs.

C.G. POSITION AT START-UP: 22.0 ins. A.O.D. (40% S.M.C.) U/C DOWN
ENGINES: Type: Olympus 320X   Ser. No.: 1. 22217
                                              2. 22215

OTHER RELEVANT AIRCRAFT CONDITIONS

TSR2 XR.219 — FLIGHT NO. 2 — 31ST DECEMBER 1964

Cockpit checks completed to Flight Reference Cards Issue 3 amended December 1964.

Fuel on entry:	F. 10800 / A. 9200 lbs.
C.G.	G. 39.4% F. 39.8%
Brake accumulators:	3200/2400 p.s.i.
Oxygen:	⅔rds/95 p.s.i.
Radio:	lower aerial selected.
TACAN:	locked-on on ground
Air Data Test:	1. 6650'
	2. 45600'
Altimeter zeros:	Main — 986 mbs.
	Standby — 987 mbs.
Engine starts:	
No. 1	T5 rising 13 secs.
	30% 35 secs.
	57%/310°C 70 secs.
No. 2	T5 15 secs.
	30%/400°C
	57.8%/284°C
Undercarriage lights:	3 Greens, Reds out.
Aileron gearing indicator	10°.
Brake accumulators:	4200/4100 p.s.i.

Cabin temperature selector in Manual for start-up, and selected to Auto Normal for taxying. This produced rather too warm air at the cockpit within five minutes, and the controller was re-set to Half Cold.

Flow distribution throughout the engine speed range was comfortable and appeared to be normal, and no sharp variations in temperature or flow sensing were noted.

Engines during cabin temperature checks:—
          70/70%   322/340°C

As with Taxy No. 12 the vibration level with No. 1 engine in the NH range 87–95% was greater than during the initial taxying series, but was not regarded as unacceptable.

Operation of the nozzle over-ride shifted the datum of the critical NH range of the vibration downwards by 2%.

Nozzle over-ride checks on Nos. 1 and 2 engines satisfactory with Aj gauges indicating SHUT on Over-Ride selection (90/90%).

Flap blow checks at 90/90%:	
20° flap	blow at mid 20° segment
35° flap	blow at mid 35° segment
Reheat lighting checks:	Double datum switches at
	Normal (100%)
No. 1	max. dry 99.0%/720°C
	reheat at 1st gutter satisfactory.
No. 2	max. dry 98.0%/702°C
	reheat at 1st gutter satisfactory.
Fuel:	F. 9600 / A. 6900 lbs.

TSR2 XR.219 — FLIGHT NO. 2 cont'd.

During engine checks it was confirmed that with No. 1 engine set above 95% or below 87% the engine vibration level reduced considerably though not to the low level of the first engine installation (1st flight programme).

In the late afternoon light with the sun low on the horizon close to the end of the runway, lighting conditions in the cockpit were poor and it was impossible to achieve sufficient instrument lighting brilliance to offset the prevailing contrast conditions. The only instruments which were readily readable under these conditions were the trim gauges on the port side and the Aj and T5 gauges on the starboard panel. C.S.I. reference was particularly difficult in its deep shade under the shrouds and under these circumstances its night illumination could not be seen.

Use of the white flood-lighting was also ineffective as the floods illuminated the rear of the pilot's elbows and cast shadows of these across the instrument panels. This inadequate lighting was a limiting feature in the flight.

When lined up on Runway 24 the sun glare at an acute angle to the windscreen resulted in an excessive mottling effect on the centre windscreen which made forward vision difficult. This resulted subsequently in visual reference being lost during the rotation for take-off, and in visual difficulties during the landing approach.

Take-off: Runway 24.
                                       Wind/velocity 250°/12 kts.

Reheat lights satisfactory and nosewheel initial lift at 120 kts., checked and resumed on passing 170 kts.

Due to loss of visual reference in rotation take-off incidence was not achieved at the scheduled speed, and unstick occurred at approximately 200 kts. This emphasised the need for incidence reference as a take-off monitor.

Double datum switches to Intermediate at 220 kts., and throttles moved back to disengage reheat on passing 2000'. Due to slowness in disengagement of the reheat stops No. 1 engine remained in reheat at the 1st gutter for a short period until this was identified and power reduced to Max. Dry Intermediate.

Heavy vibration was apparent during the initial climb and this was at first thought to be airframe buffet, but on reducing power to level at 3000' when the vibration amplitude increased, it was found that this was associated with r.p.m. reduction into the 94–90% range.

No. 1 engine was increased to above 96%, and this reduced the level to that previously noted for the climb phase. Return to below 96% and in the range 96–87% on No. 1 engine increased the vibration amplitude to a level in which vision was obscured by apparent eyeball resonance. This was intolerable and dictated the pattern of the remainder of the flight.

Level flight was established in asymmetric power at 95.5/90%, 612/560°C, and a port turn initiated after announcing the decision not to retract the undercarriage.

The vibration level even in these conditions was such as to make it immediately desirable to land, and this intention was declared. However the aircraft was not positioned at this time for a satisfactory approach, and it was also necessary to burn off some fuel to achieve a suitable landing weight.

While repositioning for the approach reheat lighting checks and sharp control inputs were carried out which, under the prevailing conditions of excessive and distracting vibration, could not be observed with the normal standards of accuracy. Response was satisfactory however.

TSR2 XR.219 — FLIGHT NO. 2 cont'd.

Reheat lighting at 200 kts , undercarriage down, flaps 20°, 2000':—

No. 1, satisfactory (1st gutter only selected).
No. 2, satisfactory (1st gutter only selected).

Sharp bank inputs port and starboard at 200 kts. in this configuration gave relatively crisp response with little apparent adverse yaw, and adequate rate.

When taking off bank at this increased rate the effects of inertia were apparent, and both stopping bank and returning to wings level resulted in inertia overshoots. Improved damping from auto-stabilisation may be expected to cover this case of sharp control demands; while conditions remained entirely adequate under smooth control input conditions in this configuration without auto-stability.

Power adjustments in configuration changes, turns etc., continued to be complicated by the essential need to maintain No. 1 engine outside the 87–94% NH range. The aircraft was rolled out of the base leg turn at 7 n.ms./1800' and set up to approach initially with asymmetric power at 200 kts., reducing to 190 kts. at short finals as this appeared to be appropriate to the required 12½° landing incidence with 35° flap.

Throughout the sortie no reference to re-trimming had been necessary, and immediately before lowering 35° flap trim displacements were made in the three axes to check trim rates, which again when observed under the prevailing adverse circumstances appeared to be satisfactory.

35° flap at 220 kts. required a very slight nose-up trim adjustment, and at some transient points in asymmetric engine adjustment there was a momentary feeling of directional trim asymmetry which was not read on the slip indicator and no adjustments were actually made.

On rolling out on to the approach the low sun position directly on the end of the runway resulted in almost complete obscuration of vision through the centre windscreen panel. The approach lights could still be seen however, and at a range of about 1½ miles the VASI's; this enabled the approach to be continued visually. Visual reference through the quarter panels remained unobstructed throughout.

Coupled with inadequate forward vision under these extreme lighting circumstances (the inadequacy being no worse than on some other contemporary aircraft in these conditions), the low relative maximum brilliance of the cockpit lighting caused difficulty in reading vital instruments.

The approach was continued with reference to the approach lighting only, and on passing this the flare and landing were carried out by feel, namely by flaring from 190 kts at an altitude judged through the quarter panel to be approximately 50 ft. This resulted in a smooth touchdown of the rear wheels followed within one second by a very violent lateral oscillation at the cockpit which persisted for approximately 4 seconds and during which positive control of the situation was momentarily lost.

The oscillation was estimated at the time to have been at approximately 4–5 c.p.s. and at least ±1g (Instrumentation confirmed ±1½g at 5 c.p.s. lateral and some longitudinal).

When the oscillation damped out sufficiently to allow the recovery of full control it was found that the nosewheel was still high although the stick had been inadvertently allowed to move forward from the scheduled position for aerodynamic drag. At this time and while still under some degree of disorientation the tail parachute was streamed without recovering reference to A.S.I., and this resulted in beak door operation at 161 kts. (Instrumentation), namely 6 kts. above

TSR2 XR.219 — FLIGHT No. 2 cont'd

the schedules speed. Tail parachute development was felt to be normal with a relatively long pause before smooth development of de-reefing. The nosewheel had been lowered to the runway before operating the tail parachute handle.

Upon development of full parachute drag wheel braking was applied gently at first and then at maximum pedal pressure for approximately 2 seconds passing 120 kts. Control of the landing roll-out was smooth and uneventful, and the parachute was jettisoned at approximately 20 kts.

At standstill the brake temperatures read 200/700°C with the starboard brake temperature gauge erratic and apparently unreliable.

Fuel: F. 7000 / A. 4200 lbs.

During the latter five minutes of the flight the pilot's cabin temperature became uncomfortably warm at Half Auto Cold, and the controller was adjusted to Full Auto Cold just prior to the approach. This maintained warm but reasonable conditions until taxying in when the temperature again rose to an uncomfortable level. Through most of the sortie the navigator quoted "cool" conditions in his cockpit.

Engines at shut down: 58/57%, 300/290°C.

With the exception of No. 1 engine and the undercarriage, all systems were serviceable at shut down.

SUMMARY

No. 1 engine vibration level became excessive in flight resulting in blurred vision due to eyeball resonance. This dictated an immediate landing.

On touchdown in a normal low rate-of-descent landing (Instrumentation 4 ft./sec.) the undercarriage lateral oscillation encountered on Flight 1 recurred with greater amplitude. This was such as to disrupt control and cause disorientation for 3–4 seconds at a critical point in the landing.

In a one-hour sortie the temperature at the pilot's cockpit rose too high for comfort at Full Cold setting.

In this configuration stability and response to controls was excellent, and allowed full attention to be given to the necessary engine-condition investigation. These control qualities also minimised embarrassment from the unfavourable visual conditions prevailing on the approach and landing coupled with the inadequate level of instrument lighting.

R. P. Beamont, Manager; Flight Operations

The BAC TSR.2 Flights 3 and 5 at Boscombe Down

In research and development (R & D) test flying it is essential to be ready to deal with the unexpected, especially where there appears to be every reason for confidence! In all human activity it is human to err and the field of aircraft design and preparation is no exception.

Nevertheless it can come as a surprise when a new aircraft which has been subjected to many years of design evolution and systems rig testing in the specialist departments, suddenly produces a fault which could result in loss of the aircraft. It can be even more surprising if it transpires subsequently that the fault had been predicted at an early stage in design but not acted on by the design authorities before the start of flight testing.

A prime example of this occurred on Flight 3 of the BAC TSR.2 supersonic

Touching down at Boscombe on a wet winter's day. A close photograph from the 'chase' Lightning. (British Aerospace)

bomber/reconnaissance aircraft in January 1965. This aircraft had already had a complicated gestation period, both technically and politically, and as mentioned previously its first flight was made with engines lacking a conventional airworthiness status. A series of catastrophic failures on test to the low-pressure (LP) compressor shafts of the Bristol Olympus 22R engines in the preceding months had culminated in three explosive-disassemblies (i.e. the engine blew up), the second of which destroyed the Vulcan bomber flying test-bed, and the last of which took the roof off the test cell at the National Gas Turbine Establishment.

The cause had been identified as instability of the LP shaft, but modified engines would not be available for some months.

Even so the first flight was required to take place without modified engines and with N_h limited by the pilot 'as much as possible' to less than 97 per cent in order to avoid the 98–100 per cent range in which all the previous shaft failures had occurred. This limitation took no account of the essential need for 100 per cent N_h to cover the one engine failure case with these initially de-rated engines, and the first flight was authorised with this risk element.

Following a successful Flight 1 on 27 September a long delay occurred until the first pair of modified engines became available, and then progress was dictated by final clearance for undercarriage retraction which was slow to come. The vibration difficulties on Flight 2 prevented retraction and this test was scheduled eventually for Flight 3 by which time exceptionally good qualities of stability and control at low speed had been established, and we went quickly to the retraction cycle test point selecting 'up' at 210 kt at 2,000 ft. After attempting and failing to analyse the rapidly changing warning lights sequence, it became clear that conventional retraction had not been achieved.

The 'chase' Lightning and Don Bowen, BAC's chief test navigator, using his back-seat periscope, confirmed that the port bogie beam had rotated to the vertical but had not tripped the uplock stage, and the leg remained down with the bogies near-vertical and 'reds' on. Hopefully 'Down' selection was made and the port bogie beam unwound itself to green lights, and the starboard did likewise to fully down and green lights.

It had not occurred to me that there might have been a miscalculation in the hydraulic force required to overcome the varying air-loads during the undercarriage cycle; but there was more fun to come!

After much head-scratching and re-testing on the ground test rig, Flight 4 was set up and a similar failure occurred, but this time to the starboard leg! Landing configuration was once more achieved safely with 'Down' selection.

This problem by now had the undivided attention of the management, and after two further weeks of high pressure remedial action by the engineers Flight 5 was scheduled to 'prove the final cure'. In the event this resulted in an even more comprehensive sequence failure with much more serious implications.

Flight 5 on TSR.2 prototype XR219 occurred on 14 January 1965, a cold winter's day with more snow forecast. The view ahead through the sharply raked windscreen was uninspiring. Grey snow-laden clouds whipped by closely overhead, and the ground seen mistily below through light falling snow was a monochrome of black winter woods and hedgerows and grey-white fields under a thin covering of snow. It looked bleak and uninviting, but in the cockpit the auto-controlled temperature was a comfortable 20°C and the work of data-gathering at scheduled test points progressed comfortably at a steady rate interrupted only briefly for periodic radar fixes from Boscombe Tower.

The test schedule called for further stability and control response investigation with undercarriage down and full 'blown' flaps in the speed range 220–180 kt IAS, then a full cycle (Up and Down) of the undercarriage and, if successful, two further cycles. In the three flights since Flight 1 the undercarriage sequence problems encountered had so far prevented clean retraction, and it was now becoming very urgent to clear this to enable the flight envelope programme to be expanded.

In experimental test flying there is seldom the high drama so set in the imagination of media men, and the work continues in professional calm much of the time. But sudden arisings such as flashing 'attention-getters' can cause an adjustment of priorities, and of course a fire warning can certainly concentrate the mind!

On this occasion, however, XR219 was flying with its already established smooth precision and with all systems functioning correctly, and the time had come for the final undercarriage tests. Calling Jimmy Dell in the 'chase' Lightning, XL629, to close in to enable John Whittaker to film the retractions, I set up the prescribed test conditions at 220 kt IAS and 2,000 ft and, giving a countdown on the radio (recorded on the continuous voice recording on-board tapes), selected undercarriage Up.

Accompanied by the now familiar slight rumblings and mild vibrations the port sequence lights flickered from green to red and went out, as did the nosewheel lights, but the starboard reds flickered momentarily and then stayed On. Don Bowen (BAC's chief test navigator) confirmed through his periscope that the starboard leg was still down, but with the bogie beam apparently stopped at near-vertical but not rotated far enough to operate the up-locks, and Jimmy Dell agreed from his Lightning. It was the situation-as-before on Flight 4 despite all the resultant remedial work. This was becoming routine it seemed — but not for long!

After reporting the details to our engineers in Boscombe Tower, I made the Down selection and from this point on the priorities changed progressively.

The nosewheel lowered correctly, the port undercarriage lowered but failed to rotate the bogies from the vertical to the landing condition with reds remaining On, and the already down starboard leg failed to rotate the bogies to the landing position also with reds On. The sortie had now gone into 'precautionary' mode.

After much radio discussion and debate in the aircraft it was decided that no further undercarriage cycling should be attempted lest it resulted in even worse asymmetries. The sortie had gone into 'emergency' mode!

It soon became apparent that despite earlier briefings on this possibility no-one on the ground was now going to advise a landing in this condition. In the aircraft we had a full appreciation of the implications. If we landed with the bogies in the vertical such that the front wheels would touch down first instead of the correct sequence with the rear wheels first, would the spin-up drag (which normally pitched the front wheels down into contact after the rears had touched down) force the bogies to reverse upside-down with consequences which could be both unpredictable and unattractive?

In only a few minutes this routine test sortie had changed into a situation demanding critical decision and one which could be fatal for both of us. The decision could only be taken on board and, as it had been in previous critical arisings in test-flying, when it came to the point I was reluctant to abandon the aircraft and consequently almost certainly ensure the loss of the whole programme. But even then there was the thought that the politicians seemed likely to 'lose' the programme for us all anyway, so why should we take the risk?

However in the four previous short test flights XR219 had shown this exceptional degree of controllability in pitch at low speed, and the thought occurred that if I could lower this big aircraft very gently on to its malfunctioning undercarriage, any adverse effects of spin-up drag at touchdown might be minimised and the aircraft allowed to settle slowly, rotating the beams backwards (against hydraulic pressure) into correct contact with the runway. It was a gamble but, using the VHF mute switch to keep Boscombe out of the conversation, I put it to Don Bowen as his chance to use his Martin-Baker Mk 5 ejection seat in the back, and he responded by saying: 'What are you going to do Bee?' I said I thought I would try a landing, and Don came back with the classic: 'You're not going to get rid of me that easily!'

By now low fuel was adding to the urgency and I gave VHF notice of our intention to set up a low approach fast enough (with this highly loaded delta wing) to give a positive flare and hopefully a gentle touchdown.

From then on total preoccupation with setting up this important approach to achieve the precise conditions for this critical landing eliminated any further considerations. The decision had been made and now we were committed, and total concentration was needed right down to touchdown.

It was an interesting moment, and I have often thought with admiration of the degree of stoicism shown by Don Bowen in staying aboard throughout those, for him, anxious moments of the long approach to the final revelation of the touchdown with nothing for him to do in the back cockpit but monitor the fuel gauges and think of what was to come.

The TSR.2 behaved as I had hoped in the touchdown with a recorded vertical rate of descent of only 6 in per sec — scarcely perceptible in the cockpit, and the bogies were seen by Jimmy Dell close by in his Lightning and by the flight test engineers near the runway, to rotate backwards into correct contact without damage.

We had saved the TSR.2 from destruction, and also the programme for a further six weeks until it was cancelled anyway by the politicians.

After all the excitement had subsided and in the inevitable period of anticlimax later that year, it occurred to the crew that no-one had bothered to acknowledge or give any formal recognition to this action. It was almost as if the general feeling among the ministries and those in authority was that if the TSR.2 had been destroyed it would have saved a lot of trouble! So the crew had to be consoled with the thought frequently expressed by Freddy Page (Sir Frederick Page, now retired Chief Executive of British Aerospace plc) in this and earlier programmes — 'Never mind, righteousness has its own reward!'

TSR.2 makes its first fast low pass at the end of Flight 10. (British Aerospace)

TSR.2 Routine flight test

The 26th of February 1965 was a significant date in the flight testing programme of the TSR.2 which was intended to provide sophisticated multirole capability for the RAF and for the Royal Australian Air Force from the early 1970s to the end of the century and beyond. On this date the prototype, XA219, was scheduled to begin the measurements of its aerodynamic efficiency in terms of air-miles-per gallon of fuel used in the low-level high-speed cruise — one of the vital design points in its specification.

As already recounted, since the first flight at Boscombe Down on the previous 27 September the rate of achievement of planned testing had been frustrated by problems with the Olympus 22R engines and by repeated undercarriage cycling malfunctions, but these had been solved, and on Flight 14 I had flown the prototype with Peter Moneypenny back from Boscombe to Warton, on the way exploring for the first time transition to supersonic flight, and also carrying out its first radar directed instrument descent through icing cloud prior to landing at Warton.

At the English Electric base the programme took on a new tempo. The main technical problems were behind us and between-flight servicing and turn-rounds now had the full benefit of the total expertise of the design office and specialist departments in all the relevant disciplines on immediate call, instead of the 200-mile pipeline from Boscombe to Warton and the 70 miles from Boscombe to Weybridge which, despite heroic efforts by all concerned, had inevitably slowed down progress for six months in the initial test programme at Boscombe Down.

Now Flight 16 was scheduled for 'Low-level performance and handling' with the specific purpose of beginning the measurements of aerodynamic drag and engine installation efficiency. If all went well it was also planned to commence detailed measurements of rate of roll and assessment of aircraft response to varying 'taileron' (roll control) inputs.

There was also an aspect new to the programme. The first nine test flights on the prototype, each providing limited but valuable information and data, had been restricted severely by technical problems which had among other difficulties prevented retraction of the undercarriage.

This had finally been achieved on Flight 10 at Boscombe and after two satisfactory Up, Down and Up cycles the speed envelope had been extended from the

With successful undercarriage retraction on Flight 10, XR219 was taken out to 500 kt on the same flight. (British Aerospace)

undercarriage limit of 275 kt right out to 500 kt IAS on that sortie with excellent controllability.

Some undercarriage damage was incurred on Flight 11 and after this was repaired Flights 12 and 13 had achieved the outstanding test points required for clearance for the planned delivery flight from Boscombe to English Electric's main BAC military test base at Warton for the full test programme to take place.

This flight, No. 14, had been fully successful with a number of 'firsts' achieved on the way to Warton, including the TSR.2's first transition to supersonic flight, and when landing at Warton we had felt certain for the first time that we had a sound, capable, practical and really impressive aeroplane on our hands.

After a routine systems check on Flight 15, XR219 was now prepared for a sortie which would depend on suitable weather over a short straight route from Lancashire's South Fylde coast across Morecambe Bay and on over the high fells of Ribblesdale and Lunesdale. The basic requirement was for steady, accurate flight at 2,000 ft which would involve flying over the tops of some of the high fells at 200 ft or less and would require some divergences from track to avoid the highest peaks while firmly maintaining the true 2,000 ft level for test accuracy. Hopefully turbulence would be encountered in the lee of high ground and TSR.2's response carefully noted.

On the day the conditions were excellent with a ridge of high pressure giving broken fair-weather cumulus with base at about 3,000 ft, and visibility unlimited in a brisk north-westerly following passage of a cold front.

For the first time since the first flight five months earlier, the sortie could be approached with increased confidence in technical reliability and with the knowledge that the TSR.2 was no longer an unknown quantity with troublesome characteristics, but was beginning to demonstrate some of its predicted exceptional qualities.

Peter Moneypenny, Warton's chief test navigator, and I began the pre-flight checks at about mid-morning and when these were completed in about 15 min I called the Tower to alert Jimmy Dell in the Lightning chase aircraft that I was about to start engines. With all systems functioning correctly I taxied XR219 out on to the north–south runway and then backtracked down the Main to the 08 end for the take-off on Runway 26 which would be in a 10 kt crosswind component from north-west.

It was a fine, sunny morning and for the first time the prototype was starting on a routine schedule of tests, fully serviceable and with no outstanding technical defects to deal with during the flight except the undercarriage landing vibrations which were yet to be cured but were already well understood. So that it was with a real sense of pleasure that we began the sortie.

Setting flaps 36° and 'blowing' (discharging high-velocity air ahead of the flap to prevent airflow breakaway), and with no over-riding engine limits following the successful modifications to the LP shafts (from Flight No. 2) maximum reheat was stabilised at 98/97.5 per cent N_h, jet pipe temperature 728/706°C, brakes were released and XR219 accelerated smoothly down the centre-line needing little steering correction. Then, with progressive stick-back from 130 kt IAS, it rotated smoothly to lift off at 178 kt IAS and 13.5° AoA.

Undercarriage Up selection at 205 kt IAS/200 ft achieved retraction and lights out at 230 kt IAS/800 ft, reheats cut and power reduced to 95/95 per cent N_h at 5,000 ft/360 kt IAS, and we turned port over the Ribble estuary towards Liverpool Bay. All systems were serviceable and descending to 2,000 ft I increased speed to 490 kt IAS to start the cruise.

With radar clearance for our first heading I rolled starboard with half stick deflection and in these clear visibility conditions confirmed an earlier impression. This aircraft did not respond to lateral control input with the conventional swept-wing adverse yaw due to aileron drag, that is briefly yawing away from the direction of turn until settling down on the new heading. Looked at closely in the comfortably relaxed circumstances of this sortie, it seemed that XR219 yawed very slightly into the direction of turn, and a repeat with sharper stick input demonstrated this clearly. The TSR.2 had a tendency in these conditions towards what became known as 'proverse' yaw.

This was unexpected and would need to be investigated thoroughly for flight safety and aerodynamic considerations, but for the present I noted on my knee-pad 'brief proverse yaw in starboard turn initiation at 495 kt IAS/2,000 ft causing mild nose-drop into the turn — check implications in IF (instrument flight) etc'.

At this early stage in the programme some of the unusual characteristics of the new aeroplane were becoming increasingly impressive. Inherent stability on all axes (with no auto-stabilisers on the prototype) was enhanced by firm short-period damping and exceptionally well harmonized control response and force-gradients; and the highly loaded delta wing purposely designed for low gust-response was proving to be exceptionally insensitive to wind gusts and turbulence in and out of cloud. Now we were about to look at all these aspects in the low-level rough-air turbulence to be expected through the Pennine valleys and especially in the lee of the high peaks.

In short, as I turned XR219 out over the sea from Formby Point and set up the first scheduled cruise heading of 028° overhead Blackpool at 2,000 ft with power set initially at 86/86 per cent, with the green and brown farmlands of the Fylde slipping by below at around 500 kt IAS, this aircraft seemed to be not so much an immense technical advance at the beginning of a critical test programme, but rather a smooth, firm, precisely controllable large jet aeroplane with thousands of hours of flying behind it. There was a sudden feeling of great confidence and enjoyment. This was a magnificent aeroplane and this was a moment to savour!

Within two minutes speed was stabilised again at 490 kt IAS by reduction to the scheduled 84/84 per cent N_h. Now to hold height and speed steady for 10 min, flying manually, and this proved to be simplicity itself. The TSR.2 slipped smoothly and accurately across Morecambe Bay's shining surface dappled with hard-edged dark shadows from the scattered cumulus clouds above.

With more time to take in small detail than in the previous often critical flights, it was notable that the fine lines round the nose radome and windscreen produced little wind noise. The engines, far aft at low cruise power and not in reheat, hummed smoothly. The cockpit, unusually spacious for a military aircraft, basically well laid out and equipped with Jimmy Martin's latest masterly design, the first zero-altitude ejection seat, seemed almost too comfortable and secure. This impression was enhanced by the contour-designed seat padding and associated parachute and escape equipment of the seat which resulted in a comfort level unusual in a military aircraft at that period. But this was no time to become too comfortable and relaxed!

As we crossed the Lune Valley south of Kirkby Lonsdale the high fells loomed ahead and on either side. The 1,700 ft Goosdale Fell to starboard, and then Leck Fell, 2,058 ft at our cruising level. Then the Calf, 2,230 ft, over to port and the North Riding country stretching away to the east with Birkdale Common rising above us to 2,300 ft.

The green pastures had given way to the all-year-round winter yellow-browns of the moors broken everywhere by criss-crossing drystone walls up to the high tops, and by the limestone screes scarring the slopes and sometimes falling away precipitously from the peaks as on the west face of flat-topped Ingleborough. It was a magical scene in the crystal clear visibility and one could almost hear the curlews.

Now XR219 was sliding across hill tops with 100 ft clearance or less and then deviating to the right a few degrees to slip by 300 ft below the crest of The Calf and along its eastern slopes at about 150 ft above the scree. All in rock-steady security more reminiscent of the scene from a seat in a wide-screen cinema than the cockpit of a fast jet!

Suddenly there was some gentle vibration roughness which had to be air turbulence on the downwind side of the fell, but it was still quite insignificant in the TSR.2 as Jimmy Dell in the following Lightning chase aircraft R/T called 'I'm pulling up because of this turbulence'. 'What turbulence?' I said, to the enjoyment of Peter Moneypenny in the back seat!

The Pennine scenery, so often cherished in many previous years of Canberra and Lightning testing, though not often at this low level, was breathtaking on this brilliant day. The aircraft seemed to slide effortlessly along the sides of ridges, across the narrow green valleys of Lune and Ribble and over some of the 2,000 ft tops at exhilaratingly low level.

This was for its time an extraordinarily precise aeroplane and it was a joy to fly. But it had not been built for pleasure and with a conscious effort of will the tests were continued.

Kendal ahead and then Appleby, the scene of parliamentary questions following the early supersonic booms from our P.1 in 1954, was coming up fast to port, and ahead looming above us ominously into a dark thunderhead was the 2,500 ft peak of Great Dunfell Pike.

The first 10 min cruise was complete. Now for the second.

The hill-slopes in front were now disappearing up into the dark grey storm cloud, but over to port the mountains of the Lake District still stood out sharp and clear with shining glimpses of the Irish Sea beyond Shap and the 3,000 ft peaks of Skiddaw and Helvellyn.

But now to turn smoothly back to the still clear weather, south-west on to heading for Warton, still maintaining the 2,000 ft/490 kt IAS test condition and continuing to weave around the highest ground where necessary. Another 10 min cruise would have us back at the coast, and then there were more tests to come.

With no necessary changes to trimming and only the smallest throttle adjustments, XR219 continued to virtually fly itself in these conditions and there was no longer any room for doubt at all. This aeroplane at this flight condition was an entirely new aviation experience. It had already shown excellent qualities in supersonic flight at altitude, and now close to its primary role at low level it only needed an added 100 kt to begin to prove its main operational design point. This I felt sure it was going to do in the very near future.

But soon, with the hill country behind, we were heading back across Morecambe Bay with Blackpool Tower clear ahead and the second cruise stopwatch time was up. Peter Moneypenny had completed the fuel flow records, the TSR.2 had seldom deviated outside ±50 ft from the datum 2,000 ft throughout and I felt that we should have good results from these tests.

Next to begin measurement of response to 'taileron' lateral control. In the previous 15 flights general handling had been established as satisfactory throughout the initial test flight envelope from 150 to 500 kt IAS, to 30,000 ft and supersonic speed at that height, and in approach and landings down to 155 kt IAS.

This was before the era of air-to-ground data transmission, but the TSR.2 prototypes were heavily equipped with state-of-the-art on-board trace-recorders and vibration sensors continuously recording over 190 data points, and with good serviceability at last the engineering test programme was now under way.

Response to lateral control inputs was scheduled in 'partial rolls' to left and right at 1G with limited stick inputs. These would be carried out in the first instance with smooth, quick inputs (but not maximum rate 'snatch' inputs) to 90° of bank and then if satisfactory to 180°.

After checking for clear airspace with Warton radar and confirming to the Lightning chase, I set up the first scheduled test condition at 3,000 ft and 450 kt IAS overhead the Ribble estuary and ran through the test points in left and right quarter and half rolls. Response as expected was smooth, linear and precise and stopping the rolling motion without inertia overshoot needed only slight anticipation. The aircraft rolled to 90° and 180° in each direction without sideslip at this moderate speed and it felt secure and totally satisfactory; so much so that I decided to look a little further and merely announced to Moneypenny that I would 'repeat that to starboard', knowing that if I mentioned what was really my intention it would result in an R/T debate with the Warton flight test engineers which I did not wish to have at that moment.

From the previous flights it was already clear that the 'taileron' differential tailplane control was providing the designed rolling power and that the lateral/directional stability characteristics were providing a large safety margin at these flight conditions, so I felt that although it was not on the test schedule a ⅓rd stick roll-rate could be sustained safely through a full 360° roll at 1G and would provide convincing evidence that we could push forward the test programme faster and with confidence in this area.

I had circled back towards Preston so as to keep in the area of the Warton base with the initially very low fuel load (still limited by the first-stage de-rated engines) now getting down towards the scheduled landing weight, and I now lined up over the Ribble heading west and called 'rolling starboard — now'.

With nose eased slightly above the horizon in a 45° port bank and trims zeroed on all axes, at 450 kt IAS/3,000 ft I moved the stick smoothly starboard to ⅓rd deflection, stopped it there and watched as the TSR.2 rolled smoothly with slip-ball dead centre right round to 340° at which point I eased off the stick back to central, and XR219 ceased rolling at wings-level smoothly and without overshoot or any signs of over-sensitivity on any axis. It was unreal and reminded me strongly of rolling the Warton fixed-base TSR.2 simulator!

When I mentioned this in the subsequent debriefing it was music to the simulator engineers!

Meantime there was an unaccustomed silence on the R/T. Then Moneypenny's voice said: 'What happened there?' and a distinctly surprised Jimmy Dell said: 'That one went right round!' 'Quite right,' I said, 'and very nice too!'

And so this fascinating and valuable sortie came to a close. I flew a practice approach in a normal visual pattern down to Finals for Warton's 26 runway for an overshoot and then climbed away in dry thrust noting adequate thrust margin at 200 kt IAS.

For the landing approach with gear down on base leg and flaps to 35° with 'blowing' at the ILS outer marker, XR219 again flew down the approach virtually without assistance, a characteristic which, with confidence, we had now come to expect of it. Over the 26 threshold at 50 ft/178 kt IAS and flare with smooth back-stick. Throttles to idling when the wheels rumbled at 172 kt IAS. A brief moment of undercarriage 'lateral' vibration, then the brake 'chute when still nose-high. Only then ease the nosewheel down with gentle forward stick to roll-out down the centre-line with scarcely any steering input needed despite a gusting cross-wind component from 355°.

The first of the main programme test flights had been completed, and the TSR.2 seemed set to make fast progress in the immense task of 2,500 test flying hours that lay ahead before entry into RAF service.

But it was not to be. Jimmy Dell and Don Knight flew seven more test sorties in the next few weeks until the planned initial programme was complete, and I had issued the first flight operations summary statement to the Ministry departments and company boards. It had been possible to report with convincing test evidence, and in exceptionally positive terms, on the success of the phase 1 tests.

The prototype was laid up for embodiment of the final undercarriage modification, which had already been proved experimentally to cure the outstanding landing vibration problem, and then before TSR.2 could be returned to flight status the Labour government cancelled the whole programme with subterfuge by an unscheduled statement in the Budget Speech on 5 April 1965, precluding any debate in Parliament. The TSR.2 never flew again.

BRITISH AIRCRAFT CORPORATION (OPERATING) LIMITED
PRESTON DIVISION

Total Flight Time: 00.48   Flight No.: 16
Take off: 10.22   Landing: 11.10   Date 26th February, 1965
(Start-up – shut-down: 1 hr. 12 mins.)

EXPERIMENTAL FLIGHT REPORT

Aircraft Type: TSR2   Pilot: Mr. R. P. Beamont
Serial No.: XR.219   Navigator: Mr. P. J. Moneypenny
OBJECT OF TEST: Schedule No.: 16
Low Level Performance and Handling

TEST CONFIGURATION:

TAKE-OFF LOADING:

Fuel: Ind. contents:		Tare Weight and Equipment 58371 lbs.	
Forward group	118000 lbs.		
No. 2. tank	4200 lbs.	Crew	340 lbs.
Aft tank	9300 lbs.	Stores	lbs.
No. 4 tank	3400 lbs.	Water	lbs.
Total ind. fuel	21100 lbs.	LOX	24
Usable fuel	21651 lbs.	Fuel	3338 lbs.
Unusable fuel	1687 lbs.		
Total Fuel	23338 lbs.	Total Weight	82073 lbs.

C.G. POSITION AT TAKE-OFF: 22.2 ins. A.O.D. (S.M.C. 40.1% U/C EXTENDED)
ENGINES: Type: Olympus 320X   Ser. No.: 1. 22210
                                                            2. 22215

OTHER RELEVANT AIRCRAFT CONDITIONS

TSR2 XR.219 — FLIGHT NO. 16 — 26TH FEBRUARY 1965

Cockpit checks completed to Flight Reference Cards Issue 3.

Fuel:	F. 11900 / A. 9200 lbs.
C.G.	G. 39.6%, F. 39.7%
Undercarriage indicator:	3 Greens
Aileron gearing indicator:	5°
Altimeter zero:	Standby 1021 mbs.
Main	1019 mbs.
Hydraulic Accumulators:	3200/3000 p.s.i.
Brakes:	F. 1450/1600 p.s.i.
	A. 1450/1450 p.s.i.
Compass heading checks:	310°/310°
Auxiliary Intake Doors:	OPEN/OPEN (Checked with crew chief)
Oxygen:	FULL/85 p.s.i.

Lower aerial selected.

A.D.C. Check:	1. 6,500'
	2. 45,500'

Engine starts

No. 1:		T_5	6.0 seconds
		30%	30.0 seconds
		Idle	58.0%/302°C
No. 2:		T_5	11.8 seconds
		30%	30.0 seconds
		Idle	58.0%/286°C
Auxilliary Intake Doors:			OPEN/OPEN (Checked with crew chief)
Hydraulic Accumulators:			4000/4000 p.s.i.
Brakes:			F. 1450/1500 p.s.i.
			A. 1450/1450 p.s.i.
Aileron gearing indicator:			5°

In D.C. throttle checks No.1 D.C. control was rendered difficult due to a sticking switch. It was possible to make contact but with heavy switch force.

Roll/yaw gearing selected to −.2° for take-off.

On taxying out difficulty was experienced in lining up at the end of 26 runway due to the relatively narrow width (50 yards), and to the need for adding differential brake input to maximum coarse nosewheel steering deflection to achieve the necessary radius of turn. The runway surface was dry and with a lower coefficient of friction this manoeuvre would not be practicable.

Nozzle override checks at 90/90% :	SHUT/SHUT
Flap blow checks:	20°: mid 20° sector
Flap blow checks:	35°: mid 35° sector

TSR2 XR.219 — FLIGHT NO. 16 — 26TH FEBRUARY 1965. — Contd.

Flap blow checks: 50°: mid 35° sector
Max. dry Normal   98/97.5% r.p.m. 728/706°C
Reheat lights to first gutter were checked on both engines against parking brake. Lights were satisfactory and the brakes held at this thrust condition.

The parking brake was released and reheat increased to third gutter and this resulted in the brakes releasing under judder conditions for 1 – 2 seconds. Fuel:
F. 10,400./A. 8,000 lbs.

During the take-off run some apparent undercarriage/airframe lateral oscillations began and, immediately prior to unstick at approximately 190 kts., had reached quite high amplitude. This oscillation disappeared at lift-off.

The double datum switches were not moved to INTERMEDIATE and the climb-out continued at max. reheat NORMAL, with undercarriage selection at 205 kts. and cycle complete with all lights out by 230 kts.

Reheat was cancelled and the climb continued at 95/95% to 5000/350 kts.

During the initial climb the Navigator reported an indicated rapid drop in fuel contents, but this was not seen on the Pilot's gauges and apparently soon stabilised at the Navigator's station.

The aircraft was turned onto 028° at 2,000' over Formby Point for the first cruise at 450 kts. increasing to 490 kts.

Stop watch: Zero,   2,000' 490 kts. 85/86% 438/456°
                                           2,000' 495 kts. 83.5/84%
                                           2,000' 490 kts. 84/84%

Height and heading holding was satisfactory in this flight condition, as was speed stability and a 10-minute cruise was maintained within excursions of approximately ±5 kts. from 490 kts and ±100' from 2,000'.

At approximately 0 + 9 minutes when approaching Kendal, it was necessary to increase indicated height to 2,300' to pass over a hill top with 200' clearance.

Moderate turbulence was encountered over hill country at the northern end of the leg, but this did not detract from flight accuracy.

A starboard turn was initiated east of Kendal at 0 + 10 minutes and during the turn at 495 kts. the tendency to drop the nose due to proverse yaw was apparent.

After roll-out on reciprocal heading at 0 + 11 minutes: 1940'/495 kts. 84.4%/84.2% 420/414°C.

A 9-minute stable run on a southerly heading was carried out with excursions from datum limited to approximately ±50' from 2,000' and ±5 kts. from 490 kts. Engine speed constant at 84/84% approximately.

Longitudinal trimming for these runs was barely necessary, but lateral/directional fine trim was required at the beginning of each run, and this confirmed the relative over-sensitivity of the rudder trimmer; minimum adjustments giving too coarse inputs resulting in relatively powerful rolling moment due to yaw.

0 + 20 minutes, end of run:

2,000'/490 kts. 84.2/84.2% 418/414°C Fuel: F: 7,550/A.4,900 lbs.

At take-off the cabin conditioning had been set at NORMAL AUTO and remained at this throughout, the cabin temperature being comfortable and not varying to any noticeable extent throughout the run.

Control conditions throughout this 20-minute cruise were virtually ideal in pitch and yaw, but tending to over-sensitivity in roll especially in turbulence and in a 180° turn at 490 kts. (Roll/Yaw gearing at –2°).

TSR2 XR.219 — FLIGHT NO. 16 — 26TH FEBRUARY 1965. — Contd.

Still with Roll/Yaw gearing at –2°, I.A.S. was set at 450 kts/3,000' and a longitudinal stick jerk recorded with damping approximately dead beat.

A port stick jerk resulted in virtually "dead-beat" damping, but the aircraft was slightly out of trim directionally and the aircraft rolled back to starboard slowly after the input.

General handling in turns and reverse turns in this configuration did not show significant difference from the zero roll/yaw gearing case, and selection was made back to zero.

Comparative handling in roll showed no significant change in this condition, and increased rate roll was investigated.

It was noted that at this flight condition (450 kts/3,000') sharp lateral inputs resulted in a momentary movement of the slip ball in the opposite direction before centring and travelling in the proverse sense. This motion could be seen on the pitot probe; e.g. with left stick input the probe moved starboard initially as the port bank came on and then smoothly back through the in-trim position to slightly slip ball left.

Use of sharper lateral control movements up to ⅓ stick deflection resulted in relatively crisp roll response and no tendency to inertia overshoot if take-off of bank was anticipated normally.

Due to the positive nature of this response, roll control was further explored through 90°, 180° and 360° rolls while maintaining slightly positive normal acceleration. These manoeuvres were smooth and straightforward in every sense, with no tendency towards inertia coupling effects in recorded roll rates up to 90°/second.

Sharp inputs to half stick deflection, checking at 90° of roll, resulted in inertia overshoots when stopping the roll.

After lowering flap 20° at 265 kts., the undercarriage was lowered satisfactorily at 210 kts. in approximately 15 seconds to 3 GREENS with no trim asymmetries; and a practice approach to 26 runway was flown with 35° of flap, fuel 6200/3900 lbs. Engine checks in the base turn: 90/90%, 552/540°C.

With wind 330°/8 kts. an overshoot was carried out from 200 kts. I.A.S. in Max. Dry Normal with satisfactory thrust margin, and the pattern rejoined for landing on runway 26.

Downwind checks:

Accumulators:	4200/4200 p.s.i.
Fuel:	5300/2900 lbs.
C.G. GL:	39%
Wind/Velocity:	355°/8 kts.

The final approach was carried out at 190 kts. with 35° of flap at approximately 2° glide slope, and the flare made to level the aircraft over the runway for a gentle touchdown with progressive reduction of power.

Touchdown:	172 kts.
Incidence:	14½°

The vertical rate of descent was low, but from the moment of touchdown a 2 – 3 second undercarriage lateral oscillation was set off which resulted in the pilot being thrown from one side of the cockpit to the other to the point of hitting the helmet on the port and starboard sides of the canopy.

The tail parachute was streamed normally, nosewheel high (Reefed selected as

TSR2 XR.219 — FLIGHT NO. 16 — 26TH FEBRUARY 1965. — Contd.

scheduled) and the lower deceleration rate was compensated for by increased wheelbraking.

Shut-down checks:	61/58.5%. 290/276°C
Hydraulic Accumulators:	4200/4200 p.s.i.
Brake Temperatures:	400°/540°C

SUMMARY

Two 10-minute low altitude cruise legs were carried out at approximately 490 kts. I.A.S. under satisfactory control conditions, which included moderate turbulence and passage at 200' over high ground.

Directional, longitudinal and speed stability/control were highly satisfactory in these conditions. Lateral control was slightly over-sensitive in turbulence and sustained turns, but this did not affect test accuracy significantly.

Auto-control of cabin temperature in this sustained high I.A.S. condition at low level was comfortable and constant.

Further investigation of roll control with variations of roll/yaw gearing settings demonstrated no significant changes from the latter, but showed that roll response up to 1/3rd stick deflection at these speeds is satisfactory and does not suffer from the effects of inertia with smooth inputs.

A heavy undercarriage lateral oscillation incident occurred following a gentle touchdown. Apart from this the aircraft was fully serviceable on landing.

The 50 yard runway width was barely sufficient for a 180° turn, at full deflection, nosewheel steering Coarse, with added differential braking.

R. P. BEAMONT,
Manager; Flight Operations

DEFECT REPORT:

Undercarriage Landing incident (vibration).
No other defects.

Celebrating the successful First Flight: Freddy Page, Air Minister Julian Amery, Henry Gardner and Roland Beamont. (British Aerospace)

Chapter Eleven

Jaguar

In the first international collaboration programme since the Second World War for the development of an advanced fighter-bomber, the SEPECAT Jaguar, a short-fall in control capability was identified and remedial action became essential.

In the late 1960s the first European collaborative organisation in the field of military aviation was formed by Breguet Aviation of France and BAC Warton with the aim of producing an aircraft which could meet the requirements of the RAF and L'Armée de L'air for a dedicated low-level strike fighter for the next two decades.

The two requirements overlapped in some respects and were not entirely identical, so compromise was necessary. To the perfectionists of both sides this was anathema, but since they were not going to get any aircraft without joint agreement the final outcome was a specification calling for high subsonic speed at low level with externally carried weapons, and supersonic speed at altitude in 'clean' configuration.

The aircraft had to have practical operational capability in low-altitude turbulence, which meant a high wing-loading; a low gust-response wing; shortfield operating capability with moderate pressure tyres for rough field and desert operations; very demanding 'state-of-the-art' weapon aiming accuracy and, for the RAF only as the French did not require it, the first inertial navigation system (INAS) to be developed for a European tactical fighter. It was also required to have two engines for single-engine safety.

It was a demanding task, not least the merging into one efficient management system of two highly independent professional organisations with strong feelings of national pride and independence. Inevitably there were clashes of philosophy and professional pride, and often what was seen as just plain obduracy on one side or the other. But under the determined leadership of Freddy Page at Warton and Henri Ziegler at Toulouse two prototypes emerged, one at Istres and one at Warton.

Breguet chief test pilot Bernard Witt flew the first aircraft from Istres on the Mediterranean Coast, followed soon after by Jimmy Dell in the second at Warton, and the test flying was divided as planned between Warton and Istres. It had been suggested by the French that the weather factor at Istres would provide significant advantage to the programme over what they claimed to be the 'bad flying weather in England', but in the event the test flying proceeded at a similar rate at both bases and there were no significant delays due to weather.

I had retired from experimental testing after the TSR.2 according to plan, but had continued to keep my hand in on 'fast jet' flying with regular Lightning production

tests and occasional Canberra and Strikemaster (for Saudi Arabia) work until 1968; and when some doubtful areas became apparent with the Jaguar I was able to take advantage of the two-seat Jaguar trainer for a personal look.

After about two years of intensive and successful testing some doubts were being raised about spoiler lateral control quality by Jimmy Dell, but these were not being supported by the Breguet pilots so the engineers, seizing on this 'pilot's indecision', took the formal view that there was no problem. In discussion Jimmy Dell said that although 'hard' evidence had not yet been established, he felt that in combined 'worst case' conditions of turbulence and heavy external stores there was the possibility of lateral PIO which at best could be operationally unsatisfactory, and at worst possibly divergent and dangerous.

I raised this at the next Warton board meeting and came up against strong resistance — there was no evidence warranting design changes it was said. Although it was my firm policy not to intervene with the chief test pilots now that it was no longer my job to do the experimental flying, I suggested to Dell that we might look at this together. He agreed very readily, and on 1 April 1969 we flew down to Istres together in the Company's HS125 business jet.

The flight across France was over total cloud cover with only a brief glimpse of Mont Blanc's snow fields before we finally saw the cloud breaking ahead with the runways of Istres bathed in morning sunshine and the channels and lagoons of the Camargue shining to the south-west.

Our flight was to be in the first French dual-control two-seater, EO-1, and for my first on the type I would fly in the rear seat which had the 'instructor's' controls fully representative of the front seat, but with rather restricted vision when in the nose-high landing condition.

Kitting-up took only a few minutes — flying overall, lifejacket, 'bone-dome' helmet and radio and oxygen mask and leads. It was hot in the Mediterranean sun and I dispensed with the proffered 'G' suit, preferring my own traditional 'G' protection of a wide leather, brass-buckled belt which I had used with good effect in the Second World War and on through 20 years of Canberra, P.1 and Lightning testing.

Jimmy Dell started the engines, giving a briefing on the basics of flap settings, engine speed, response to use of elevator at V_1 and V_2 (the speed at which the pilot can elect to abandon take-off or continue, and the take-off safety speed), climb-out safety speeds etc, and then said: 'You've got her'. We had worked together for so long that we had total confidence in each other — a pleasant feeling that added to the pleasure of this interesting occasion.

Taxying out along Istres' winding perimeter tracks showed that even with my straight-ahead vision limited by the front pilot's helmet to either windscreen quarter panel, the Jaguar was simple to taxy with its quiet, responsive Turbomeco Adour engines, and smooth progressive pedal brakes and well developed nosewheel steering.

Immediate line-up and 'clear take-off' came from the Tower with confirmation of no other traffic, and after stabilising at 'max dry' and checking engine conditions and systems, the throttles were moved into maximum reheat and the brakes released. Acceleration was modest on this hot day by comparison with a Lightning (but indeed few other fighters could match that aircraft on take-off), but steering the centre-line was smoothly achieved with nosewheel steering until rudder power took over at around 60 kts.

Smooth elevator response raised the nose progressively to airborne after V_R (the speed at which the pilot 'rotates' the aeroplane in pitch for take-off) and the Jaguar immediately felt solid, secure, smooth and unexpectedly quiet (by comparison with the robust roar of a Lightning's two Avons in reheat!).

Climbing out from the Istres circuit we turned west towards the coast with the instantly recognised Camargue spreading out below. This Jaguar flight was a fascinating experience, but I would have been equally fascinated to be down there among the bird-life and wild horses of the Camargue on this brilliant day.

Levelling at 10,000 ft and cancelling reheat, with Jimmy Dell commendably silent and letting me get on with it, the Jaguar felt pleasantly responsive, crisp and unfussy in pitch and yaw at low and moderate speeds, and just slightly imprecise in roll, though not to an unacceptable extent. So, increasing speed to Mach 0.9 at this height I looked carefully at response and damping again in pitch and yaw which were both precise with dead-beat damping from small, sharp control inputs.

Then the roll axis, and this was a surprise. The air was non-turbulent at 10,000 ft and I had not expected quite the positive impression that occurred next. Sharp spoiler inputs gave good responses but the reversals did not stop the rolling motion dead-beat. There was in fact a need to correct and correct again to stabilise the lateral plane.

Spending some time looking at this it soon became apparent that the lateral damping even in the dead-calm air prevailing at this height was far less than precise, and that although it was not dangerous in these conditions it did raise a serious question about possible deterioration in turbulence or combinations of adverse conditions such as underwing stores.

The rest of the sortie was devoted to general handling within the cleared subsonic flight envelope, and finally some simulated low-level attacks down to 100 ft over the Camargue marshes, keeping a vigilant lookout for the flickering formations of wild-fowl disturbed by our noisy intrusion. As a naturalist and countryman I began to resent my own presence! It was turbulent low down over the marshes in the hot midday sun and although the Jaguar's control in pitch and yaw was excellent for the precision required in attack manoeuvres, the lateral lack of precision was outstanding. This would not be an acceptable standard to offer for evaluation in the forthcoming combined Services team trials.

We flew back to Istres where, as we joined the circuit Jimmy Dell said: 'If you are happy go ahead and land'. I already felt at ease with this fine, smooth and quiet small aeroplane, and with Dell's briefing on the appropriate numbers I curved the Jaguar responsively and accurately into the base leg and down on the final approach at 180 kt with flaps at 50°. The approach was steady and undeviating and, with throttles closed over the threshold and an easy responsive flare, the soft-action undercarriage rumbled smoothly on at about 145 kt. I streamed the drag 'chute still nose-high, and then lowered the nosewheel into runway contact with gentle forward stick.

This was a simple, pleasant aircraft, easy to fly with great potential for its main operating task of low-level attack. In this flight it had seemed almost impervious to the rough air around Istres which had severely shaken our HS125 on arrival. But there was already no doubt in my mind about the lateral control. Dell's concern needed reinforcing. The Jaguar needed roll auto-stabilisation.

Further discussion with the French flight test authorities merely produced a Gallic shrug of indifference. Their prototype was shortly to be handed over to the Centre d'Essai en Vol (CEV), the French government test centre, where it was expected that the British Boscombe Down pilots would also take part in the trials.

I believed it essential that the hand-over should not be made without a full briefing to the customer authorities on this lateral control aspect, primarily for reasons of safety but also as a matter of policy. It was essential that SEPECAT, the Jaguar international management agency, should reveal to the customer its full updated knowledge of the aircraft before handover.

I reported this situation at the next meeting of the Warton board, and met with a surprising reaction. Warton, led first by Teddy Petter and subsequently by Freddy Page, had always followed a policy of listening to the pilot, yet here in this first-ever international programme they appeared to be backing away from this tradition.

Recounting my experience and supporting Jimmy Dell's view, I said that there was sufficient evidence to demand further work on the lateral spoiler control system and, if necessary, to introduce a roll-stabiliser (I knew that Warton aerodynamics department had identified this potential problem and were already scheming an auto-stabiliser system in case one became necessary).

The reaction was swift and, in comparison with our normally calm and balanced debating atmosphere, surprising. The existence of a problem was fiercely denied by the Project Office, as it was said no evidence had been produced to support such a view.

I listed the many recorded relevant reports from Warton pilots (though none from the French) and unusually found myself in full opposition to one of my colleagues, saying that there was indeed evidence of a possibly vital shortfall in control quality, and that remedial design action was essential together with full accounting to the authorities on both sides of the Channel. My colleague seemed to be about to have a stroke, but the Chairman, Freddy Page, said: 'This matter will be dealt with outside this meeting'.

Later that day and after a further very detailed interrogation with me (Freddy Page's

Flying experimental Jaguar BO-8 with Tim Ferguson at Warton on 5 April 1973. (British Aerospace)

pilots had to be sure of their facts), he issued a memorandum confirming authorisation of an experimental status roll-stabiliser for urgent trial installation, and this was put in hand immediately.

At about this time a near-panic reaction came from the Breguet test centre at Istres. In their first official trials with the Jaguar CEV pilots had encountered 'near-catastrophic' PIO when they flew into very severe Mistral turbulence over the mountains while carrying a heavy centre-line store — here was that 'combination of worst conditions' which had eluded us up to then! But the solution was already on the way.

I flew six further two-seater sorties in the roll-stabiliser development programme including four from the front cockpit, variously in Jaguars EO-1, EO-2 and BO-8 with Paul Millet who had taken over on Jimmy Dell's retirement, Jesberger of Breguet Dassault, John Cockburn and Tim Ferguson. In the last two flights I took part in the final evaluation of the optimised production-version roll-stabiliser system. The first of these (in XW556) included general handling throughout the low-speed and high-speed envelopes, and the last was devoted to simulated attacks at low level with Warton airfield as the target. The transformation was complete. The Jaguar now had the crisp, responsive and well-damped controls on all axes that were essential for its demanding task.

I reported to the Board:

'At low level, moderate to severe turbulence was encountered and lateral damping assessed at 460 kt IAS down to 150 ft.

'With roll-damper off lateral damping in gusts was poor to the point of disrupting tracking accuracy, but switching in roll-damper immediately reduced these disturbances to an acceptable level.

'. . . the aircraft is now therefore considered to have fully acceptable characteristics of stability and control for the primary task'.

It had taken four years from the first recognition of this problem to achieve a satisfactory solution, and now the Jaguar was fit and safe to go into service. But as with most of their new aircraft the conservative RAF viewed their new strike fighter in 1975 with less than great enthusiasm initially. The Jaguar was a 'Pussy Cat' said the Lightning and Phantom pilots in Germany, and 'it needed reheat for taxying!'

But eventually in the 1991 Gulf War they said that Jaguars had a 100 per cent sortie rate record in 617 war flights with very high target accuracy and a nil loss rate. 'It was', said the chief of the Airstaff, 'the most cost-effective aircraft in the inventory!' Those in the teams who had striven with the development programme in the 1970s had cause to smile.

A production Jaguar at Warton in the early 1970s with production flight test engineers and ground staff. The author is in the centre. (British Aerospace)

Chapter Twelve

Light and vintage aircraft

In the 1970s and 1980s I became involved in testing very light aircraft as President of the Popular Flying Association (PFA), and in display flying vintage aircraft as a member of the Shuttleworth Collection Committee. Some of these fascinating activities are described in the following chapter.

The assessment of home-built aircraft for the Popular Flying Association (PFA) in the period 1977–81 produced some interesting episodes. By definition the 'home-built' category covers airframes designed and built by the amateur owner without benefit of factory facilities; or else those designed professionally and then constructed by the home-builder. This activity included the home assembly of factory-produced kit-sets and also in a few cases the end-products of apprentice training schemes, and it was with one of the latter that some interesting flight test situations occurred.

The Petrel was a two-seat design development of the single-seat Procter Kittiwake, aimed at providing simple side-by-side seater training with a tricycle undercarriage and adequate if not exceptional performance with a Rolls-Royce Continental O-240-A 130 b.h.p. engine.

Selected by British Aerospace at Warton to form the basis of an apprentice exercise,

Flying the rotary engined Vickers Gunbus at Wisley. The aircraft is now in the RAF Museum, Hendon. (British Aerospace)

The author about to make the Petrel's first flight. (British Aerospace)

the design was found to be incomplete and further design work was carried out by Warton designers in a number of areas including the aileron control circuit, control column geometry, fin and tailplane stiffness and pitot-static system. They also added some innovations including toe-brakes, a redesigned canopy, electric fuel booster pump and glassfibre wingtips.

Construction was mainly done by apprentices at Preston under the supervision of the training manager, Sumner Miller, and when the aircraft was eventually rolled out in February 1979 it was virtually a new type.

With responsibility delegated by the Civil Aviation Authority (CAA), the PFA monitors the design, engineering and flight testing standards of all conventional aircraft in this category up to 1,500 lb all-up weight, covering the initial Permit to Fly and the ultimate Flight Certificate. During the 1970s the author carried out the PFA tests for a number of these interesting little aeroplanes including the 'BAe' Petrel.

The Petrel ready for take-off at Warton. (British Aerospace)

Engine running began on 26 February 1970 and was completed satisfactorily but a number of items required further attention before flight including canopy locking, seat position and cushioning, parking brake lever and artificial horizon.

Taxying tests began on 9 May and these were extended to a take-off with 10° flap at 50 kt IAS, a level flight at 50 ft for about 600 yd to check aileron and rudder responses, and then conventional hold-off and landing. All of these points were responsive, well-damped and satisfactory, but as the nosewheel finally touched (in a 5–8 kt crosswind from starboard at 50°) a sharp jolt and judder was felt from the nosewheel steering through the rudder pedals. In further tests this was found to be an unsatisfactory characteristic of the direct ungeared connection between the nosewheel and the rudder pedals, but was accepted for further test flying.

By now a new atmosphere had become apparent around this project. What had been scarcely noticed as merely a commendable Board decision to approve a practical training scheme for the apprentice school was suddenly seen to be a first-flight test programme on an aircraft which had been partly redesigned at Warton but which had not been subject to the standard and strictly formal and progressive company procedures of design approval, quality control, final ground testing and Airworthiness clearance, but which nevertheless would now seem to be a 'Warton' responsibility if anything untoward occurred! So the Airworthiness Department under Glen Doe became deeply involved in a last-minute reappraisal of the programme, finally giving a verbal clearance-to-fly towards the end of the month.

The first flight on 25 May proved to be a classic example of the effects of incomplete coordination or diffusion in the line of design responsibility. The aeroplane could virtually only be flown in left-hand circles even with nearly full right stick, and left to its own devices stick-free it would roll away to port smartly on to its back!

Rather urgent rigging checks revealed a 1½° twist in the port wing (trailing edge up) which had somehow escaped inspection and quality checks, and this was ultimately corrected by shimming the rear spar attachment. The aircraft continued to provide interesting episodes for a while however, such as on Flight 2 when total ASI failure resulted in a handling sortie conducted without speed reference by co-ordinating pitch attitude with engine power settings in the same manner as similar arisings had been coped with successfully with Lightnings and Canberras in past years, though at somewhat higher speeds!

With the little Petrel this proved a trickier procedure owing to the very small usable speed (and incidence) range; but by Flight 4 with a nearly in-trim aeroplane, good progress was possible with certificate testing and after Flight 6 recommendations were made for a final modification standard. Extracts from the flight reports tell their own story:

PETREL G-BECA — FLIGHT 1 — WARTON 25 MAY 1979
One crew
Fuel:	Full/Full
Centre of gravity:	25.4% e
Take-off mass:	1,517 lb
Weather:	5/8 strato-cu/2,000 ft
	W/V 240/8 kt
	OAT + 11°C
	QFE 1,000 mb
Runway:	26
Flight time (1st take-off to last landing):	56 min
Engine time:	1 hr 14 min
Stop watch zero at **start up**	

0 + 5 2,400 r.p.m. for cockpit contamination checks
0 + 9 **Taxy** OP 28 OT 48 CHT 120

The elevator trimmer was difficult to see and not comfortable to reach, being too far aft between the seats. The parking brake lever was impossible to operate, either ON or OFF, with harness top straps tight.

The nosewheel steering was found to feel heavier than previously and this was probably due to the new aft-adjusted seat position. It was also too direct above low speed, and this was particularly noticeable on take-off when excessive force was needed to steer resulting in over-correction up to approx 40 kt, after which the pedal forces reduced suddenly to light as the nosewheel lifted at 45–50 kt.

Take-off: flap up
Brakes slipping at 2,100 r.p.m.
Port tank selected (F/F)

Excessive right pedal force was needed to track the centreline on the take-off run up to 40 kt+, reducing above this.

Smooth response in pitch to airborne at approx 55 kt. Immediately the aircraft became heavily left wing low at 60 kt+, requiring about half right stick for wings level at 70 kt on the climb.

This condition increased linearly with speed up to 95 kt where the force to hold lateral level was considered limiting with nearly max. right stick applied and little margin of right roll control remaining. In this condition the aircraft would roll powerfully to the left, stick-free. After levelling at 1,500 ft this was further investigated and it was seen that over the range 60-95 kt the slip ball required a light right–pedal force to centre, but that use of up to full right rudder did not provide sufficient rolling moment to reduce the left wing heaviness by more than about 25 per cent.

With the need to fly left-handed (with right throttle) this asymmetry restricted the flight to engine checks and brief flap assessments prior to circuit work.

Loud side tone on 130.8 and reported distorted aircraft transmission by ATC.

Tail trim operations excessively coarse resulting in jerky overcorrections for smallest movement.

0 + 26 Max level (2 minutes)
(with 3/4 right stick aileron to trim)
2,800 r.p.m./95 kt/1,200 ft 47 70 210

Immediate drop in CHT on reducing to 2,300 r.p.m..

Slow for flaps; necessitating slackening off top harness to operate flap selector lever (seat too far back) 65–70 kt.

Flap 10°: lever force acceptable. Slight nose-down trim change. Handling good to
          60 kt.
Flat 30°: heavy nose-down trim change, just trimmed out with full nose-up
          elevator trim at 2,100 r.p.m./65 kt. Handling good.

0 + 30 Vision forward and all round very good with high quality transparencies.

No noticeable windscreen or canopy draughts or wind noise. Engine noise and vibration levels low.

0 + 31 Fuel 85 per cent/Full. Starboard tank selected to check transfer, and selected back to port after 2 min because of the lateral asymmetry.
While holding wings level with approx 8–10 lb right stick at 90 kt it was noted that pedal-free the starboard rudder pedal led the port by about 1 in (slip ball slightly left of central).

0 + 37 Approach
2,300 r.p.m./65 kt/700 ft OP 48 OT 70 CHT 170
Flap 10°; R/W 26; W/V 290/6 kt; Fuel 80 per cent/Full.

The left wing asymmetry tended to mask the control qualities in the approach, but pitch and yaw response were excellent and resulted in smooth flare and touchdown at 55-45 kt with about ½ right stick to maintain wings level.
Undercarriage was soft and dead-beat, and steering of the landing roll adequate but again with excessively heavy nosewheel steering pedal forces. Wheel braking was adequate but not powerful.

Summary
The flight duration was limited by the pilot's ability to continue to hold out-of-trim lateral forces. This severe asymmetry tended to mask what are probably satisfactory basic characteristics of stability and control, and limited the scope of the test programme.

Engine installation suitability was excellent in the conditions tested and noise and vibration levels were low. No fumes of any description were noted in the cockpit throughout.

All flight instruments and controls functioned satisfactorily except the radio which produced unacceptable side tone in reception and heavy distortion in transmission (to Warton ATC).

The aircraft gave an immediate impression of sound quality and good workmanship and should be straightforward and pleasant to fly when modified in the lateral case.

Better cockpit finishing would improve its appearance.

Defects
Defects requiring correction before next flight:

1. Heavy left-wing-low trim asymmetry.
2. Heavy nosewheel steering forces possibly exaggerated by the now too far aft seat-back (following the recent adjustment). Investigate implications of gearing change.
3. Radio defective.

Additionally attention should be given to investigating a gearing change in elevator trimmer operation.

R. P. BEAMONT
25 May 1979

This was not a very satisfactory first flight! But after further rectification work a further five test flights showed that it had at least reached a safe standard.

The author flying the Procter Petrel over Warton. (British Aerospace)

PETREL G-BACA — FLIGHT 6 — 19 SEPTEMBER 1979
Summary at the completion of the first phase of flight testing

In its first six flights the aircraft has been shown to have generally pleasant flying characteristics, and the engine and fuel system have not been faulted.

The engine installation is smooth and quiet, and the canopy/windscreen configuration does not produce significant airflow noise or draughts.

The nosewheel steering is undergeared and rather coarse in use but this can be accepted with practice. A strong kick-back occurs through the rudder pedals from the nosewheel caster-action in crosswind conditions, and this will probably define the max usable crosswind as 15 kt component.

Directional and lateral retrimming has not yet achieved stick-free trim in cruising flight which must remain the desired target, but the out-of-trim lateral forces are now small.

Although negative longitudinal static stability was found unacceptable initially, this has been adequately restored (one crew) by fitting forward ballast. Further flying is required to assess the aft CG case with two crew (plus the forward ballast).

In all flights to date the aileron control has proved only marginally acceptable for continued test flying due to excessive forces and low response rates. While safe to fly under supervised conditions, this roll control is in fact inadequate for recovery in rolling pull-outs and pilots should be reminded of this prior to each flight. Remedial action is needed in order to obtain a normal 'touring category' clearance for this aircraft.

Performance is modest reflecting the weight/power relationship, but is quite adequate for the 'air experience' role envisaged for this aircraft.

Stalling, slow speed handling and particularly the approach and landing are straightforward and pleasant with the exception of poor lateral control in turbulence.

Cockpit instrumentation has been satisfactory so far, but extensive IF assessment has not yet been undertaken.

Recommendations
1. Improve lateral and directional trimming to achieve in-trim conditions with stick and rudder free at 80 kt IAS.
2. Improve aileron power/reduce aileron force gradient.
3. Assess aft CG case with two crew.
4. Improve operation of elevator trimmer, if practical, by introduction of a trim wheel.
5. Pending investigation of increase in rudder area no spinning is to be undertaken; and in the event of this clearance being a future requirement an anti-spin 'chute to be fitted.

R. P. BEAMONT
21 September 1979

Testing a Minicab
The first light aeroplane tested by the author for the PFA was Gardan Minicab G-AWEP, built by enthusiast Stan Jackson, superintendent of the plating and processing department of the great English Electric (later British Aerospace) factory at Preston. This aeroplane was a remarkable example of the quality which can be achieved by a combination of skills, knowledge, enthusiasm and dedication, and yet in its test programme and a decade of subsequent pleasure flying 'Echo Papa' gave no serious problems at all and a remarkable level of reliability.

Basically of wood and fabric construction and with a Rolls-Royce Continental C90 engine of 90 b.h.p., the Minicab weighed under 1,100 lb with fuel and one crew and

Stan Jackson starting his Minicab for its first flight. Author in cockpit. (British Aerospace)

'Echo Papa' airborne at Samlesbury. (British Aerospace)

it was a delightful if rather delicate aeroplane both to fly and maintain. In the air it was much affected by gusting winds and general turbulence and in the hangar it was prone to all-too-easy damage from spanners dropped through its fabric or unauthorised boots climbing over it!

Nevertheless, with sparkling performance, light control harmony, well-damped and stable flight characteristics and the ability to land with full flap into a 10 kt wind in under 50 yd (and sometimes across the main runway at Warton in crosswinds which would otherwise have been too strong for it), it was one of the most pleasurable aeroplanes in 40 years.

Used frequently for home-to-work commuting between Samlesbury aerodrome and Warton, it began and ended the day on a high note and sometimes gave moments of unusual fascination, such as when meeting and joining formation with a skein of pinkfoot geese heading into a stormy sky over the Ribble estuary at 45 kt one winter's morning on the way to work over the rush-hour traffic jams.

Its first flight was an interesting and pleasurable experience.

MINICAB G-AWEP — FLIGHT REPORT NO. 1 — SAMLESBURY
21 JUNE 1969

Fuel:	11 gal
crew:	1
Weight:	1,026 lb
CG:	15.03 in
Weather:	Wind 90° 15–18 kt gusting ⅞ths/2,500 ft
Visibility:	10 miles
Take-off:	Runway 18
Engine:	start satisfactory on first swing after two primes. 1,200 r.p.m., oil pressure 32 p.s.i., oil temperature 30°F, cylinder head temperature 90°C.
Altimeter set:	996 millibars.

On the ground, stationary and while taxying, the fresh air provided by the new air vent on the port rear cabin window was satisfactory.

Run-up checks
Idling: 600 r.p.m., 95°F, 30 p.s.i., Cylinder 150°C
Full power 2,250, 110°F, 35 p.s.i., Cylinder 200°C
No 1 Mag switch off, 2,200 r.p.m.
No 2 Mag switch off, 2,250 r.p.m.

At the end of these engine checks the cylinder head temperature was 230°C, and a fairly strong hot engine smell was present.

While taxying at approximately 1,000 r.p.m. the cylinder head temperature dropped quite rapidly and had levelled at 155°C on reaching the runway.

Prior to take-off checks
Idle 600 r.p.m., 150°F, 18 p.s.i., Cylinder 155°C Max power 2,250 r.p.m., Suction 4.25 in

With max throttle set and trimmer neutral, flaps up, the tail was lifted smoothly with gentle forward stick movement and lift-off occurred after less than 200 yd at approximately 45 kt.

500 ft   70 kt, 2,250 r.p.m., 170°F, 32 p.s.i.
                Cylinder 210°C

Longitudinal control light, responsive with good damping. Lateral control light, responsive with good damping. Directional damping less good with tendency for the slip ball to wander.

Engine noise and vibration levels in max power climb moderate and satisfactory. Cruise at 1,000 ft/2,000 r.p.m.

After two minutes, ASI 81 kts. Trim (elevator) at the zero notch as for take-off. Noise level low and pleasant. Cabin air fresh with port vent open.

After three minutes cruise in these conditions, ASI 86 kt, 2,000 r.p.m., 180°F, 30 p.s.i., Cylinder 170°C, Suction 8.5 in. Power reduced to 1,850 r.p.m. and speed stabilised at 70 kt in slight turbulence.

Control checks
The pitch control was satisfactorily responsive and well damped, and lateral displacements resulted in good response coupled with a slight recovery tendency i.e. positive rather than the more normal neutral stability. This was not an adverse feature as it contributed to maintaining wings level, hands off.

Response to rudder input resulted in adequate control in yaw but in less satisfactory damping, and in the prevailing turbulence as well as following deliberate rudder inputs, rather low weathercock stability was noticeable. The slip ball was active throughout the flight and fairly continuous small amplitude rudder co-ordination was necessary to maintain slip ball zero, especially in turbulence. It was also noted that full power acceleration in take-off, climb or level flight required left rudder to counteract propeller torque. In smooth air control harmony was excellent, but in turbulence and in manoeuvre the need to co-ordinate with rudder was noticeable.

In deliberate Dutch roll oscillation the lack of weathercock stability was noticeable, damping being 'soggy' with failure of the down-going wing to recover, and side-slip remaining on initially pedal-free.

In the initial climb and subsequently whenever maximum power was used a heat source was noticed under the legs and this became quite uncomfortable when combined with solar radiation.

The fresh air vent provided adequate cooling air and was clearly very essential under these circumstances. No oil or petrol fumes were present and the hot engine smell became less apparent as the flight progressed and was no problem.

Slow down 1,000 ft clean configuration.

IAS was reduced to 55 kt where slight wing rocking occurred accompanied by reduced control responsiveness.

Slow down 2,100 ft, 15° flap. Very slight nose down trim change.

42 kt slight buffet and slight nose drop.

Slow down 3,100 ft, full flap at 50 kt. Slight nose down trim change.

At 40 kt slight wing drop and further nose down trim with tendency to yaw to starboard.

Recovery commenced from 39 kt.

In these tests the variation of trim with flap was no more than 1–2 lb on the stick and scarcely required trimmer adjustment. Engine control at low speeds remained smooth and excellent, and there was no sign of plug roughness on opening up after 1–2 minutes at tick-over.

Max level 1,000 ft:

After one minute at 2,250 r.p.m., ASI 105 kt increasing, 180°F, 32 p.s.i., Cylinder 195°C.

A very slight nose-down trim adjustment was necessary between 80 and 100 kt.

Throughout these checks the elevator trim tab control range was adequate for the very small adjustments necessary, but the slack and stretch in the cable made trim adjustments rather imprecise.

A normal approach was made for landing 1 with power set to control the descent at 60 kt initially, reducing to 55 kt to set take-off (15°) flap.

The slight nose-down trim change resulting required a small nose-up trimmer adjustment, and the final approach was flown at 55 kt to threshold for a touchdown at approximately 42 kt on the main wheels before closing power. This landing was relatively smooth and the subsequent roll-out was controlled reasonably easily, though the relationship between the foot position on the rudder pedals and the heel position on the brakes was not easy to achieve smoothly, largely due to the incorrect position of the starboard brake pedal relative to the starboard rudder pedal.

In take-off 2 the lift-off was achieved in approximately 150 yd against a 15 kt wind and an approach set up with 2 notches flap (30°). This required the elevator trim tab setting back 1 in from neutral on the wheel.

The approach was pleasant and satisfactory at 50 kt and power was cut during flare for a three point touchdown at approximately 40 kt.

After taxying, engine checks before shut down:

2,250 r.p.m., 190°F, 32 p.s.i., Cylinder 185°C.

Summary

The engine, fuel and electrical systems functioned completely satisfactorily, and the engine was smooth, responsive, remarkably quiet in the cruising range and generally conducive to confidence.

The flying controls with their previously noted low static friction were pleasant and responsive in flight; and positive longitudinal stability, slightly positive lateral stability, and positive but low weathercock stability added up to pleasant control harmony and an easily flown aeroplane.

Minicab 'Echo Papa' over its Samlesbury base. (British Aerospace)

The latter characteristics of low weathercock stability necessitate rudder co-ordination for accurate flying and result in a less than crisp aeroplane directionally. This is an area which could be improved with advantage. Take-off presents no problems but the landing with sensitive longitudinal control and relatively nose-high attitude coupled with vision distortion through the windscreen transparencies, is not easy to get right first time and is likely to require practice.

With the elevator tab trim wheel set at the neutral notch very little retrimming is required in flight, but the trimmer range at 'Full Nose-up' is not quite sufficient to trim out full flap in the forward CG case with one crew.

Flight time 25 minutes.

R. P. Beamont

Testing a Fw 190 Scale Replica

Two dates — 13 September 1943 and 30 March 1980 — had a certain similarity for the author as both involved flights in 'Focke-Wulf Fw 190s'. The early date concerned the first Focke-Wulf to be captured intact when it landed in 1943 at Fairwood Common in South Wales, and the second was a surprisingly close half-scale replica built in 1979 by Mike Searle of Aero Services Ltd at Elstree and registered G-WULF. There the similarity might have ended for the wood and glassfibre construction replica weighed only 1,010 lb with its 100 h.p. Continental O-200-SA engine, while the original weighed 8,600 lb and had around 1,700 h.p. from its fan-cooled BMW 801-D 14-cylinder, twin-row radial engine; but there turned out to be other interesting similarities.

The author about to fly the replica Fw 190, Leicester.

The replica, G-WULF, designed by War Aircraft Replicas of the USA, had a span of 26 ft and a length of 16 ft, so it was a very small aeroplane indeed and gave a first impression on close acquaintance that it had escaped from a model aircraft rally. In general appearance it was an almost true replica of the real thing with wing, rear fuselage and tail, undercarriage and under-fuselage bomb/long-range tank rail all looking accurate. The cockpit area was realistic also with a true-looking windscreen and canopy profile, but the rear half of the canopy let the accuracy down as the transparency was cut off just behind the dummy armour plate where, on the original, an outstanding feature was the long clear-view rear canopy extending halfway to the tail.

Forward of the windscreen the engine cowling was a clever simulation of the original with the exhaust system terminating realistically in four ejector stubs a side, three of which were dummies. Only a look through the nose intake revealed not a lusty twin-row radial engine but the O-200-SA 'flat-four' which was well cooled without benefit of the original's fan cooling.

The propeller was of wood, three-bladed, and skinned in GRP (glassfibre-reinforced plastic). Finished in black, with a well-proportioned black spinner painted with the white spiral of the period, it all looked very realistic. Only a long critical look revealed two basic dissimilarities; the wing had noticeably less dihedral and the cockpit/windscreen was slightly further aft than that on the original. Nevertheless without another aircraft to give it scale the replica did look very like its exciting original and in flight the sight of it seemed likely to give cold shivers to Second World War veterans!

Walk-round checks showed a high standard of skinning and detail finish and commendably low static friction on all controls and absence of noticeable backlash. The tailwheel was steered through conventional springs and the retracting undercarriage was noted to have a comfortably simple linkage and geometry. It was thought likely to be prone to the accumulation of mud/grit from the wheels (shod with go-cart tyres) and that this would need to be the subject of regular maintenance checks.

The replica Fw 190. (Philip Jarrett)

Climbing into the cockpit of this aircraft was for this low-aspect-ratio pilot akin to pulling on rather tight trousers, and in fact getting out of it subsequently was the only difficult part of the whole operation! However once I was seated in the comfortable semi-reclining seat with the feet resting on the rudder pedals virtually under the rear of the engine, it proved to be a comfortable cockpit with all controls and switches within easy reach. Of particular interest was the stick grip which, while providing a reasonable representation of the shaped grip of the original Fw 190, was in practice an American P-86 style stick and very comfortable in use.

My report to the PFA recorded the following:
'The flying controls were free of noticeable static friction and backlash, and the throttle and fuel cock were well positioned and easy to operate.

The rudder pedals were found to have a noticeable amount of fore/aft spring-loaded free play when both pedals were equally depressed (not brake pedal rotation). This proved to be undesirable in taxying and take-off/landing run control, as it reduced direct feel of tailwheel steering. With no parking brake, starting and ground-running required restraint by brake pedal operation which proved adequate.

View ahead was largely obscured by the high nose and safe taxying required swinging the nose (as did the original FW 190). Tailwheel steering was adequate once the fore/aft rudder pedal movement had been allowed for.

With cold outside air temperature (OAT +6°C) the small windscreen and canopy misted quickly with canopy shut, and the absence of a fresh air vent was noted.

When checking the movements needed for activation of the manual undercarriage emergency DOWN selection it was felt that this was likely to be a difficult operation.

At full power acceleration was brisk but there was no tendency for self-lift of the tail which needed light but positive forward stick to achieve take-off attitude. Prior to this [the] total lack of forward vision resulted in some slight veering about the runway centre-line.

Unstick at approx 55 kt and initial climb held at a comfortably steep angle at 70 kt. Undercarriage retraction complete in 9.5 sec. Red and green indicator lights satisfactory. No noticeable trim change, noise or buffet associated with undercarriage down, or when retracting.

Three-axis control responses, 1,000 ft/100 kt: Pitch — light, positive and dead-beat. Aileron — light, crisp and dead-beat. Rudder — very light and powerful, but well damped.

Aileron/elevator harmony excellent, but rudder lighter and out of harmony. However it was very soon apparent that with excellent weathercock stability and crisp response and damping in all axes, rudder co-ordination was seldom necessary and its lightness was not noticeable except when deliberately assessing sideslips, etc.

Rolling power was high with 360° barrel rolls executed smoothly at 100°/sec+, and about 2.5 lb to full stick deflection.

Stick force per G was light at 1.5 lb/g estimated but with no noticeable static friction or backlash and with dead-beat damping these low values were very satisfactory for fighter-type manoeuvrability. Crisp 'hesitation' rolls were practicable.

At all speeds above 100 kt, r.p.m. needed controlling against overspeeding and this was easy to manage with smooth, responsive throttle but had to be remembered.

IAS increased to 165 kt (never-exceed speed 175) in shallow dive with only moderate increase in noise level, and all control responses as before though heavying slightly. Noticeable in mild turbulence that tracking accuracy remained dead-beat and excellent.

2,000 ft: 9.5 gal, slowdown to 'clean' stall.

As IAS reduced below 60 kt for the first time in the flight a nose-up trim adjustment would have been needed for stick-free trim, but was not made. Stall 42 kt. Slight buffet from 43 kt. Left wing smooth roll away, checked instantly by small forward stick.

Repeat gear down. Effects of gear lowering at 70 kt hardly noticeable. Stall buffet as before 43 kt; left wing drop at 42 kt.

Throttle response at stall good.

From 70–160 kt the aircraft remained in lateral and directional trim controls-free and needed hardly any pitch adjustment.

Longitudinal static stability was positive and well damped throughout the speed range 42–160 kt.

Sideslips — 1,500 ft. 1.3 Vs (stalling speed) power on. 9 gal.

Left and right rudder. Strong weathercock stability and light aileron force to hold (positive lateral stability, sideslipped wing rises).

During all low engine-power points the undercarriage warning horn operated correctly with acceptable noise level in the headset.

Right-hand circuit and approach to runway 28.

At 70 kt and below the very nose-high attitude was restrictive and confirmed that straight-in approaches would be unsuitable for this aircraft below about 80 kt (which would result in the complication of losing excess speed on the flapless aircraft during final approach).

On overshoot from 100 ft/70 kt about ⅔ throttle gave good response and a steep climb while retracting undercarriage from 80 kt — time 12 sec.

Left-hand circuit and continuous curve approach at 70 kt maintained vision of the threshold until rolling out and flaring at about 10 ft when all forward vision was lost, direction having to be maintained by alternate side viewing of the runway edges.

Control in the flare was precise on all axes and it was easy to hold level as speed bled off slowly in a long float until gentle touchdown, but in the initial roll-out some veering occurred due to the restricted vision references coupled with rudder pedal 'sponginess'.

Mike Searle flying his Fw 190 replica. (Philip Jarrett)

After a second take-off:
From 2,000 ft/90 kt.   Left turn dynamic stall. 7 gal.
Power increased to achieve 3G/70 kt in level turn. Left wing drop with short buffet. Stopped immediately with slight forward stick.
Repeat in right turn with same result. If stick held at wing-drop the incipient spin would develop but was controllable with forward stick. This was not investigated beyond ½ turn.
Wing-overs from 120–60 kt and loops from 160 kt were smooth and elegant, but if pulled too tight below 75 kt would depart left-wing with recovery as above.
Engine smooth and responsive with stable indications and good cooling throughout.
No fuel or other fumes were noted throughout this 1.10 hr flight, and radio performance on 122.25 with RAF inner helmet and 1945-standard mask/headset, clear and satisfactory.
Final left-hand continuous curve approach at 70 kt satisfactory.
Roll-out and flare over threshold at 67 kt and long 'blind' float before gentle touchdown on final landing. Braking action smooth, but difficult to prevent veering until slow speed for the reasons above.

Conclusions
G-WULF has been described by Mr R. I. V. Walker (the PFA's chief engineer) as well-built to professional standards. Flight experience supports this and the aircraft has exceptional control qualities for any aircraft in this category. It is a pleasure to fly and

well within the capabilities of suitably experienced 'tailwheel' pilots, with the one exception that forward view is not merely restricted but is non-existent for straight taxying and in straight-in approaches. This aspect will need to be covered in Pilots' Notes and by strict supervision of conversion training. It could use a wing-flap system.

The aircraft was not found to have any other vices although its tendency to roll out of looping plane manoeuvres into incipient spin if uncorrected needs taking account of in planning flight demonstrations.

Full performance measurements were not made on this flight but there is a comfortable excess of power for missed approaches without swing or trim changes. One-minute stabilizations at 1,000 ft showed 135 kt at 2,500 r.p.m. and 150 kt at 2,750.

Its mini-fighter style qualities are enjoyable and confidence-making to a point which might cause inexperienced pilots to exceed their own capabilities and this must be guarded against.

In all a very attractive high-performance single-seat aeroplane with high quality and predictable control characteristics, generally symmetrical trimming and a smooth engine installation helped undoubtedly by the three-blade propeller; but an aircraft which needed supervision in conversion training due to severely limited forward vision in its necessarily flapless approaches which tended to result in excessive threshold speeds, long floats and hold-offs and therefore relatively lengthy landing runs particularly if associated with wet grass. This was a fun aeroplane of high quality and a credit both to its designer and to owner and builder Mlke Searle.'

Flying First World War fighter 'Scouts'

For ten happy years I was a member of Alan Wheeler's team of 'ancient pilots for ancient aeroplanes' at Old Warden, and flew the Shuttleworth Collection's Bristol Fighter, Sopwith Pup, Royal Aircraft Factory S.E.5a, Avro Tutor and Hawker Tomtit on display days. These historic biplanes are maintained meticulously in splendid

The author prepares to display the Shuttleworth Bristol Fighter at Old Warden.   (Shuttleworth Collection)

The author displaying the Bristol Fighter at Old Warden. (Shuttleworth Collection)

condition by the dedicated work of mostly retired engineering enthusiasts, and flying them is a rare privilege and sometimes rather a mixed blessing!

Although the safety record at Old Warden is remarkably good, there is always the possibility of engine failure on a 70-year-old aeroplane, so every minute of every flight has to be conducted with the possible need for a forced landing very much in mind. This means all the time keeping within gliding distance of fields or open spaces identified as large enough and smooth enough to land on without breaking or seriously damaging anything.

Another study of the Bristol Fighter.
(Shuttleworth Collection)

The author taxying the Shuttleworth Collection S.E.5a. (Shuttleworth Collection)

Then the weather. All tailskid or tailwheel aircraft must essentially avoid crosswind take-offs or landings, especially the latter, and this can prevent a display if the wind is too strong or gusting or not in the right direction. A further and major consideration can be a critical change in wind conditions after take-off and if the aeroplane can no longer land back because of adverse winds then a diversion to another airfield may be necessary, although this judgement can only be made by the pilot in the light of prior briefing information as he has no radio and cannot check that his diversion airfield still has suitable weather!

Fuel state of course comes into this and he will have made sure before take-off that there will be enough if he has to divert.

Then the characteristics of the aeroplanes have to be considered. Few realise that the simple, basic aeroplanes of the past were considerably more difficult to fly accurately than their modern counterparts, and in fact the safe landing of a Sopwith Pup or an S.E.5a even in good conditions was quite problematical in the First World War and still is today!

The author low-flying the Shuttleworth S.E.5a.

The lovely vintage 1916 Sopwith Pup. (Steven Jefferson)

Not all of the vintage biplanes were difficult in this sense though, and the Avro 504 and Bristol Fighter were exceptional in their inherent stability and responsive controls which made their landings straightforward, safe and delightful as long as they too were made strictly into wind.

The Bristol Fighter is perhaps the most popular to fly of the First World War aeroplanes with the Shuttleworth pilots. Its great Rolls-Royce Falcon engine chuffs away like a vintage Bentley and is precisely responsive to throttle without ever missing a beat. Once the pilot becomes used to leaning out to look at the grass ahead between the port undercarriage wheel and the port engine cowling in the total absence of direct forward vision until the tail is raised, the take-off run is held straight with light and responsive rudder until the wheels stop rumbling with hardly a touch of the firm, responsive elevator

A unique formation of two Sopwith Pups led by the author in the Bristol Fighter. The Pup pilots were Neil Williams and Desmond Penrose. (Shuttleworth Collection)

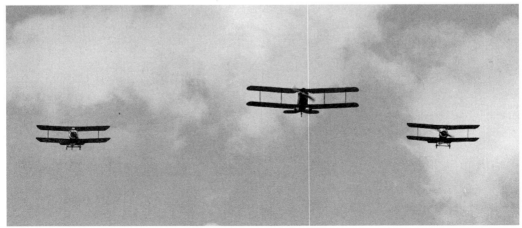

Forty years after the author's first Avro Tutor flight; the Shuttleworth Collection Avro Tutor at Old Warden in 1976. (Steve Jefferson)

and the Bristol sails into the climb at 65 m.p.h. rather like a two-winged lift!

At cruising revolutions there is less noise from the engine than from the buffeting wind round the minuscule windscreen, and when the throttle is closed for the glide approach the evocative 'wind in the wires' sound predominates.

The flying controls are not in conventional harmonization, but the light and responsive rudder and firmer but precise elevator give very satisfactory controllability to this quite heavy and inherently stable aeroplane. However, the ailerons let it down as with most aircraft of the period, being increasingly heavy with speed and virtually solid when diving above 130 m.p.h.

Although the Bristol had a fine operational record it must have been heavy work in air-to-air combat as the author found one day when 'dogfighting' the German LVG C.VI flown by Desmond Penrose. In a diving and turning 'combat' the two were evenly matched, but with aching arms and shoulders I found the very slow response in roll, even with bootfuls of rudder to help it with rolling moment-due-to-yaw, distinctly inhibiting when trying to get on the LVG's tail. After about 5 min of that all over Old Warden we gave it best, and I cooled off in the refreshing side-slipped breeze as I approached and landed the Bristol over the hangars and down the hill into a southerly wind.

Despite its age the Bristol always felt 'solid' and a real aeroplane, and when I switched off and climbed down it was with a sense of not only enjoyment but achievement for once again I had not 'bent' this historic aeroplane — then a voice from the crowd said: 'That was a very gentle dogfight. Was there something wrong?'

In contrast to the Bristol Fighter the S.E.5a was perhaps the best-handling fighter on either side in the First World War for it not only had excellent pitch and yaw control and inherent stability on both axes, but it also had light and responsive ailerons up to the quite high speed for its period of 130 m.p.h. Above that the ailerons heavied considerably, but with its maximum speed of 132 m.p.h. and a dive capability above 200 m.p.h. its general performance was probably superior to that of any other fighter in 1917/18.

Its 200 h.p. Wolsley Viper engine gives it a throaty roar and take-off in 40–50 yds, a high rate of climb and a ceiling above 20,000 ft, and every flight in the S.E. was immensely enjoyable except for one aspect. It was totally unforgiving in the landing!

With its high undercarriage, short-coupled fuselage and landing wheel axles tethered to the undercarriage 'vee' struts only by 'Bunjee' rubber cords without benefit of any shock absorbers, every landing had to be a perfect three-pointer with the throttled engine at tick-over, or else any deviation such as tail too high, too much throttle, rough uneven grass, gusting wind, etc, would send the S.E. off into its first bounce — which would not be the last! The determined pilot would then grit his teeth, pull throttle and stick hard back and then wait for the second, higher bounce, and the third and then hopefully the last as the S.E. subsided finally on to the grass.

Occasionally it would not do this and would drop a wingtip into the turf with damaging results, so all pilots became very wary of this unforgiving characteristic. The other option open to the pilot was to ram open the throttle during the first bounce and go round to try it again, but most probably with similar results! After many safe landings in the S.E. this happened to the author once just after what had seemed to be a perfect three-pointer and then, while concentrating on holding straight on the ground the main wheels were felt to encounter a slight bump or ridge, and off we went. Three 'kangaroos' later and now fully stalled we did not drop a wing but settled with relief back on to wheels and tailskid with wings level. As the 'Ace from the Base' climbed down from the cockpit the inevitable voice from the crowd said 'Do S.E.s always land that way?' I said 'Nearly always,' but I don't suppose he believed me.

The third historic biplane was in my experience something of an enigma.

The pretty little Sopwith Pup has often been recorded through 70 years as being the best-handling First World War One (fighter), and yet in my book it was in some ways the worst! But the reasons behind this anomaly are I believe to be found in timescale rather than quality.

In 1916 when the Pup first entered service with the Royal Flying Corps it did indeed set new standards of agility and performance as compared with the ponderous Vickers Gunbus, de Havilland D.H.2s and R.E.8s of the early war years, and its pleasantly responsive elevator which allowed accurate control in pitch and especially in precise landings, made it relatively safe to operate and quick to gain the confidence of the pilots.

It did, however, have one major disadvantage. The Pup is inherently unstable directionally, requiring continuous co-ordination with rudder by the pilot to keep it straight. This, while continuously feeling with the left hand for the correct balance between the fuel and air levers in order to keep the 80 h.p. Le Rhone rotary engine from a 'lean mixture' engine cut which can be reset in flight, or a 'rich mixture' cut which cannot, all adds up to a quite intense workload!

However the Pup's directional sensitivity goes some way to easing this problem, and as it continuously develops sideslip one way or the other the pilot is subjected to icy cold blasts asymmetrically round the minuscule windscreen, i.e. left cheek = left yaw and vice versa. Therefore in the interests of mitigating supreme discomfort he soon learns to use these blasts of cold air on one side or the other as a sideslip indicator, and co-ordinates with rudder to keep the air pressure equal on either cheek and to keep the Pup flying straight as a bonus!

In no way can the Pup be said to be as nice to fly as the S.E. and the Bristol, but it has a determined personality and can certainly be described as a challenge!

Chapter Thirteen

The decline of an industry

No-one at management and board level in the aircraft industry in the three decades from the end of the Second World War in 1945 could fail to notice a pattern emerging in the 1950s and 1960s of ill-judgement and faulty decision-making at the highest levels which, if not reversed in time, seemed bound to result in the gradual run-down and decline of this once vital and powerful element in British industry. By the 1990s this decline had indeed happened with the constriction of the once multi-company industry to only one Corporation, and with the by then essential selling off (to foreign buyers where they could) of most of the remaining elements of British Aerospace's loss-making civil airliner business except for the successful activity of the design and production of wings for the European Airbus series.

At this stage Britain's sole remaining stake in the development of major aircraft for its own requirements lay in the European collaborative programme Eurofighter 2000; a programme dogged with political, administrative and serious technical difficulties which had, by the spring of 1995, already been faltering in the pipeline for over 15 years without even beginning the vitally important stage of its long and intensive main flight test and development programme. At the time of writing in March 1995 the ever-increasing delays to and costs of this programme were said by government sources to be 'the cause of concern and continual review'.

Without Eurofighter the British industry has no other high-performance military aircraft programme in sight, and of course our capacity to 'go it alone' in the design, construction and development of high-performance aircraft in this country has long since been lost. It is said that international collaboration is essential 'to maintain stability' in the costly major aircraft programmes of today, and certainly Labour Prime Minister Harold Wilson found this to be true when in 1964 he tried unsuccessfully to cancel Concorde, having forgotten that the French were equal partners. So he cancelled TSR.2 instead, which proves the point.

In a 40-year association with the aircraft industry, mostly at management and later board level, I witnessed many examples of strange, inexplicable and often downright incompetent decision-making at procurement level, and of course some also by the contractors. Often no single centre of influence seemed to be to blame, but in the 1960s we all shot ourselves in the foot!

As a specialist there were many 'behind-closed-doors' policy meetings that I did not attend, although I saw the working papers. But also as a specialist there were many decision-making meetings which I did attend and sometimes the conclusions reached and decisions taken were frightening in their lack of understanding and incompetence.

For example, based on a courageous decision by Teddy Petter, chief designer of English Electric at Preston, and backed by the main board, not to be deterred by the government opt-out of research into supersonic flight in 1947, English Electric had put forward a proposal for a supersonic research fighter on which the Air Ministry finally based a requirement, F.23/49, and contracted with Warton for two experimental prototypes and a structural-test airframe. This, the P.1, began the first British fully supersonic flight research programme in 1954 which, by 1958, had reached twice the speed of sound with the P.1B/Lightning development.

The handling and performance of this series of swept-wing fighters proved to be superior to those of any other fighters in their class in the world. The RAF squadrons converted with ease to the Lightning from 1961 onwards in place of their still excellent but subsonic Hunters, and they soon began to establish a great reputation for this fighter which remained in service for 27 years until 1988, despite having been declared about to be made redundant and replaced by Phantoms by the end of the 1960s!

The American Phantom had a more up-to-date and advanced technology radar weapons system compared with the Lightning though in other respects its performance was inferior, but it was purchased because 'the RAF has no requirement to develop the Lightning', according to the message spread from the MoD at the time. English Electric could never understand this ruling although it was aware that the Lightning was not proving popular with RAF engineers due to maintainability problems. These were resolvable and did not affect the advanced performance capability of the aircraft in any way however, and it seemed inconceivable that such a world-class and superior fighter should not be developed to its maximum potential just at the point when the taxpayers' money had been shown to have produced world-acclaimed results!

With the confidence of 15 years of Canberra success and in parallel ten years of successful P.1 and Lightning supersonics behind them, Warton were not prepared to accept what appeared to be a crastly inept Ministry policy, and the Project Office continued to work on developing the potential of this fine aeroplane to improve its capabilities for the RAF and to give it a positive ability to break into export markets, especially the Gulf States.

As long ago as 1957, soon after the first flight of XA847, the first true Lightning, I had recommended in strong terms to the Warton Board 'that we won't stand a cat in hell's chance of exporting the Lightning unless we double the fuel capacity'. This did not receive a rapturous reception in some quarters but it was well taken by the more intelligent, and by 1962 Warton was proposing a major modification to the fuel system for the final (Mk 3) production series which would more than double the internal fuel capacity with scarcely any loss of performance.

The Ministry did not want to know and rejected the proposal, but then towards the end of the Mk 3 production run they suddenly required all the Mk 3s to be retrofitted with the increased fuel tankage! This of course at heavily increased cost to the taxpayer.

But this was the key to exports and English Electric quickly put in hand major additional developments for ground-attack weapons and reconnaissance cameras, all company-funded with no support from the government.

While these were being test-flown successfully major interest was established in Saudi Arabia, and with remarkable speed and against maximum in-country American competition a contract was signed between the Government, English Electric and Saudi Arabia for the provision of a new 'supersonic' defence system with all-through training and the supply of Strikemaster jet trainers and English Electric Lightnings, the fully developed 'export' Mk 53s and 55s. The numbers were substantial and the task formidable and politically loaded. This contract, 'Magic Carpet', began in 1965 the truly massive programme for the support of the Royal Saudi Arabian Air Force which continues in 1995 as 'Al Yamamah', now with Tornado fighters and fighter bombers, and has over three consecutive decades been recorded as Britain's largest-ever export contract, worth many billions of pounds to this country and providing secure employment for many thousands of people at home and abroad.

This could never have happened without the English Electric-inspired modifications to increase the Lightning's fuel and military capability, yet at one stage in the early 1960s the MoD was actively opposing any such action or support for it.

Quite coincidentally our friends and neighbours at that time were Harold Watkinson (Viscount Watkinson of Woking) and his family. We saw each other often and one day Harold asked me to talk to him privately. He was Minister of Defence at that time and knew that I was involved with Lightnings though we had not talked about it. On this occasion he said that he was getting briefs from his 'advisers' (Air Ministry Operational Requirements (OR) Branch) which seemed to be diametrically opposed to 'his information from Warton' about the future potential of the Lightning in the RAF, and asked what I thought.

I gathered that the OR were telling him that the Lightning had no potential for ground-attack or reconnaissance, or for any future development at all. I gave the view, which I had expressed earlier in the week to the chairman of English Electric, Sir George Nelson in the presence of my chief, Freddy Page, that, with the modifications to increase fuel and the successful development testing of rocket launchers and bomb pylons (which I was doing myself) together with an advanced Vinten camera reconnaissance pack, and the optional alternative reinstallation of the 30 mm cannon (which had been deleted by Air Ministry two years earlier and then suddenly reintroduced by them!), the Lightning would prove to be an excellent low-level, fast reconnaissance aircraft and a practical ground-attack fighter within the limitations of its armament in addition to its primary role of high-performance interception which would not be downgraded in any way.

Harold Watkinson was puzzled about this apparent contradiction. Who was he to believe if not the Air Ministry's own specialists? Not for the first (or last) time OR had got it wrong, but English Electric's unsupported initiative paved the way for and secured the great Saudi contract.

But the harm had already been done to the future of the RAF Lightnings, and no further government funds were provided for improving that fine aircraft or extending its weapons capabilities. Though 'programmed to phase out in 1969', after only eight years of service, the Lightnings were actually retained in RAF front-line service until 1988 when they were still, after 27 years in squadrons being acclaimed by their pilots (many of them second-generation) as being 'able to see off anything we meet in the skies of Europe'.

Over many years it was apparent that there was often fault on both sides, the contractors or the government customer; and in some cases when the faults were in both organisations momentum ground to a halt and programmes failed. The BAC TSR.2 strike/reconnaissance bomber for the 1970s and far beyond was a case in point.

In 1959 the government reversed their own defence policy decision of 1957 that there would be no future requirement for supersonic aircraft for the RAF after the Lightning, by introducing operational requirement OR339 (later updated to OR343) for a low-level, deep-penetration, supersonic strike and reconnaissance aircraft required for service by 1970. It was to be a dense, highly sophisticated aircraft with the most advanced state-of-the-art navigation and weapons systems, and it had to be capable of operation off restricted runways and by 'normally trained' crews. In other words although it would have exceptional performance the pilots would not have to undergo a special, higher level of training other than in flight at high speed/low level.

This was seen as a major task in industry and only one company, English Electric, appeared to have all the necessary experience and capability to undertake it. There was no other company with the up-to-date experience of 20 years of continuous jet bomber and Mach 2 supersonic fighter design and production, and in addition English Electric had already put forward a design study for such an aircraft to replace their own Canberra under the project heading P17. This design was based so much on the logic and experience gained from the Canberra and P.1 that Warton felt totally confident of their technical capability to do the job while realising that some administrative expansion would be needed to manage and monitor essential sub-contract work.

It was something of a surprise to learn, however, that as a fundamental condition of the Ministry contract the work would not be placed with one company, but that industry must form a consortium of no fewer than three major companies to undertake the work. This was the only major new military contract in sight, so the new proposition had to be taken seriously. But the industry did not welcome the proposal. English Electric wanted the lead as of right from its experience. Vickers wanted the lead because it was a long-established aircraft constructor dating back to the beginning of the century (in contrast it said to English Electric, the 'newcomers in the North'). The proud independence of de Havilland and Hawker precluded them from competing — many said they would not have been able to tackle it anyway.

After heated debate and under continued government pressure, English Electric and Vickers agreed to form a consortium, the British Aircraft Corporation. Then the vital question of a new engine was resolved by the MoD who ignored BAC's strong recommendations for a new-generation Rolls-Royce engine in favour of the Bristol Olympus which they, the Ministry, claimed was 'already a going concern'. It was not of course and the Olympus development for TSR.2 was an entirely redesigned engine which, in the event, gave a great deal of trouble in the critical years of testing the prototype TSR.2.

Then came another bombshell. English Electric were informed that Vickers were to be given design authority as the 'main contractor'. English Electric would be in a subordinate role (to Sir George Edwards, managing director of Vickers) but the TSR.2 design starting point was to be English Electric's P17! This seemed to many at Warton and elsewhere to be an untenable position loaded with potential pitfalls, personality clashes, culture differences and major administrative blockages.

The programme would be a hard nut to crack by one company which knew what it was doing, but to force two strongly independent organisations into a shotgun marriage purely at the whim of some Whitehall or St Giles Court genius who in all probability would not have to carry the can for a disastrous result, seemed to stretch credibility beyond all reason.

It is a historical fact that it was actually done, and that after four years of exemplary effort and dedication to the principle 'the RAF needs TSR.2', the massive administrative difficulties were worked through, personality clashes subdued (or where necessary resolved by firing!) and a prototype emerged which seemed to have great potential. It did, however, have technical defects which delayed first flight, many of which resulted from design/engineering constipation in this immensely and unnecessarily complex new manufacturing organisation.

Throughout the four years 1960–1964 there were many examples of serious planning being frustrated by 'don't want to know' attitudes somewhere in the internecine management system. They were mostly sorted out in the end but often only after delays which accumulated and became all too apparent at the much delayed flight test stage.

One example was the planning for the flight testing venue which would not only involve positioning the aircraft and full technical support, but could require moving specialist personnel away from their normal and important priorities. The prototype was in-build at Weybridge in 1963 — where would it fly? Weybridge, ridiculous with its very short runway leading straight into the village. Wisley had no room for an emergency stop which could have the prototype across the busy Portsmouth road in the event of an untested drag 'chute failure during the runway trials.

Where else? Boscombe Down? Warton? Both runways were adequate but Boscombe would need a whole new manufacturer's flight testing set-up many miles away from both contractors' bases. However, Warton's runway and full operating and test and specialist facilities were all suitable and first-class.

We were getting into the last year before flight and there was not a sign of discussion or planning on this issue. My department and all the others associated with flight testing needed to know. Freddy Page could not help he said, so I went to see the Vickers management and all became clear — Weybridge saw the flight-testing as being within their sovereignty. It had to be first flight from Weybridge or Wisley they said. The rules of MoD approval-to-test which I understood well would not permit either however, and it was apparently unacceptable to Vickers for the prototype to fly at Warton even though I was the designated pilot! So with six months at most to go a whole new team of administration and technical facilities had in the end to be set up 'on neutral ground', at Boscombe Down. This unsound decision alone added at least six months to the delayed first flight and to untold increase in programme costs. In another indication of mutual lack of confidence in the conduct of the programme the BAC main board posted a Weybridge production expert, Charlie Houghton, to the Warton Board with a brief to 'sort out' the Preston production works. I doubt if many people at Warton or Preston felt the need to be sorted out in this respect after our recent record with over 1,400 Canberras for 15 air forces and over 300 Mach 2 fighters for the RAF, which compared rather favourably with the record at Vickers over the same period with the failed Swift, the failed Valiant V-bomber, the failed Vanguard turboprop airliner and the less than fully successful BAC One-Eleven 'bus stop jet'. The earlier Viscount had of course been a major success. But Houghton was soon seen to be of good value and a respected member of our team. Less than a year later he was retired from our board to return to Weybridge, saying before he left: 'You people know the job better than I do!'

And then came perhaps the key point in the relationship. With the rapid increase in pressures of the period before first flight in clearing all the remaining technical problems, it was apparent that Warton's experience and expertise in high-performance aircraft was being relied upon more and more at Boscombe and more remotely even by Weybridge. It had also finally got through that the TSR.2 flying programme could never be done at Wisley and would inevitably become a Warton responsibility. Weybridge retained nominal, and often querulous, authority over what was still going on at Boscombe, even on one occasion actively trying to interfere with operational flight planning decisions which they were not in any way qualified to do.

Then it was formally announced that Freddy Page would take over responsibility for TSR.2 flight development (2,500 test hours planned for the next four years) from the day when I would land the prototype at Warton on delivery from Boscombe. In fact from a few weeks before the first flight at Boscombe Down, Page and Warton had already been in practical day-to-day charge.

So the saga of TSR.2 came to its end, after some very successful flight testing, on Budget Day 1965 when cancellation was announced without warning by the Chancellor, Dennis Healey.

A miracle had been achieved by the many brilliant engineers and able, dedicated and loyal people at all levels of the scrambled-together organisation, and it is to their lasting credit that despite all the immense difficulties a fine aeroplane was produced which showed briefly its enormous potential and put the wind up the American aircraft industry. That of course is another story.

The cancellation of TSR.2 was the pivotal point. Before that date the British aircraft industry was a world leader in supersonic technology with the capacity to design, build and deliver the supersonic aircraft needed for UK defence and export customers. After the cancellation this capacity was allowed to fade away. No new all-British supersonic design has been produced for the RAF in the 30 years since 1965. The capacity is no longer there and will not return in the continued absence of a national will to meet our own defence requirements from our own industrial resources.

The argument that single nations can no longer have such capacity 'to go it alone' is clearly refuted by the technical successes of the Swedish SAAB supersonic fighter programmes, and the Rafale of France. But with the hindsight of 30 years it can now be seen clearly that while the cancellation of TSR.2 was the pivotal point in the run-down of the British aircraft industry, that run-down began inevitably with the crass government decision five years earlier to force amalgamation in the industry. This action emasculated the best in the industry and left no single company able to undertake sole responsibility for new high-performance projects. British industry has built no all-British new supersonic fighter or bomber designs to meet the specific needs of the RAF since the Lightning of 1957 and the TSR.2 of 1964, and the subsequent international collaborative programmes have resulted — and always will result in compromises.

In 1960 the leaders should have been allowed to lead, and the losers to fall by the wayside to reduce the overmanning and over-capacity of the late 1950s. But the British technology and drive that has sustained the immensely valuable Al Yamamah programme for so long, and the now obvious (in 1996) dependence on British technology to save the Eurofighter 2000 by drastic redesign of its flying controls computers are the clearest possible indicators that British innovative design and engineering skills are still there, and that with the reincarnation of confident support from government leading to a return to industrial 'clout', this country could be able once again to compete in this field with France, the USA and Sweden. There are no other contenders, although the remnants of the Russian aircraft industry still have the potential to spring surprises in the future.

Chapter Fourteen

Retrospect

A major milestone occurred 20 years after I had initiated test flying at Warton and following 21 years of continuous test and demonstration flying on the Company's products.

When I retired from test flying and flew my last Lightning test on 28 March 1968 it had been my own decision. I had begun to notice that although at age 48 I continued to enjoy it all, I was now finding that when flying at Mach 2 I was tending to run out of our Irish Sea supersonic test run before I had completed the test schedule — which I would normally have finished with minutes to spare! It was time to make way for the younger and very capable test pilots in the team who had for years seen their chances of promotion frustrated — 'Will Bee ever give up?'

I maintained my licence and continued to fly in general aviation for many years, but for a long time it was difficult to accept that I could no longer take a Lightning on the flight line each day and, after completing its experimental or production test schedule, wring it out over the sparkling Irish Sea or the glistening slopes of the Lake District as only a Lightning could be flown.

Often a call from the 'Ops Room' to the board room that an aircraft was ready for me had resulted in excusing myself from a meeting if the subject under discussion had not been in one of my areas of direct responsibility. It had always been a remarkable (and enjoyable!) contrast to leave the hot, stuffy board room and only minutes later, concentrating only on the professional drills and technicalities of supersonic flight, soar up through any weather, summer or winter, into the brilliant sky and cold, clear limitless visibility above cloud. Then when the tests were complete I would dive back into the Warton circuit and up into an invigorating roll or 'roll off the top', or more often to concentrate hard for an instrument descent through dense cloud steered by the calm voices of Warton's professional radar recovery and approach controllers onto the instrument landing system (ILS) for a 'coupled' automatic ILS approach to the airfield. Sometimes not breaking out of cloud until at only a few hundred feet, with the approach lights appearing out of the murk and the runway lights ahead. It was always wonderful and so much more than the 'just a routine test' as so often quoted for the media. Then back to the board room where the same discussion as like as not would still be in progress!

It was inevitable that these contrasts should leave me with a different and necessarily unique dimension in taking part in board-room debate, and I only hope that this aspect did not show. At least I remained on the Warton board for a decade after retiring from test flying!

It had been a wonderful 40 years. The high point was unquestionably my seven years with the world's finest air force, and the very highest point of that period the terrifying but proud months of the Battle of Britain when it was only the fighter pilots who could save this country from invasion. They did not fail.

Regrets, very few. In retrospect how much more one could have achieved in the Battle of Britain had one had the experience that had been accumulated by 1944 after four further years of combat flying.

Then there was a missed opportunity in 1960. With the formation of the new conglomerate, the British Aircraft Corporation, I was told over the telephone by English Electric chairman Viscount Caldecote that as a fundamental arrangement of the new corporation my name had been put forward for MoD 'Design Authority' for flight testing the new supersonic strike aircraft for the RAF, TSR.2, and that this post would be as deputy chief test pilot of BAC. The TSR.2 was by a considerable margin the most important new development in the aircraft industry at that time, and when I queried the level of this appointment the explanation was given that Sir George Edwards was appointing his airliner experienced pilot Jock Bryce as chief test pilot of the new corporation 'because the future of BAC lay', he said, 'with the Weybridge designed civil airliner projects'. This was entirely questionable as it seemed from Warton that the future much more clearly lay with English Electric's highly successful and profitable military aircraft programmes.

This proved to have been a totally accurate prediction when in the 1980s British Aerospace's main civil businesses were finally sold off, having come close to bankrupting the entire corporation, leaving Warton as the sole centre of future British military aircraft design, production and export sales.

Nevertheless in 1960 with strong advice from my long-time colleague and chief Freddy Page, as a loyal 'company' man I accepted the 'deputy' proposition against much protest and advice from friends everywhere and took on the TSR.2 programme which proved in the event professionally satisfying.

But when Jock Bryce retired from test flying four years later the mantle of BAC chief test pilot was passed on to the Weybridge Division deputy chief test pilot, Brian Trubshaw, who subsequently made a splendid job of testing the Concorde and was then advanced to full member of the main BAC board.

My post of 'Deputy' quietly faded away with the TSR.2's political cancellation in 1965, though I scarcely noticed it as I still had much to do on the many Warton programmes as a divisional director.

My wife, Pat, who throughout the 50 wonderful years of our marriage has been totally staunch and supportive during very many crisis periods, both company and family, was incisively clear in her views; 'You must be mad,' she said, 'if you don't insist on CTP'! She was proved quite right of course.

Another event in the 1970s posed a not unexpected dilemma. The very important Saudi Arabian Defence technical and training programme had been initiated by English Electric in 1968, and another company had been contracted to carry out in-country administration and in-the-field servicing. By 1970, however, this part had got into difficulties. The initial deliveries from Warton of Lightning supersonic fighters and Strikemaster jet trainers had been completed and flying training on the desert airfields was progressing well, but many aspects of the administrative support was not satisfying the Saudi authorities.

Matters came to a head when the British government was informed by the Saudi

The beginning of the great Saudi Arabian defence contracts 'Magic Carpet' and 'Al Yamamah' in 1966. The Saudi evaluation mission at Warton with Pakistan Air Force advisers. RSAAF chief test pilot Capt Hamdan, later C-in-C of the RSAAF, with author at left centre. (British Aerospace)

A RSAAF Lightning Mk 53 over the desert near Dhahran. Note the Vinten reconnaissance pod forward of the ventral tank. (British Aerospace)

government that unless the maintenance and administration tasks were transferred *in toto* to English Electric 'the British would be phased out and the whole future programme would be handed over to the Americans' whom we had so far beaten comprehensively in fierce competition. With this massive multi-billion-pound export contract with enormous future potential clearly in jeopardy, the British government took over the administrative contract responsibility and, with EEC's reluctant agreement, subcontracted the administration and servicing programme to Warton as additions to Warton's main contract for the supply and technical support of aircraft and in-country flying training to operational standard.

At this stage there was a great deal of departmental shuffling at Warton with the aim of channelling many of our best people away from their already important specialist tasks to 'hold the fort in Saudi'. I had kept my head down, knowing very well what was going on from my regular quarterly board-report visits to the Saudi Air Force headquarters and to the main air defence bases at Riyadh, Dhahran, Tabuk and Khamis Mushayt. But one day in a meeting of the Warton Board the subject was raised urgently of a name for someone to take over in-country as Director of Operations, Saudi Arabia. Pointing to me, the chairman said: 'According to Riyadh they want Bee — he can do no wrong!'

The prospect of that particular task did not surprise or worry me at all as I had seen much of it at first hand and how it had been mishandled in the past four years, but it also occurred to me that I already had as much responsibility as I could reasonably handle at Warton, and in the Munich and Turin Panavia Tornado programme at the same time. So I did not immediately show enthusiasm. But that night and the following day the chairman, the managing director and finally the chief executive all said: 'You've got to do it Bee'.

After sleeping on it, thinking it through thoroughly and consulting my never-failing oracle of sound, pithy common sense, the long-suffering Pat, we concluded that it was

The Panavia Tornado prototype on test from Warton, 1975. (British Aerospace)

not on — something would have to give. Next day I put it to Freddy Page that my priority post as director of Tornado flight operations, together with my then still current Warton board responsibilities for airfields (2) and ATC management, flight operations, flight test engineering and the publicity/public relations department, would leave no reasonable margin for giving adequate time or priority to the major crisis in Saudi Arabia.

Freddy Page's response was simple. 'You can recruit staff as necessary, set up your headquarters in Riyadh, have a 125 (business jet) at your disposal and commute between Riyadh, Munich, Turin and Warton as necessary.' Although this implied either tremendous confidence in my ability or sheer desperation (I was not sure which), I realised that spreading one man over so wide a field of active, urgent day-to-day operations and decision-making would have the inevitable result of spreading the supervision too thinly.

But being essentially a team-man I was not about to refuse a new responsibility without debate. So I tried a diversionary tactic. No mention had been made of relevant emoluments at this stage so I said to the Warton Saudi programme director, who had now come on to the scene, that I would certainly have to offload something and that I would expect the international rate for the job in Saudi Arabia covering the new task, separate from and in addition to my current salary as a director of the Warton Division and of Panavia Flight Operations (a salary level which was not by any means in the international class at the time in any case!).

That, it appeared, was different! The next day Atkin said: 'You've priced yourself out of the job,' which was what I had intended. Apparently I was expected to take on this immense new task without any increment in pay! But I have often wondered how the future would have developed had I taken on the Saudi task on the conditions offered at what proved to be the commencement of the immensely successful Al Yamamah defence programme which has since then been renewed over three consecutive decades as Britain's most valuable-ever export contract.

These were but a few aberrations in 40 years of rewarding work beginning in the world's finest air force and continuing for 33 years in the most successful design and manufacturing team in post-war British aviation. The aviation world has produced outstanding leaders and high quality people of dedicated skills, loyalties and professionalism and I have been privileged to work with one of the most successful teams of all, English Electric, in the 1940s, '50s and '60s.

There were of course some disappointments and though these were far outweighed by the immensely positive side of serving in RAF Fighter Command and, post-war, taking a close personal part in the evolution of Britain's first jet bomber series, the Canberras, and our first truly supersonic fighters the P.1 and P.1B, at the end of it all some more negative aspects were still memorable.

In the autumn of 1944 when I had just come to the conclusion of my fifth year of war flying and somewhat surprisingly safely to the end of my third tour of operations, with a fighter wing whose morale was so high that we felt that we were winning the war on our own; and when I had just learnt that my own immediate future could either mean continued service (but on staff duties) in the RAF or transfer back to Hawker for an experimental test flying post which could continue if I wished after the war ended — a uniquely assured prospect at that time of universal insecurity — it was a frustrating blow to find myself suddenly completely out of the running, incarcerated in a German prison camp and eventually totally cut off from any joint celebration of what we all felt had been a hard-won victory. Six months later, by the time the Russians had released the aircrew prisoners from my Luckenwalde camp near Potsdam in June 1945 and we had reached home bedraggled but still hopeful, the celebrations had all been forgotten and the country was in egalitarian political fervour with only one thing in mind — a general election! It was indeed an anticlimax.

Then, 33 years later after three decades of success mounting on success which had brought the EEC Preston and Warton team from a little-known Lancashire locomotive engineering works and subcontractor to Handley Page for Second World War bomber production in the 1940s, to the leading establishment in British aviation for military aircraft and our sole producer of military supersonic aircraft, my retirement took place in an atmosphere of total preoccupation with management musical chairs. Now was the time it was said to be 'off with the old, on with the new'.

At the end of the 1970s some senior managers were suddenly moved from Warton to corporate headquarters at Kingston to meet the demand for major administrative expansion resulting from the great Tornado contract for NATO on top of the vast and continuing Saudi Arabian defence programme. This opened the floodgates for a new generation to take over at Warton and grab what they could with humourless ruthlessness.

The old loyalties to 'the company', the RAF and the country which had been the mainstay of company morale for over three decades of great success were swept aside by an inrush of stone-faced young 'new management' intent apparently only on 'what's in it for me?' Long and successful specialist experience was now held to be of no consequence in the lemming rush to establish the new order, and the only goal was said to be cost-effectiveness by total dependence on computerisation with senior posts staffed by accountants and engineers and other specialists relegated to minor roles if not dispensed with entirely. This was the new enlightened policy.

When my 32 years at Warton came to an end there was an extraordinary surge of warmth and friendship from long-servers at all levels of the company from shop-floor to engineering and specialist departments, but only cold indifference from the 'new-generation' management, most of whom I had myself in the recent past actively supported in their selections to the Board.

Then came the day in August, a Monday, when I drove in from our Samlesbury home to park outside my office in Flight Operations with the realisation that this was for the last time. I had said most of the goodbyes the previous week; there was now, and most important of all, just the pilots and Flight Operations staff. Nothing at all had been said of the traditional farewell lunch in the directors mess, and then a message came from the new chairman's secretary saying that a recently appointed sales director who was taking early retirement would be 'lunched out today' and the chairman wanted Mr Beamont to be there as well.

I said that I had arranged to lunch with the pilots and did so. I picked up my briefcase at 5pm after saying farewell to my long-time and faithful secretary and strong support, Chrys Butcher, locked up and looked out across the airfield to the Ribble Marshes where I had watched the waders and wild fowl for 30-odd years from the ground and from the air, for the last time. Flying was finished for the day and the last engines silenced. The call of a curlew came down the wind.

Had it all been worth it? Yes indeed it had.

But now a new chapter was opening with time at last for family, for the hills and moorlands, and for the sparkling waters of salmon and trout rivers. Time perhaps to write of some of these experiences for the interest, but hopefully not boredom, of generations to come for whom there will always be challenges and the satisfaction that comes from facing them, and for some, the lucky ones, the challenge of the skies.

Testing at the cutting edge

Some of the incidents described in these pages have been lighthearted, some routine, and some unexpected and concentrating the mind. They have been just a few of the infinite variety of events which, together with the intensive routine testing, go into the clearing to a safe and efficient standard of a modern high-performance aircraft, and make test flying not only a vital part of the evolution of an aeroplane, but for the experimental test pilot a most fulfilling occupation.

Every so often among the hundreds of hours of routine testing there comes an unexpected crisis, or a planned and essential high-risk test on the cutting edge. These challenges ensure that the work can never become dull or, in that currently fashionable term, boring.

The Warton legacy. Left to right, the English Electric Mach 2+ Lightning, 1957; the BAC Mach 2.5 TSR.2, 1964; and the 50,000 ft + English Electric Canberra, 1949. (British Aerospace)

In the high-technology world of today the experimental test pilot's task, though different in detailed respects from the past, remains essentially as it always has been to confirm the suitability or otherwise of the aeroplane for its designated task. The test pilot is its final inspector and critic, and this is never going to make him popular in some quarters.

In the words of John William Dunne, aircraft designer and test pilot in 1913: 'The aeroplane does do these things, and if the theory does not give warranty for the practice it is the theory that is wrong'.

'Integrity — The cornerstone of our profession in that the test pilot's job is determining truth.'
(Society of Experimental Test Pilots, California, USA, 1995)

Appendix One

English Electric Company Ltd
'First time' speeds in a British aircraft.
The P.1 and Lightning Development Programme, 1954–1963

Date	Aircraft	Altitude (ft)	Speed (Mach)	Place	Pilot
11. 8.54	P.1 WG760 *(1st British supersonic level flight)*	30,000	1.02	Boscombe Down	R. P. Beamont
10.10.54	P.1 WG760	30,000	1.13	Warton	R. P. Beamont
3.11.54	P.1 WG760	30,000	1.14	Warton	R. P. Beamont
12.11.54	P.1 WG760	30,000	1.22	Warton	R. P. Beamont
28.2.57*	P.1 WG760 (R/H)	33,000	1.45	Warton	R. P. Beamont
28.2.57*	P.1 WG760	36,000	1.53	Warton	R. P. Beamont
15.5.57*	P.1B Lightning XA847	41,000	1.62	Warton	R. P. Beamont
17.5.57	P.1B Lightning XA847	40,000	1.73	Warton	R. P. Beamont
4.6.57	P.1B Lightning XA847	40,000	1.75	Warton	R. P. Beamont
23.11.57	P.1B Lightning XA847	44,000	1.83	Warton	R. P. Beamont
17. 2.58	P.1B Lightning XA856	40,000	1.86	Warton	R. P. Beamont
16. 9.58	P.1B Lightning XA847	40,000	1.88	Warton	R. P. Beamont
16. 9.58	P.1B Lightning XA847	40,000	1.9	Warton	R. P. Beamont
15.10.58	P.1B Lightning XA847	42,000	1.92	Warton	R. P. Beamont
25.11.58	P.1B Lightning XA847 *(1st British flight to Mach 2)*	44.000	2.00	Warton	R. P. Beamont
3. 4.63	Lightning F.2/3 XN734 *(Fastest flight in Lightning)*	39,000	2.105	Warton	R. P. Beamont

*Possibly equalled by the Fairey FD.2.

Appendix Two

'First flights' of English Electric prototypes and major type-variants by the author in the period 1949–1968.

	Date	Aircraft type (powerplant)	Serial
1.	13.5.49	B.3/45 Canberra B.1. prototype (RR Avon RA2 engines)	VN799
2.	9.11.49	B.3/45 Canberra B.1 2nd prototype (RR Nene engines)	VN828
3.	8.10.50	Canberra B.2 1st production aircraft	WD929
4.	15.7.52	Canberra B.5 modified with RR Avon RA7 engines	VX185
5.	12.6.52	Canberra T.4 trainer prototype	WN467
6.	12.8.52	Canberra PR.3 1st production aircraft	WE135
7.	23.7.54	Canberra B.8 interdictor prototype (converted from B.5)	VX185
8.	4.8.54	P.1 Lightning prototype (AS Sapphire SA5 engines)	WG760
9.	18.7.55	P.1A 2nd prototype with guns and ventral fuel and, later, reheat. Also foot-pedal wheel brakes.	WG763
10.	4.4.57	P.1B Lightning, 3rd prototype (RR Avon 24R engines)	XA847
11.	5.9.57	P.1B 5th prototype, engine development aircraft	XA856
12.	3.4.58	P.1B Lightning, 1st pre-production aircraft	XG307
13.	6.5.59	Lightning (P.11) T.4 trainer prototype	XL628
14.	20.9.59	2nd T.4 Trainer prototype	XL629
15.	30.11.59	1st production Lightning F.1	XM134
16.	16.8.60	1st production Lightning F.1A	XM169
17.	9.1.62	Lightning F.3 development prototype. New fin	XG310
18.	17.4.64	Lightning F.6 development prototype	XP697
19.	27.9.64	TSR.2 prototype	XR219
20.	24.11.65	Lightning F.6, 1st production aircraft	XR768
21.	29.8.67	Lightning 55 Trainer prototype/1st production aircraft (for Saudi Arabia)	55–711

Bibliography

Hawker Aircraft Ltd experimental flight test records. Langley Airfield 1939–44. Via Frank W. Mason

Author's flight test reports. English Electric Co. Warton and Samlesbury 1948–74. Via British Aerospace.

Author's flying log books.

Supersonic Flight Richard P. Hallion. Smithsonian Publications.

Typhoon and Tempest Frank Mason. Aston Publications.

Index